SECRET

Southern California

A Guide to Unique Places

Kathy Strong

First edition

Information and recommendations listed in this guide
book were confirmed at press time. We recommend,
however, that you contact establishments to obtain
current information before traveling.

Excerpts from Louie, Take a Look at This!: My Time with Huell Howser, by Luis Fuerte (as told to David Duron), used with permission of the publisher, Prospect Park Books.

ISBN: 978-1-54396-629-9 (print)
ISBN: 978-1-54396-630-5 (ebook)

An imprint of PS Wish You Were Here Travel
http://pswishyouwereheretravel.com/

Manufactured in the United States of America

To John, my traveler in life.

For Brent and Trevor, my sons: Thank you for your love and inspiration every mile of the way. May you always find happiness on the roads you choose to travel.

For all my fellow travelers and "secret sharers" who agree with this book's philosophy:

"All the secrets of the world worth knowing are hiding in plain sight."

— Robin Sloan, Mr. Penumbra's 24-Hour Bookstore

CONTENTS

FOREWORD

Travel has always been my happy place. When I reflect on the most memorable times of my life, thus far, travel is by far the common denominator. I recall my first family trips as a child, sleeping huddled on a pile of blankets in the back of the Dodge to awaken in the early hours at a mountainside café that served stacks of country pancakes. I remember being a young, carefree adventurer staying in tiny inns across Europe or hopping around the Caribbean discovering new islands—all on a nonexistent budget. And, when my two sons arrived, taking my children with me on discoveries of everything unique and exciting and witnessing their amazement at every turn. My urge to unearth that new adventure or find is just as fervent today, fueled by my traveling friends' advice and discoveries.

One major discovery stands out. With all my travels through the years, there is nowhere I have been on earth that is more precious in my memories than right here, where I grew up, in Southern California—a destination filled with beauty, wonder, diversity and so many sweet surprises. Although I have enjoyed sharing these discoveries in eight previous editions of SOUTHERN CALIFORNIA OFF THE BEATEN PATH, as well as in countless articles and travel columns, I have concluded that many of the most inspiring and unique discoveries within my writing actually came from my readers who live and visit here, as well as from my many knowledgeable friends in travel.

And, so, I thank each and every one of you who have taken the time to share your secrets for all to discover in SECRET SOUTHERN CALIFORNIA. I dedicate this book to my very special secret-sharing friends. May you never keep a secret that is just too wonderful to spill!

Fondly,

Kathy

INTRODUCTION

California, specifically Southern California, ranks as one of the top tourist destinations in the United States; more than 260 million vacationers choose SoCal each year to sample its world-renowned attractions, year-round sunshine, celebrity haunts, Mediterranean-style beaches, mysterious deserts and mountain playgrounds. These visitors spend more than $126 billion once they arrive. Also, nearly 40 million people reside within the state, many savoring weekend escapes in their own backyard—a bounty of diverse scenery and happenings all just a few minutes or few hours away from home!

Secret Southern California was written for all of these adventurers, those coming from both far and near who seek truly unusual getaways. Secret Southern California is a totally updated guide that is a spin-off from the popular Off the Beaten Path Southern California, editions 1-8, by Kathy Strong. Still a guide to those hard-to-find spots, even in the most obvious destinations, this book is for the traveler who seeks something more than the usual: side-road explorations, "living" history lessons, new adventures, cutting-edge experiences and even secrets shared by locals and travel experts who know their destination best. No matter what your interests are, from Hollywood-movie-great haunts to lush, palm-lined Indian canyons or speakeasy bars, Secret Southern California will grant you some new ideas for your next vacation or weekend escape.

Come along and discover those secrets that just have to be shared—especially when they are tied up in adventure, fun and anything but the expected. If you think you know everything about your favorite destinations in Southern California, consider this an opportunity to add a few more favorites to your list. For those who seek intrigue, pleasant surprises, let's-not-tell finds and off-the-beaten-path treasures, this is just for you!

The Making of a State

When James Marshall discovered gold at Sutter's Mill in 1848, the story of what makes California unique really began. California became the "promised land" for those seeking opportunity. No journey was too tough to stop the great migration of dreamers who made their way to find riches in the foothills of the Sierra. Even when the riches were depleted, the migration continued, first by train, with completion of the transcontinental railroad in 1869, and later by automobile, along historic Route 66.

Marshall's discovery epitomized the American dream: Anyone could find riches, whether these came from shiny minerals hidden in the earth or from hard work, determination and ingenuity. Movie studios, airplane factories, vineyards, and orange groves filled the environs of Southern California. As one historian wrote, "California was founded on gold fever, but it has since thrived on land fever, oil fever, and Hollywood fever." That sums it up—and the fever that afflicts present-day adventurers to California continues.

Fun California Facts

- California is the nation's third largest state. It has 1,264 miles of coastline bordering the Pacific Ocean. The state is 560 miles wide and contains 158,706 total square miles.

- The Salton Sea in the Imperial Valley is the largest lake in the state. The Salton Sea is 30 miles long and 14 miles wide at its widest point.

- The highest point in the state is Mount Whitney in the southern Sierra at 14,496 feet high; it is also the tallest peak in all the forty-eight contiguous states. At 282 feet below sea level is Badwater, the lowest point in the entire Western Hemisphere. The two locations are just 60 miles apart.

- How did California get its name? There are several theories or lore. In one story, Hernando Cortés uttered the Latin words callida fornax, meaning "hot furnace," when he first landed in Baja California. Another story relates that Cortés named the land after a sea-formed arch, using the Spanish words cala (cove) and y (and) and the Latin word fornix (arch). The most popular explanation is from Garci Rodríguez Ordonez de Montalvo's sixteenth-century Spanish romance Las Sergas de Esplandian. The novel refers to Californe, a mythical island. It is thought that the early settlers, with their Spanish heritage, may have named the state after this island.

- California has several nicknames. Everyone has heard California referred to as the "Golden State," but how many of these other nicknames have you heard? America's Number One Market, Cornucopia of the World, El Dorado, Eureka State, Gateway to the Pacific, Grape State, Land of Discoveries, Land of Gold, Land of Living Color, Land of

Promise, Land of Sunshine and Flowers, Sunshine Empire and Wine Land of America.

- The first state flag was of homespun cloth decorated with a red star, a grizzly bear and a red flannel strip along the bottom, with the words above it reading "California Republic." The flag design survived and in 1911 became official.

- How many state symbols do you know?

  Tree: Redwood

  Flower: Golden poppy

  Fish: Golden trout

  Marine mammal: Pacific gray whale

  Animal: Grizzly bear (now extinct in California)

  Bird: California valley quail

  Colors: Blue and gold

  Fossil: California saber-toothed cat

  Insect: California dog-face butterfly

  Reptile: California desert tortoise

  Rock: Serpentine

  Mineral: Gold

  Gemstone: Benitoite

- State sport: On Aug. 20, 2018, surfing became California's official state sport. After all, what represents the California Dream more than surfing?

- State song: The official song of the state might surprise you: It's "I Love You, California," written in 1913 and finally adopted by the state in 1988. Most people think the song is "California, Here I Come," written in 1924 with words by Al Jolson.

- Population: California is a big state. The 2000 census shows California as containing eight of the thirty counties in the United States with populations of more than one million persons.

- The state's capital is Sacramento, but it wasn't always so. In 1777 Monterey was proclaimed the capital of what was then Spain's California territory. The capital moved northward to four other state cities before becoming permanently situated in Sacramento.

Visit California: **https://www.visitcalifornia.com/**

CENTRAL COAST

You could say that the entire Central Coast of California is an off-the-beaten path destination. Filled with gently rolling green hills studded with oaks, plains covered with wildflowers, rich remnants of California's beginnings, sweet-smelling citrus groves, verdant fields of twisting grapevines and unparalleled Mediterranean-like ocean scenery, discoveries lie around each and every corner. From Hearst's elaborate San Simeon palace on a hilltop to a sprawling cowboy movie ranch near Thousand Oaks, the area boasts variety and abundant off-road adventures. Here, you can explore small late-nineteenth-century towns with pioneer stagecoach stops, as well as big and little cities that boast hidden historical gems, wineries, surf-crashing scenery and charming getaway retreats.

San Luis Obispo County

https://www.slocal.com/

San Simeon

Scenic, two-lane Highway I leisurely twists down the rocky Pacific coast of northern San Luis Obispo County. You'll want to stop at various points along the thoroughfare, regarded as one of the most beautiful highways in the world, to linger over a romantic sunset or to watch sea otters at play.

California is blessed with many fascinating museums and a few "castles," but one castle museum stands out from the rest—not just for its history and treasures, but also for the magnificent coastal journey that leads to its hilltop splendor. The town of San Simeon boasts the magnificent home of William Randolph Hearst, the **Hearst San Simeon State Historical Monument**, which attracts more than one million visitors annually. Known affectionately as Hearst Castle, the state treasure offers an assortment of day tours imparting interesting history and facts in and around the museum and grounds—and awe-inspiring vistas from its glorious hilltop perch.

AUTHOR'S TIP:
TOUR IN THE EVENING

*Although the castle schedules a wide variety of day tours, the most unique offerings at the castle are the **Evening Tours**, offered each spring and fall. The evening "living history" tours, which last more than two hours and take in highlights of the day tours, are really a step back into the glamorous 1930s, a chance to experience firsthand the opulent lifestyles of the celebrated guests and occupants of the "Enchanted Hill." While guests tour the softly lit grounds and environs of the estate, docents in authentic 1930's costumes assume a variety of guest and staff roles. "Guests" in satin cocktail gowns and suits stroll the rose-filled gardens; "butlers" serve appetizers to "guests" playing cards in the Assembly Room; and a "starlet" lounges on the 400-year-old bed in La Casa del Mar. The evening is not over until you've viewed a "movie" in the castle's theater, a Hearst Metrotone newsreel recounting some of the important events of 1933. Evening Tours of Hearst Castle are available on certain weekends only. Reservations are recommended. http://hearstcastle.org/*

The oldest native of San Simeon, J. C. "Pete" Sebastian, died several years ago, but he left behind a legacy worth exploring. Sebastian took over **Sebastian's Store** (established in 1852) from his father in 1948, but he worked as a child with his father in the store when the Hearsts were setting up the castle and later worked as a landscaper on Hearst's castle grounds. He remembered how the castle grew in concept from a few bungalows to replace the tents to the most opulent private residence in the country. The tiny grocery store across from San Simeon Bay saw customers such as Winston Churchill and Cary Grant and witnessed the unusual unloading of ranch cattle from ships, which involved the cows "swimming" ashore to waiting cowhands. This oldest operating store in the state was kept open during the Depression by purchases inspired by Hearst's generosity; he asked Sebastian to supply all the needy families in the area with food and groceries and to bill him for the costs. Visit the vintage store today and pick up some snacks for a picnic along the driftwood-strewn beach just across the way. The tiny wooden structure is packed with food, gifts, mementos and nostalgic memories of an era gone by. Sebastian's is located at 442 San Simeon Road.

Historic **Piedras Blancas Lighthouse** first guided mariners along the rocky coast here in 1875. The Bureau of Land Management now manages the lighthouse as a historic park and wildlife sanctuary accessed by guided tours only. A variety of tours are offered year-round, including sunset and whale-watching tours as well as guided tours of the restored lighthouse and surrounding buildings. **http://www.piedrasblancas.org/tours.html**

Cambria

Pine-covered hills cradling a two-winged artists' hamlet make up the village of Cambria just south of San Simeon. The charming alpine-like village on the sea was originally settled in the early 1860s when William Leffingwell built the area's first sawmill, now the site of **Leffingwell's Landing** on Moonstone Beach. Visitors touring Cambria's **Moonstone Beach** Drive today will find a romantic strip of intimate inns with cozy fireplaces, small bistros and windswept views of a shimmering expanse of green water met by fudge-colored sand. Stroll down this beachcomber's paradise and collect polished pieces of jade, agate and quartz and explore tide pools; or watch the sun set into the Pacific from giant log benches offered along the way.

Fiscalini Ranch Preserve in Cambria is within walking distance of overnight accommodations, yet feels so very far from everything. The preserve, once owned by the ranching Fiscalini family, grants nature lovers 430 acres of preserved natural beauty to explore, highlighted by a dramatic ocean bluff that runs more than a mile along the shoreline. The rocky coast rises to a 400-foot ridge with breathtaking views of migrating whales, birds and playful otters before sloping southeastward to the willow-edged creek. Each spring, the meadows boast beautiful wildflower displays. The preserve is free and open every day from dawn to dusk. **http://www. ffrpcambria.org/ranch.html**

LOCAL'S SECRET: COVELL'S CLYDESDALE RANCH

"Cambria has its jewels like Moonstone Beach, Fiscalini Ranch and a quaint downtown, but when I discovered Covell's Clydesdale Ranch **(https://www.covellscaliforniaclydesdales.com/home.html)** *on the hilltop overlooking the ocean, I fell in love! Riding a Clydesdale on a guided trail ride through a private forested ranch where you can see a herd of more than 80 Clydesdales horses roaming free is just amazing! I love beautiful scenery and horseback riding, and when I found this unique combination with a beautiful Pacific Ocean backdrop, I knew I had found a true local's secret. I'm not sure where else in the world you can do this, but the experience is like 'off-roading on a couch' and not to be missed."*

– Hilary Townsend, Founder, Townsend Public Relations,
http://townsendpr.com/

Along this scenic drive is an intimate oyster bar and shellfish restaurant that is popular with local residents and anyone who is lucky enough to discover it. **The Sea Chest** at 6216 Moonstone Beach Drive serves dinner only from 5:30 p.m. each evening (closed some Tuesdays). The petite restaurant, surrounded by lavender geraniums and ice plants, displays a combination of Victorian gingerbread trim and nautical touches outside, and inside offers informal, intimate seating, skylights, greenery and spectacular ocean views. Enjoy the oyster bar and incredible seafood dinners. **http://www.seachestrestaurant.com/**

Turn from Moonstone Beach Drive into Cambria's newer West Village, where you'll find a variety of antiques stores, art galleries, specialty shops, pubs, delis and boutiques. Also, directly off Main Street in the West Village, is a landmark affectionately known as **Nitt Witt Ridge**. Beer cans, abalone shells, toilet seats and even the kitchen sink are embedded in this rather unique "castle" that looms over the colony of Cambria. The cliffside house built by the late "garbage man" Art Beal has caused debates for years. Beal spent more than fifty years constructing his home out of all forms of "recyclables" that ranged from inlaid tiles to any imaginable salvaged item. Called a "Poor Man's Hearst Castle," Beal once worked at the San Simeon castle, salvaging some items for his own creation. New owners took over the property and are now conducting public tours of the Registered California Landmark. The 40-minute tours are free, but there is a suggested $10 donation. Call 805-927-2690 for tour information.

Take your car and follow Main Street down to the East Village of town to discover more galleries and shops, fine restaurants and intimate lodging. The East Village was the original downtown of Cambria built in the 1860s, although many of the original structures were destroyed in the great fire of 1889.

In addition to pine-studded hills and ocean vistas, Cambria is surrounded by working farms and ranches. To enjoy some of the country pleasures of the area, take Main Street to Santa Rosa Creek Road at the lower end of the East Village. This idyllic country road is lined with working cattle ranches, orchards and farm stands. About 5 miles east along Santa Rosa Creek Road is **Linn's Fruit Bin Farmstore**, a family berry farm that produces mouthwatering olallieberry pies and jams, as well as unforgettable chicken pies prepared with whole chickens. The small berry farm has grown to include a popular restaurant and a gift shop with well-chosen country crafts, kitchen items and other food treats on Bridge Street in Cambria. http://www.linnsfruitbin.com/

About 4 miles south of Cambria on Highway I is a cluster of weathered buildings situated among pastures of grazing cows and rolling green hills. These remnants of a town that grew around a mid-1800s creamery form the town of **Harmony**. The dairy ceased operation more than fifty years ago, but the town has managed to avoid ghost-town status, boasting some eighteen permanent residents (give or take a few) with new town owners working diligently to bring back the historic creamery and its artsy environs, as well as the petite Harmony Post Office that closed in 2008. Park anywhere on the main street of town and wander the intimate assemblage of artists' warehouses and studios, which features glass and pottery works. Weddings are held almost every weekend in the small, adobe-walled chapel in Harmony. http://harmonytown.com/

Morro Bay

South of Harmony on Highway I, 576-foot-tall **Morro Rock** signals the gateway to the tiny coastal town of Morro Bay. Named by Juan Cabrillo, the monument has been a landmark and navigational guide to the bay-hugged community for over 400 years. Quarrying to build jetties and breakwaters in the 1930s was responsible for the dramatic shape of the rock, which is now a protected home for the endangered peregrine falcon.

Pine- and eucalyptus-studded **Morro Bay State Park**, on the edge of town, unveils some of the best hidden views of Morro Rock. The park is popular camping site and features a pristine saltwater marsh that supports a thriving bird population. Biking, kayaking, fishing, hiking and bird watching are popular here.

Head to the Embarcadero area of town to get a close-up view of the extinct volcano peak and to "reel in" the color of the bay's active fishing industry. **Dorn's Original Breakers Cafe,** the original 1940's Breakers Cafe, is a perfect spot to enjoy the local ocean offerings and an idyllic view of the bay and Morro Rock. Operated by third -generation family members, the cafe at 801 Market Street is located in the 1918 real estate office of developer A. Manford "Pickhandle" Brown, who sold bay lots for $160. The intimate bistro overlooking the bay features a full bar. Be sure to order some Morro Bay oysters, an ocean farming tradition since the early 1990s. **www.dornscafe.com**

Whet your appetite by dropping by the historic Fisherman's Wharf, a colorful spot to watch the fishermen in action hauling in the day's bounty of prawns and halibut to seabass and crab. Morro Bay's **Mural Mile** is a great way to learn about the city while touring. Take a self-guided tour of the downtown and waterfront areas and view murals depicting Morro Bay's natural beauty, its history and its famous sea life. Request a copy when stopping into the Morro Bay Visitors Center at 695 Harbor Street.

At the foot of Morro Bay Boulevard is a unique staircase consisting of forty-four steps, each 44 inches wide. The **Centennial Stairway** offers excellent photographic opportunities and dramatic views of the Embarcadero. While here, play a game on the city's **Giant Chessboard**, inspired by the open-air boards seen in Germany. Local residents designed and cut the 2- and 3-foot-tall chess pieces, each weighing between eighteen and thirty pounds. The chessboard is available for matches from the City Recreation and Park Department; call (805) 772–6278. Before beginning a game, get plenty of rest—it is estimated that during an average game, a player will lift more than 1,000 pounds!

Beach-going in Morro Bay is plentiful. Head to **Morro Strand State Beach** with one of the longest sandy stretches in the county for challenging surfing waves, as well as gentle bay canoeing. If you are traveling with your four-legged pal, drop into **Toro Creek Beach**, an off-leash dog beach with white sand located along the Strand between Morro Bay and Cayucos.

LOCAL'S SECRET: LAID-BACK GOLF

"A really sweet Stay & Play can be found up in Morro Bay. The eponymous golf course has a really, really (yeah, really) laid-back vibe, which is well-paired with the continual views of the Bay below and Pacific beyond. For the Stay portion: The Inn at Morro Bay is literally right across the street; or, if you want to mix in some rough with your rough, a lot of folks camp at the grounds adjacent to the course and then simply stroll up to the clubhouse with their sticks."

– Judd Spicer, golf writer and radio host,
https://www.juddspicer.com/ and
https://www.1039espn.com/shows/the-press-box/

Follow the boulevard south to view another state park of distinction as well as a much smaller bayfront community. South Bay Boulevard twists through rocky hills a short distance to the community of **Baywood Park**. Turn east on Santa Ysabel to reach the little town center on the sparkling bay. A handful of artists' galleries, boutiques and small cafes fill the tiny downtown located in the "Valley of the Bears," or **Los Osos Valley**.

From Baywood Park travel the small residential lanes to Los Osos Valley Road on the way to **Montana de Oro State Park**. Begin what the local chamber of commerce calls the Scenic Seven Mile Drive when you see the restored white, one-room schoolhouse surrounded by a grassy park on the right, and follow Los Osos Valley Road to Pecho Road about a mile ahead. At Pecho the roadway begins to unfold the charms of the scenic drive: magnificent rocky shore scenery, miles of deserted sandy beaches met by deep blue waters and nearly 8,000 acres of hills, including 1,347-foot Valencia Peak. Naturalists and backpackers enjoy the solitude and freedom found along the park's trails.

The name Montana de Oro, Spanish for "mountain of gold," comes from the brilliant yellow and orange wildflowers that cover the slopes of the state park each spring, but could easily stand for the similarly colored monarch butterflies that at times populate the eucalyptus groves along this route. The park road twists and turns past enormous sand dunes that flow down to the Morro Bay Sandspit, past dense groves of eucalyptus and gentle open hills until it dips down to **Spooner's Cove**—a rocky, cliff-protected beach that boasts isolated beauty. Although Hollywood has used the cove for filming several movies, the romantic cove is still quite off the beaten path. Swim, sunbathe, fish or hike through the state park; foot and horse trails, isolated strands of beach, tide pools and vista points are all plentiful. Spring wildflower viewing is spectacular.

Just a few yards away from the **Spooner Cove Ranch House** (the park headquarters, containing interesting exhibits) is a newer addition to the park, the **Holloway Garden**. Holloway Garden showcases many of the plant species that grow wild throughout the park; one garden bed is specific to the plants used by the local Chumash Indians. The AT&T-funded "boardwalk" trail from here crosses the dunes and provides access to a sandy beach without disturbing the dune flora. http://www.parks.ca.gov/?page_id=592

Avila Beach

Find more of the coastal pleasures of San Luis Obispo County by heading south on 101 and taking the San Luis Bay Drive exit. A little over a mile down the country road, turn right at **See Canyon**. The twisting canyon road, shaded by trees and dotted with apple farms, has been a major apple-producing area since the beginning of the twentieth century. Follow this country path past a selection of long-established stands offering several varieties of the fall- and winter-harvested fruit, some rarely found in supermarkets. The well-signed Gopher Glen along here offers samples, recipes and home-made cider.

Venture toward the Pacific Ocean on San Luis Bay Drive and follow it all the way to the **Port of San Luis Obispo**, with its small marina, fish market and restaurants, as well as beautiful Avila Beach that is ideal for sunning and swimming. Close to the town of Avila at 1215 Avila Beach Drive is the area's original 1897 hot mineral springs resort, **Sycamore Mineral Springs**, nestled among oaks and sycamore trees. The totally renovated resort boasts redwood tubs situated privately along paths under the trees and filled with natural soothing mineral water. Tub sizes vary from intimate tubs for one or two to the Oasis, which can hold up to forty people. The recreational offerings at Sycamore include sand volleyball courts, a heated swimming pool and a body care center specializing in massages and herbal facials. The hotel offers many deluxe accommodations, with several newer suites that cling to hillsides, with private hot tubs on balconies, fireplaces, romantic high-stepping beds and separate sitting areas. The spa at the inn is not fancy, but the technicians are top-notch and add the right blend to leisurely soaks in the tubs to make the relaxation experience complete. **https://www.sycamore-springs.com/**

Near here, make a stop at **Avila Valley Barn**, offering a bounty of local produce, homemade pies and jams, handmade ice cream, pressed apple-cider and a menagerie of friendly farm animals to feed and pet. **http://avilavalleybarn.com/index.html**

Pismo Beach

A little farther down Highway I is the city of Pismo Beach, once known for its prolific clamming industry. The clams are no longer as plentiful, due to the endearing but hungry sea otters, but the same stretch is now notable as the only remaining vehicle-allowed state beach in California. Dune buggies mesh with cars, horses and people on the otherwise tranquil sandy way. Each fall and winter, between mid-October and mid-March, the butterfly finds its home in Pismo Beach in the **Monarch Butterfly Grove** at **Pismo State Beach** with hundreds of monarch butterflies clustering in the limbs of eucalyptus trees and Monterey pines; these "butterfly" trees follow a trail north of Grand Avenue on Highway I to the border of neighboring Grover Beach.

AUTHOR'S TIP: FOLLOW THE MIGRATION OF MONARCHS

There are various locations in Southern California that attract the majestic monarch butterfly. If you want to get up close to the beautiful insects, check out these areas during migration season—generally October through March:

Morro Bay State Park, Morro Bay

Pismo Beach State Park, Pismo Beach

Camino Real Park, Ventura

Point Magu State Park, Malibu

El Dorado Nature Center, Long Beach

Monarch Hot Springs, Desert Hot Springs

Monarch Butterfly House on Ocean View Avenue, Encinitas

La Jolla Shores Drive, La Jolla

Plan a docent-led tour of the newly opened **Pismo Preserve** that offers more than ten miles of ranch roads and trails with panoramic vistas of the coastline all the way to Point Sal. The 900-acre coastal conservation area is ideal for hiking, horseback riding and mountain biking.

Dinosaur Caves Park, part of an 1840's land grant, in Rancho Pismo offers inspiring vistas of Pismo Pier and surrounding hills. However, its history as a roadside attraction is just as fascinating. Once known as the Caverns of Mystery, the "mysterious" caves beneath the park can still be explored by kayak via offered tours.
https://centralcoastkayaks.com/activities/cave-excursion/
https://www.pismobeach.org/288/Dinosaur-Caves-Park

The small town of **Oceano** has at least one famous inhabitant, the **Great American Melodrama and Vaudeville** at 1863

Pacific Boulevard. Boo the villain and cheer the hero at this late-1800s-style melodrama that also boasts live revues with song, dance and comedy acts. The melodrama hosts more than a half-dozen shows per year and offers hot dogs, sandwiches, popcorn, pretzels, beer, wine and soft drinks, of course. **https://www.americanmelodrama.com/**

Oceano Dunes, located a few miles from Pismo Beach, Oceano is the only California State Park where vehicles may be driven on the beach, with four-wheel drive recommended. Named a "vehicular recreational park" by the state, this unusual slice of California coast sees more dune buggies than surfers and a tow truck stands by in case you get stuck. The 1,500-acre dunes also contain some sensitive ecological areas which happily remain off limits for motorists navigating the sand the waves.

More dramatic dune scapes, nature hikes, and rich history are all a short ride away off Highway 1 on Oso Flaco Lake Road. The 3-mile-long country lane cuts through plains of broccoli and artichoke crops, while ahead lie views of the creamy white-sand mountains of the **Guadalupe-Nipomo Dunes National Seashore.** The Guadalupe-Nipomo Dunes is the largest remaining dune system south of San Francisco and the second largest in the state of California, encompassing an 18-mile stretch of coastline. A small dirt parking lot is provided at the entrance to Oso Flaco Lake; no vehicles, camping, diving or fires are allowed inside the preserve. From the parking area you may embark on nature hikes in the dunes, along the shore and by the lake. Guided trips are offered at times. The dunes may also be appreciated from Point Sal Beach farther down Highway 1 off Brown Road. The 9-mile drive turns to a climbing dirt road through rural hill country to this isolated white-sand beach nestled in the steep hillside.

Paso Robles

San Luis Obispo County's northern territory, inland a few miles from the ocean, offers its own diverse charm and beauty. Highway 101 cuts through these small agricultural towns; take the off-ramp into the rural town of **San Miguel**, about 8 miles north of Paso Robles. **Mission San Miguel Arcángel**, founded in 1797 as the sixteenth of the California missions, is the small town's best-known landmark. The present-day parish church, with a moss-covered tile roof and graceful olive trees guarding it from the roadway, boasts many of its original decorations intact and stands as one of the most authentic reminders of California's mission days. **http://www.missionsanmiguel.org/**

About a half-block down from the mission lies another historic treasure, tucked away on the old highway. Follow Mission Street south to the sign marking the entrance to the **Rios-Caledonia Adobe**. The broken concrete highway, which follows the original dirt stagecoach road, parallels the railroad tracks and leads to a parking area where the foot trail with a self-guided tour begins. You will pass vintage gas pumps, an old-fashioned rose garden, hewn timbers used in the construction of the adobe, a water storage tank and pump and a wishing well with cactus garden before reaching the adobe, which dates from 1846. This inn and stagecoach stop on the old mission trail stands as an excellent example of California's Mexican-era architecture. Using Indian labor, Petronillo Rios built the two-story adobe as his residence and headquarters of his sheep- and cattle-ranching operations. The roof was constructed of handmade tiles; the rafters were fashioned from pine poles secured with strips of rawhide. From 1860 to 1886 the adobe was used as an inn and stagecoach stop for the San Francisco to Los Angeles route; later it was utilized for various businesses, private homes, and even an elementary school. Restoration began on the deteriorating adobe in 1968, thanks to the combined efforts of the Friends of the Adobes and San Luis Obispo County. The whitewashed adobe structure has an upper-story veranda wound in ancient lavender wisteria. Stroll around the exterior and inside to discover a saloon, complete with a poker game in progress and beer selling for a nickel; a Wells Fargo outlet with safe and stacked traveling trunks; the old primary grades schoolroom that was used during the construction of the San Miguel brick school in 1887; and more. **http://www.rios-caledoniaadobe.org/**

A few miles south of the adobe is the city of **Paso Robles**, formally known as El Paso de Robles, or "the Pass of Oaks." Rolling green hills spattered by blossoming almond groves, acres of grape vineyards, impressive ranches and ancient oaks compose the countryside that envelops the Victorian-flavored city. Known in the 1800s for its mud baths and natural hot springs, Paso Robles' ever-expanding wine industry now attracts more than one million visitors each year to the county's own "Little Napa." Without a doubt, one of the biggest agri-bounties of the area is its proliferation of quality wineries that dot hilltops and are secreted down rural country lanes. In fact, the last ten years has seen the region's vineyard acreage double, bringing the total number of wineries to more than 200 in the region with 40 wine varieties grown, simply translating that wine-lovers have even more reasons to linger longer in pastoral Paso Robles and "plant" their own loyalties to an ever-impressive wine region.

Allegretto Vineyard & Resort, part of the Ayres family collection, is one of the newest lodging choices in the city with 171 guest rooms, a boutique spa, pool and cabanas, manicured gardens and a 12,000-square-foot piazza. Drawing inspiration from the surrounding countryside, Douglas Ayres built and designed the Allegretto in the style of an Italian vineyard estate, filling the corridors with art and artifacts from his many travels. The Tuscan-style resort on 20 acres of vineyards and fruit orchards does a great job capturing the essence of Paso Robles: history, food, wine and beauty. **https://www.allegrettovineyardresort.com/**

AUTHOR'S TIP: WORLD'S FIRST SONIC LABYRINTH

The Allegretto Vineyard Resort has recently created the world's first Sonic Labyrinth 'Sound Circle.' Designed to provide guests a tranquil space with a distinctive series of sounds created by wind instruments, the addition of the labyrinth deepens the resort's existing wellness offerings, utilizing music and space as a way to compel guests to slow their pace and become more mindful. Activated by motion sensors, the Sound Circle creates a series of soft, soothing tones that evolve as you walk through the labyrinth. The original, handcrafted wind instruments were fashioned from European clay and contain three chambers that impart a unique harmony.

Spend a leisurely day or two touring the area's many fine wineries, down rural country roads and highways and lined in colorful roses. To obtain a map to Paso Robles' "wine country" area, visit **https://pasowine.com/**.

AUTHOR'S TIP: TAKE A DISTILLERY (AND WINE) TOUR

*Those in search of wineries tucked away down winding country roads and over the rolling hills of Paso Robles are likely to stumble upon a new form of tasting and touring—the **Distillery Trail**. And to visitors' delight, many of these distilleries operate out of existing wineries, so you get two experiences in one—if you dare. The reason makes perfect sense: the main component in the brandy, vodka, vermouth and gin you will taste is the discarded grape juice used in making wine. Several distilleries have opened around the region, offering visitors tours and tasting rooms for sampling smooth and sophisticated, one-of-a-kind spirits—that are a sure-fire win for those want to shake up their tasting pallet. A handy touring map gives visitors a self-tour highlighted by peaceful rural drives that reveal a bounty of agri-treasures discovered amid lush green hills dotted with grazing cattle and laid-out ranches.* **http://www.pasorobles-distillerytrail.com/**

After exploring the grape-draped countryside of Paso Robles, take a tour of the vintage downtown area on both sides of the main thoroughfare, Spring Street, and all around Thirteenth Street. Quaint residential streets with gingerbread-adorned Victorian homes and businesses dominate this area, which boasts an old-fashioned city park and small-town boutique shopping. **Paso Robles Downtown City Park** reveals the city's historic beginnings with the 1907 Carnegie Library, gazebo that hosts musical events and the **Paso Robles Inn** that saw the likes of Clark Gable and Theodore Roosevelt in its beginnings as a hot mineral water retreat.

Just south of Paso Robles, the Old West town of **Templeton** beckons, its vintage Main Street lined with small shops and quaint restaurants. The surrounding Templeton coun- tryside offers myriad tree-shaded drives, rolling green hill scapes, country wine-tasting stops and orchard sampling. Off Templeton Road, discover **Happy Acres Family Farm**, a 54-acre working dairy goat farm with a "happy" goat herd made up of four unique breeds totaling over 200 head. Happy Acres' goat milk is all natural and hormone-free and used by the farm to produce an array of dairy products such as fresh goat milk, cheese, ice-cream, lotion, soap and other skincare products. **http://www.happyacresfamilyfarm.net/index.html**

Follow Vineyard Drive out of town; soon you will spot the **Turley Wine Cellars**, one of the area's pioneer wineries begun more than sixty years ago with vines from the 1850s that are still producing fruit. By focusing on old vine vineyards, Turley's goal is to preserve California's unique winemaking culture. **http://www.turleywinecellars.com/**

Antiques hunters may want to follow El Camino Real in town south to the adjoining community of **Santa Margarita**. The rural country route passes by the tiny residential-farm com- munity of Garden Farms and on into the main street of Santa Margarita. Plan to take a trek through the historic **Santa Margarita Ranch**, with winetasting at the ranch's nearby **Ancient Peaks Winery** that harvests vineyards from ranch soil populated by ancient oyster shell beds. The 1772-established ranch has a fascinating past, evidenced by Indian artifacts, antique water tanks and the state's oldest stone and mortar structure, an Asistencia established by Father Serra. For more adventure beyond tasting the latest vintage, check out ziplin- ing and nature/wildlife tour experiences on the historic ranch. **https://www.margarita-adventures.com/**

The tiny downtown, only a few blocks long, hosts a few inter- esting antiques shops. Santa Margarita is also composed of rural farming areas and horse country, offering country drives out its remote roads; cross over the railroad tracks in town on Estrada Avenue (Highway 58) to begin a back-road drive through gently rolling hills, passing by spectacular spring meadows of purple lupine, the county's official flower, and cows grazing under shady oaks.

San Luis Obispo

San Luis Obispo, about 8 miles south of Santa Margarita on Highway 101, is the county seat and home to a branch of California Polytechnic State University. The friendly, tourism-oriented community of more than 40,000 people is embraced by green hills and clean air, and blessed with abundant charm and natural beauty. Begin your exploration of San Luis Obispo at its historic core, downtown. Get off Highway 101 at the Marsh Street exit or Monterey Street exit and follow the streets to the old mission area around Monterey and Higuera Streets.

San Luis Obispo was founded in 1772, when Father Junípero Serra established the **Mission San Luis Obispo de Tolosa**, the fifth in the network of California missions. The picturesque mission, an active parish church, sits in the heart of the historic downtown and is fronted by **Mission Plaza**, an idyllic creek-side public square, as well as the meandering San Luis Creek, which provided the early water supply for the mission. The plaza, with grassy park areas and graceful arbors, is the site of many community events throughout the year and is an informal gathering spot for picnickers and downtown shoppers. Scenic pedestrian bridges cross over the creek from the plaza to quaint downtown shops and creek-fronting bistros; several interesting sites are nestled around Mission Plaza's borders.

AUTHOR'S TIP: IN THE PINK

San Luis Obispo is famous to some people as the home of the **Madonna Inn**. *The fairy-tale, stone- and gingerbread-adorned hotel that aligns the freeway at the southern gateway to town is instantly recognized by its themed color pink, which continues throughout the ornate lobbies, restaurants and shops. The rooms are each one of a kind. They are themed to keep the fantasy alive. Did you know that the Caveman Room at the Madonna Inn was carved out of solid rock? It is just one of the hotel's many unusual, world-renowned guest rooms. Even if you aren't staying, you have to stop and look. Tourism officials will tell you to see the mission, the art museum and the Victorians, but you haven't seen the city until you see the men's restroom at the Madonna Inn! The men's restroom at the Madonna Inn ranks very high on the "must-see" list, but I don't want to spoil the moment for you. Just trust me, then get in line. The Madonna Inn is located at the Madonna exit off Highway 101.* **https://www.madonnainn.com/**

San Luis Obispo is the original home of another famous lodging establishment, the former Motel Inn. The Motel Inn, on the far end of Monterey Street, was actually the first "motel" in America. The "motor hotel" was born in the early 1920s when the automobile became the popular mode of vacationing. Today, the original inn has been incorporated into the popular **Apple Farm** hotel and restaurant. **https://www.applefarm.com/**

Across the street from Mission Plaza, at 696 Monterey Street, is the **History Center of San Luis Obispo County**, situated in the city's Carnegie Library. The structure, constructed in 1904 from sandstone and granite quarried from nearby

Bishop Peak, houses fascinating county historical exhibits that trace the area's growth from the Mission, Rancho, and Early American periods through the present. With a sense of San Luis Obispo's beginnings in mind, take a tour, either guided or self-guided, of the city's many historical structures. **https://historycenterslo.org/walkingtours/**

Exploring the quaint, restored streets of downtown San Luis Obispo and wandering its boutiques are a favorite pastime in the city. The 1884-constructed Sinsheimer Bros. building at 849 Monterey was a mercantile store operated by pioneer merchant A. Z. Sinsheimer. Boasting the only "iron front" on the Central Coast, it is an excellent example of the Italian Renaissance construction of the time. One block up from the mission, parallel with Monterey Street, are Palm Street and rich remnants of the city's original Chinese area. The **Ah Louis Store** at 800 Palm Street was built by Ah Louis, the patriarch of San Luis Obispo's Chinatown. The colorful landmark store served the needs of the Chinese laborers working on the railroads in the late 1800s.

Blooming old-fashioned gardens and lawns with a white Victorian gazebo mark the city's **Jack House and Garden,** the home of prominent citizen Robert Edgar Jack and his family, built circa 1875. The stately Victorian, located downtown at 536 Marsh Street (situated in one of the city's most unusual yet secluded public parks—the Jack House Garden) was deeded to the city in 1974. The interior of the elegant home, complete with original Jack family furnishings, art and books, has been entirely renovated in the style of the period and stands as one of the Central Coast's most outstanding "living museums." The idyllic nineteenth-century gardens of the estate, with a full catering facility, stage area and unique gift shop, are open for informal picnicking; docent-led tours of the two-story Victorian house are offered year-round for a nominal charge. **https://www.slocity.org/**

government/department-directory/parks-and-recreation/
jack-house-and-gardens

AUTHOR'S TIP: STICKY TRADITION

*Smack between two retail stores is a part of downtown San Luis Obispo that isn't featured in the tourism brochures, yet word of mouth manages to lure the visitor to this brick-faced alley. Old advertising signs? Hidden treasure? A historic happening? Not a chance. We are talking "ABC" bubble gum. ABC, meaning "already been chewed," gum is dribbled, spit, artistically designed, spelled, squished, draped—well, you get the idea. A walk along the shopper's alley from the parking area to the main shopping drag on Higuera Street will reveal all the splendor of **Bubble Gum Alley**. Local historians will tell you that the gum craze began in the 1960s when a few kids with nothing to do started putting their gum on a wall, and it just caught on. When you look at the immense collection of bubble-gummed sayings, initials, designs, and "statements" in this city full of history, culture, and beauty, do you see an artistic form of graffiti or a personal identity statement? Everyone has his or her own opinion, including me. I must confess that you will find my name and my sons' names lovingly swirled in the pink gooey stuff.*

If your visit to San Luis Obispo includes a Thursday evening, then set some of your evening aside to take in San Luis Obispo's nationally renowned **Farmers' Market** downtown. Each Thursday evening, four blocks of Higuera Street right downtown are closed to automobiles, and the tiny area is filled with colorful stands of farm-fresh produce and fruit, flowers, tempting food stands with barbecued specialties, entertainment and special events. The small-town extravaganza attracts from 5,000 to 7,000 people, who come to eat, socialize, buy the area's offerings, shop in the downtown stores and simply take in an old-fashioned piece of Americana that has come vividly alive.

LOCAL'S SECRET: DESIGN VILLAGE HIKE

"The rural borders of Cal Poly's university campus offer an "education" in natural beauty and student creativity. Discover Cal Poly's working ranchland by going up Brizzolara Creek. Hikers and mountain bikers can explore the interesting **Design Village** *designed by architecture students. You can also cross over the ridge to the Poly "P" or take the 6.5- mile Great Loop that drops into Stenner Creek Canyon."* http://designvillage.wixsite.com/designvillage

– Bob Kitamura, University Architect & Executive Director Emeritus, Facility Planning & Capital Projects

If you bring the children along on your visit, downtown San Luis Obispo delivers an original offering. Follow one-way Higuera Street and turn right at Nipomo. The **San Luis Obispo Children's Museum** at 1010 Nipomo Street was established through a tireless community effort with city cooperation. What began as an old transmission shop is now a wonderland of hands-on fun. Kids discover hours of imagination-inspiring entertainment that ranges from being an astronaut to "experiencing" a hurricane. The museum schedules a variety of special events and regular open hours. **https://www.slocm.org** /

LOCAL'S SECRET: ARRIVE HUNGRY

"There are so many great places to dine in San Luis Obispo, but one of our favorite places to eat in San Luis Obispo is one you might over-look. It is the **Spirit of San Luis Restaurant** *at the airport. The food is consistently delicious (especially the pancakes), the staff is friendly, brunch is served Sunday until 3:00 and it IS such fun to watch the planes come and go. You might even get lucky and spot a wild bunny in the bushes surrounding the windows!"* **https://www.sloairport.com/ dining-options/**

– Janice Kitamura, San Luis Obispo resident

From San Luis Obispo, head south on Route 227 (Broad Street) in town past the airport, and commercial development gives way to rolling green hills and cattle country. Shortly, Corbett Canyon Road intersects, veering southeast through velvety hills filled with grazing cows and oaks. Follow the winding road to explore the backroad vineyards and wineries of the lush **Edna Valley**. The bounty of hidden wineries makes for a wine-rich day of exploration and beauty. A wine trail map is available at the website: **http://www.slowine.com/taste/ orcutt-rd-corbett-canyon-wine-trail.php**

Photo by Derek Thomson, unsplash.com

LOCAL'S SECRET: EDNA VALLEY FROM ON HIGH

"My favorite thing to do to heighten my appreciation of the absolutely beautiful little valley I live in is take a short hike (1.8 miles) up nearby **Islay Hill***. At the top, you can soak up a breathtaking view of the entire Edna Valley. After the hike, you, of course, reward yourself by stopping at your favorite wine tasting room in the Edna Valley."* http://www.slowine.com

--Vicki Carroll, President of Hospice du Rhone,
https://www.hospicedurhone.org

Arroyo Grande

Eucalyptus groves and ranches lead to the charming old-town section of Arroyo Grande. The village's Branch Street makes for a pleasant old-fashioned stroll past small shops and restaurants located in quaint late-1800s structures. The "back" street of Branch is **Olahan Alley**, which follows picturesque Arroyo Grande Creek. Walk down Traffic Way to Olahan Alley and stroll the expanse of this back area, acquiring a century-old glimpse of the rear portions of the brick and stone structures with vintage lettering. Steps at both ends lead down to a tree-filled picnic area by the creek, and the alley passage leads to an old-fashioned gazebo and swinging bridge. Nearby, is the one-room **Santa Manuela Schoolhouse** built in 1901. The restored school is filled with books, maps, photos and blackboards; it is open for touring most weekends.

AUTHOR'S TIP: SWINGING BRIDGE

The 171-foot swinging bridge down Olahan Alley was built in 1875 by the Short family to connect their land on either side of Arroyo Grande Creek. The restored bridge spans the creek from downtown to a residential area. The only bridge of its kind in California, the structure is supported by four large cables and literally "swings" without much motion 40 feet above the picturesque creek. **http://www.arroyogrande.org/176/Swinging-Bridge**

Before you leave the historic village, stock up on Arroyo Grande's delicious berries and other fruit and produce by heading for its agriculturally rich fields. Fair Oaks Avenue off Highway 101 leads past vast leafy fields to Valley Road.

Santa Barbara County

https://santabarbaraca.com/

Highway I going south arrives in the tiny agricultural town of **Guadalupe** in northern Santa Barbara County. With just one main street and a sprinkling of Victorian homes, the small commercial stretch holds a surprising bounty of locally revered restaurants, mostly situated in the interesting historic brick edifices that line the main street. Most importantly, the town is the gateway to the **Dunes Center** which promotes the conservation and restoration of the **Guadalupe-Nipomo Dunes**, a National Natural Landmark. Stop in the Dunes Center to learn more about this natural treasure and take a docent- led tour. The Dunes Center promotes the conservation and restoration of the Guadalupe-Nipomo Dunes ecosystem through education, research and the support of cooperative stewardship. **http://dunescenter.org/**

Courtesy of Guadalupe-Nipomo Dunes Center

AUTHOR'S TIP: UNEARTH HOLLYWOOD TREASURES

These precious dunes on California's scenic central coast are the second largest in the coastal area of the state, spreading from Santa Barbara County to Pismo Beach in San Luis Obispo County. Although natural treasures abound within these dunes, it is the cinematic history that might be even more fascinating. It was here that Cecil B. DeMille's 1923 epic silent movie, "The Ten Commandments," was partially filmed. Archaeologists, historians and film buffs have been combing the sands that still hold the dissolving plastic-and-clay set that was dumped into trenches and buried by sandstorms decades ago. In 1983, a group of determined film buffs–inspired by a cryptic clue in DeMille's posthumously published autobiography–located some of the remains of the set, however, in late 2017 a perfectly intact 300-pound plaster sphinx head was unearthed by archeologists excavating the Cecil B. DeMille filming site. In all, 21 sphinxes graced the immense movie set; today, only a fraction of the treasures have been uncovered.

Open agricultural fields, rolling green hills and horse pastures dominate the drive on Highway 1 between Guadalupe and the junction of Highway 135 to Lompoc. This·backcountry stretch takes in the 1906 old town of **Orcutt**. Orcutt, named after William Warren Orcutt, was founded at the height of oil production in the Santa Maria Valley and was soon became a center of trade and shipping. Hungry meat lovers head to Orcutt for its legendary **Far Western Tavern**, moved here from its original Guadalupe location. As one of the foremost "Santa Maria–style" barbecue restaurants in the Central Coast, the restaurant's barbecue extravaganza features meat open-roasted over oak logs and side dishes that ultimately include the local pinquito bean, garlicked French bread and salsa. **https://farwesterntavern.com/**

AUTHOR'S TIP: FEAST ALA SANTA MARIA

*Santa Maria is the home of the Santa Maria Tri-Tip Barbecue. The tri-tip cut of beef is pretty hard to find outside California, and **Santa Maria** has perfected the barbecue creation using special seasonings on the triangular beef cut and an oak-pit fire. You can find the entree on most dinner-house menus in the Central Coast and even at spontaneous "parking-lot" barbecue pits.*

Lompoc

Drive by the rich farm and horse land of the Santa Maria Valley as Highway 135 eventually winds past Vandenberg Air Force Base and distant shuttle launch platforms, leading to Lompoc. A trip to Lompoc, once the state's flower seed capital, is a feast for the eyes and nose each late spring and early summer. Interestingly, 80% of the state's cut flower production comes from California, and over half of that comes from Santa Barbara County. In addition to flowers, the region now boasts vineyards which flourish in this lush, fertile valley.

Follow the city's North H Street to Ocean Drive (Highway 246) and turn west to discover miles of aromatic fields of sweet peas, larkspur, petunias, asters, marigolds, zinnias and other bright blooms along the highway and off various country roads. More than eighteen varieties of flowers are produced, processed and distributed each year; each May through June the area's fields are transformed into a magnificent living patchwork of dazzling color. Catch the annual

Lompoc Flower Festival held each June, which boasts guided tours through acres of flower fields, entertainment and arts. http://www.lompoc.com/FlowerFieldBrochure.pdf

Old Town Lompoc is often overlooked in search of blooms, but it is also "blooming" these days—in art. Take time to view the 40 murals that are hidden down alleys and on street corners and building sides. This outdoor art gallery curated by the Lompoc Mural Society is part of the movement to revitalize the historic old town. In addition, the **Old Town Heritage Walk**, a one-mile self-guided tour, showcases the city's history and architectural gems dating back to 1876. View the Mural Tour Map and Heritage Walk Guide at **https://explore-lompoc.com/directory/heritage-walk-lompoc/**.

LOCAL'S SECRET: EXPLORE THE BEACH CAVES

*"I love Jalama Beach in Lompoc! For centuries, part of **Jalama Beach County Park** was a Chumash Indian settlement called "Halama." But during Spanish rule of the area, villagers were taken to La Purisima Mission... Eventually, as more locals took to the beach for leisure, its value as a recreational gem was recognized. The Atlantic Richfield Company made things more official when it donated 23.5 acres to Santa Barbara County in 1943. To this day, the county runs the Jalama Beach County Park. One of the most spectacular attractions are the **Beach Caves** that can be accessed along the sand – during low tide – about a mile north up the beach."*

– Susan Bejeckian, Principal, SA/SB Public Relations,
https://somervillepr.com/

Highway 246 traverses bright-hued flower fields to Lompoc's hidden gem, **La Purisima Mission State Historical Park**. Turn onto Mission Gate Road, which leads you about 1 mile into the Lompoc countryside. Nestled among rolling hills and natural parkland is this sprawling California mission, one of only two in California operated by the state instead of the church, and number eleven in the chain of missions. A trip to La Purisima Mission is the opportunity to walk back through time and truly experience mission life as it might have been in this serene 2,000-acre pastoral setting with 25 miles for hiking and horseback riding.

The mission was founded in 1787 by Padre Fermin Francisco de Lasuen on a site across the valley from today's mission. In 1812 a severe earthquake, followed by a period of heavy rains, placed the once prospering mission in a hopeless state of disrepair. The new mission was relocated to its present site in La Canada de los Berros (the canyon of the watercress) because of the fertile soil and plentiful water supply for good crop production. Financial hardships, Indian revolts, and the secularization of the missions meant the eventual downfall of La Purisima, which went into ruin and private use through the years.

In 1934, the Civilian Conservation Corps stepped in to turn the mission ruins into the restored mission you can see today. The immense cultural restoration project of the chapel, support buildings, mission gardens and even the water system has been noted as "the largest and most complete historic restoration in the West" by Sunset magazine. Indeed, as you walk through the gardens and buildings on the sprawling acreage filled with orchards, gardens, and trees, you will be impressed by the authenticity of each carefully handcrafted replication. Stop by the visitor center for a self-guided tour pamphlet of the buildings and grounds. A leisurely visit might take about two hours and involves less than a mile of walking. The beginning of your stroll actually takes you across the original El Camino Real, the "Royal Highway," which veered through this canyon on its way to Mission San Luis Obispo. You will also see livestock in rugged corrals here. Displays in the various adobe structures, including the mission itself, are filled with exhibits of living history. All that is really missing are the padres, soldiers and Indians that made the mission come to life in the early 1800s. **http://www.lapurisimamission.org/**

AUTHOR'S TIP: GHOSTLY SIGHTINGS

La Purisima Mission does feel alive as you wander the grounds: The state park has been so carefully preserved that you can almost see the padres and Indians working the fields, grinding the corn and sleeping in their rooms. Well, one ranger there claimed he really did see a former padre in his bedroom. The ghostly apparition of a long-departed padre first appeared to him one night in the monastery building when the ranger entered to retrieve an article of clothing. The ghostly vision, dressed in nightclothes, was sitting on the edge of the bed in the bedroom known as the Captain's Bedroom. Both the ranger and the ghost were startled upon the encounter, but they must have worked things out, inasmuch as the ranger witnessed the ghost many times since and often discovered the covers of the bed messed in the morning. The ranger believed the ghost is that of Padre Mariano Payeras, one of Father Junípero Serra's successors.

Santa Ynez Valley

Following Highway 101 southward, you could easily miss the tiny town of **Los Alamos** at the northernmost point in Santa Ynez Valley. Surrounded by ranchland and pastures, the population 1,890 town has an Old West feel and a laid-back charm. Looming over the 101 at the entrance to town, is the newly renovated 1950's Skyview Motel. Now named the **Skyview Los Alamos**, the boutique hotel offers just 33 rooms with a restaurant, Bates, named after the famous Bates Motel in "Psycho." **https://www.skyviewlosalamos.com/**

For years, the **1880 Union Hotel** in town was the draw with funky rooms and old-fashioned bar, but only the saloon is open to the public today; the hotel is available for events.

AUTHOR'S TIP: FEED 'BIG BIRD'

Just outside of Solvang is a stop sure to get your attention—the large birds of OstrichLand. Peruse a gift shop with all things ostrich and emu related or purchase some eggs. But, for sure, partake of the ostrich and emu feeding. **https://www.ostrich-landusa.com/**

The roadway connects with nearby Buellton, then heads on to California's haven for windmills and wooden shoes—**Solvang.** Solvang means "sunny field" in Danish, and the small, European-like village is indeed enveloped in the sunny fields of the Santa Ynez Valley. The village was founded in 1911 by Danish Lutherans who were seeking a refuge for their way of life; today, the popular tourist destination with windmills, able skiver and wooden storks perched on rooftops boasts a healthy population of Danish-speaking natives. Most California tourists know of Solvang's Old-World shopping and bakery offerings, but a few worthwhile discoveries lie off the main beat of the village.

For a tranquil country canyon drive, turn on Alisal Road in town off the main thoroughfare, Mission Boulevard, and head south. A great bike or car ride, the country road slides downhill into the canyon filled with oaks. Along the shady road is the **Alisal Guest Ranch and Resort**, tucked away past the golf course, sycamore groves and grazing cattle and horses.

The Alisal, whose name means "sycamore grove" in Spanish, was once a prosperous cattle ranch; the resort's owner purchased 10,000 acres of the ranch in 1943 to winter his cattle, but decided to open the ranch to a few guests in 1946. Today, the family-oriented guest ranch offers endless daytime recreations such as swimming, games, horseback riding through the century-old oaks, golf on the 6,286-yard course, tennis and sailing, windsurfing and fishing on the resort's one-hundred-acre lake stocked with bluegill, catfish and largemouth bass. Children's programs are offered year-round. Nighttime recreation includes square dancing, guest talent shows, movies and romantic hay-wagon rides. https://alisal.com/

AUTHOR'S TIP: VISIT THE FALLS

*Shortly after the Alisal Guest Ranch, Alisal Road turns west, leading to the petite **Nojoqui Falls County Park**. Up the park road, you'll discover picturesque **Nojoqui Falls**, whose delicate watershed over limestone walls is even more spectacular after a hearty rainfall.*

Solvang is an ideal central touring location for all points in the Santa Ynez Valley. In just a couple of days you can sample the diversity of the valley and take in a bounty of roadside fruit stands along the way. Six communities and, within them, six distinct personalities, dot the oak-studded valley. Famous residences from the late Michael Jackson's Neverland Ranch to President Ronald Reagan's Rancho del Cielo have brought some notoriety to the area. But, it was the 2004 movie

"Sideways" that put the local, prestige wine industry on the map, capturing the area's rural allure imbued with ample sophisticated pleasures.

The tiny township of **Santa Ynez** near Solvang, just off Highway 246, is an authentic slice of the Old West. Set in the heart of horse country, its main downtown streets feature 375 horseshoes embedded in the pavement. Stroll along the historic Horseshoe Walkway to the Maverick Saloon, a colorful watering hole with live entertainment populated by local wranglers. The western-flavored main street, Sagunto Street, offers a small assemblage of gift shops. Also, along here are the **Santa Ynez Valley Historical Museum and the Parks-Janeway Carriage House.** The interesting museum hosts exhibits of Chumash Indian days, valley cattle brands and "living" pioneer-house rooms, as well as vintage clothing, dolls, china and antique memorabilia from the valley's earlier days. A charming garden courtyard offers machinery and farm equipment, as well as the turn-of-the-twentieth-century Santa Ynez jailhouse. The carriage house is considered one of the finest in the West and boasts more than thirty carriages, wagons and carts, in addition to stagecoaches, buggies and more. An excellent reference library with one-of-a-kind books and papers is located at the museum, as is a small gift shop. The first county branch library ever established in California is nestled between the carriage house and the museum. The library, built in 1912, is also the smallest facility in the state still serving as a public library. **https://www.santaynezmuseum.org/**

AUTHOR'S TIP:
THEATER UNDER THE STARS

Solvang is a romantic place, full of star-filled skies on summer nights in Santa Ynez Valley. A special treat each June through October is the town's professional theater offerings at the **Solvang Festival Theater**. *This half-timbered, open-air theater seats 780 guests for productions by the well-respected, Santa Maria–based Pacific Conservatory of the Performing Arts (PCPA). Though summer evenings in Solvang can be a little chilly, cozy blankets can be rented and hot drinks are sold at refreshment time. So, enjoy a combination of my favorite activities—superior plays, starry skies and cuddling with a favorite person—all at the festival.* **https://www.solvangfestivaltheater.org/**

The abutting towns of **Los Olivos** and **Ballard** serve up rustic charm with in-town tasting rooms, a handful of art galleries and a few inns. Make sure you stop for lunch in the area, at well-known bistro such as **Los Olivos Wine Merchant & Café** or **Sides Hardware and Shoes**—just a few steps from the town's famous flag pole. As the valley's oldest community, Ballard warrants a drive through its country lanes. Curve around the Ballard Store on Cottonwood to School Street, aptly named for its charming red schoolhouse. The **Ballard Schoolhouse**, with its steeple and white gingerbread, was built in 1882 and has been in constant use since 1883.

Foxen Canyon, just past the now closed Mattei's Tavern off Route 154, leads to prize-winning wineries nestled in rolling hills with panoramic vistas of ranch land. A turn on Zaca Station Road leads to the **Firestone Vineyard**, up a twisting lane overlooking acre upon acre of growing grapes. The sophisticated block- and wood-constructed tasting room offers tours from the lobby about every thirty minutes, with wine tasting following. North on Zaca Station Road, connecting with Foxen Canyon Road once again, the vineyard-lined canyon drive leads to the more intimate **Zaca Mesa Winery**. The wooden barn-like tasting room is nestled in the green hills among oak trees dripping in moss. Two large picnic areas with tables make for a good cheese-and-bread break in this pastoral, backroads setting.

Other notable wineries on the Foxen Canyon "wine trail" include the **Cambria Winery and Vineyard** and **Fess Parker's** own winery and vineyard. Cambria's attractive tasting room is open to the public on weekends and holidays and may be visited upon appointment on weekdays. Part of the original Tepusquet Vineyard that was planted in the early 1970s, the property is known for its outstanding Chardonnays and Pinot Noirs, which thrive on the soil and climate of the area. The winery is located at 5475 Chardonnay Lane, Santa Maria (off the Betteravia exit. Following the Foxen trail toward Ballard once again, you will reach Fess Parker Winery & Vineyard at 6200 Foxen Canyon Road. The interesting tasting room is full of Parker's coonskin legacy and wine souvenirs. **https:// www.foxencanyonwinetrail.net/**

Santa Barbara

The lush Santa Ynez Valley connects with Santa Barbara and points south by way of a pastoral, view-granting road that twists gently and often steeply through the hills. The **San Marcos Pass** meanders by picturesque Lake Cachuma and past flowing fields of spring and summer poppies and lupine. The orange- and purple-splashed hills cradle Arabian horse ranches, and the rocky cliffs that approach Santa Barbara give awe-inspiring views of the Pacific Ocean and the Channel Islands in the distance. The same pass, State

Highway 154, was traversed in 1856 by Frémont's California Battalion headed to Santa Barbara, ten years before the road was graded for wagon use. Along the way stop at **Vista Point**, with expansive views of the green valley studded with oaks and longhorn cattle. The view turnout is just below Cold Spring Bridge; Stagecoach Road, right after the bridge, leads to rustic **Cold Springs Tavern**, an out-of-the-way tavern that attracts a colorful cross-section of people. A little farther the winding pass deposits you directly in town, with convenient freeway on-ramps going north and south. **https://www.cold-springtavern.com/**

Just north of Santa Barbara is the connecting University of California community, **Goleta Valley**. As you turn off the Los Carneros exit on 101, fragrant lemon orchards lead to the area's historic park, offering a restored depot, a railroad museum, and a living museum in a restored home. The mustard yellow with brown trim Victorian **South Coast Railroad Museum** was built in 1901 by the Southern Pacific Railroad and moved to this site at Lake Los Carneros County Park in 1983, along with the Southern Pacific car that sits in front. Visitors to the museum will see working railroad communications and signaling equipment, and assorted memorabilia. **https://gole-tadepot.wordpress.com/**

A stroll through "Polly's Posey Patch" in back of the depot leads to the rural, tree-shaded grounds of the **Stow House**. The rambling white Victorian house, with lots of ginger-bread, French doors, shutters and a brick-stair front entry, was built in 1872 by Sherman Stow and given to the county of Santa Barbara in 1967. The impressive residence, originally surrounded by the La Patera Ranch, was reconverted to a Victorian home with lovely furnishings, wall coverings, rugs and artwork to serve as a museum as well as the headquarters for the Goleta Valley Historical Society. The house and adjacent Sexton Museum barn, which houses farm artifacts, are open on weekends year-round. **http://goletahistory.org/gallery/stow-house/**

AUTHOR'S TIP: OCEAN GLAMPING

The secreted northern Santa Barbara beach life is celebrated with some exclusive resorts, such as The Ritz-Carlton Bacara that dangles over the Pacific with outstretched vistas. A different take on overnight luxury is also situated directly along this slice of coast: **El Capitan Canyon**. *Some people call it "glamping," but I call it nature's most luxurious form of roughing it. El Capitan Canyon has running water, cushy willow beds, down-style duvets and, yes, a roof over your head. Nestled in oak and sycamore groves along El Capitan Creek, campers are treated to unique hotel amenities, such as bird serenades with your morning coffee.* **http://www.elcapitancanyon.com/**

On June 29, 1925, a giant earthquake shook **Santa Barbara**, and a city of not terribly unusual architecture crumbled in part. The months of rebuilding that followed brought an amazing architectural transformation to a city that was already blessed with inspiring ocean and mountain beauty. Through a carefully reviewed plan, Santa Barbara emerged in the following years like a charming Mediterranean village nestled between the verdant Santa Ynez Mountains and a sand-drenched stretch of the Pacific Ocean. The historical significance of Santa Barbara in Southern California is monumental, its structural treasures waiting for discovery on almost every downtown city block.

Santa Barbara is largely a city that can be explored on foot. In fact, the city has been designated a Gold-Level Community by Walk Friendly Communities. The Carrillo Street exit on

Highway 101 going south is a perfect starting point for exploring these downtown treasures. A 12-block area makes up the core of these historical finds and composes a self-guided walking tour, appropriately named the **Red Tile Tour**. **https:// www.santabarbaracarfree.org/wp-content/uploads/red- tile-walking-tour.pdf**

The Santa Barbara Historical Society oversees three highlights on the Red Tile Tour: the Santa Barbara Historical Museum, downtown, and the Fernald House and adjacent Trussell-Winchester Adobe, a short drive away. The hacienda-style museum, located at 136 East de la Guerra Street, was built in 1964, with a U-shaped central courtyard. The structure was constructed of 70,000 adobe bricks made on the site; the floor tiles were made for the museum in Mexican villages. The roof tiles, 16,000 in all, were also handmade in Mexico. Mementos include those of the stagecoach days and belongings of pioneer Santa Barbara families; also here is the research-abundant Gledhill Library, full of vintage photographs, maps, scrapbooks, rare books and official papers. The Covarrubias and Historic Adobes share the courtyard and historical park of the museum. The Fernald House and Trussell-Winchester Adobe are located at 414 West Montecito Street. The Fernald House is a fourteen-room Victorian mansion boasting period furnishings, distinctive gables and a handmade staircase. The adjacent home was built of adobe bricks and timbers from a wrecked ship, the Winfield Scott.

El Presidio de Santa Barbara, a state historic park at 123 East Canon Perdido Street (the intersection of Santa Barbara and Canon Perdido Streets), is the second oldest building owned by the state of California and the oldest residential structure in the city. Founded in 1782 as the last in a chain of four military fortresses built by the Spanish along the coast of Alta California, the site was blessed by Padre Junípero Serra prior to establishment of Santa Barbara's well-known Mission in 1786. Although the white adobe structure, with red-tile roof, chapel, excavation research and gardens, sits in the heart of downtown Santa Barbara, it is often overlooked by the visitor.

The Presidio, arranged in an expansive quadrangle, served to protect the missions and settlers against attack by Indians as well as to provide a seat of government whose jurisdiction extended from southern San Luis Obispo County to and including the pueblo of Los Angeles. It also served as a center for cultural and social activities, mirroring life as it was in early Santa Barbara; the most prominent structure was the Chapel, Santa Barbara's first church. The Chapel, as well as the Padre's Quarters, has been rebuilt with careful authenticity. Only two sections of the original Presidio quadrangle remain: the Cuartel, the guard's house, which is maintained as an interesting gift shop and museum with a model of the original Presidio layout; and the Canedo Adobe, a soldier's residence, now used as offices for the Santa Barbara Trust for Historic Preservation. A complete restoration of the entire Presidio quadrangle is planned, with authentic reproduction as it was in the 1790s.

AUTHOR'S TIP:
LEGEND OF THE LOST CANON

Perhaps an urban myth, but one worthy of historical status after 150 years of retelling, is the legend of the lost cannon, or the naming of the street in downtown Santa Barbara, Canon Perdido. It all started in 1848 with five mischievous teenagers who decided to steal and hide a 10-foot Spanish cannon that had washed up on west beach after an 1847 shipwreck. In the middle of the night, with the aid of a team of oxen, they towed the cannon to the foot of Santa Barbara Street, where the oxen gave out, forcing them to bury the evidence in sand. The theft was taken seriously by the American military, with a resultant edict by a Colonel Mason that if the cannon was not found, *all males twenty years or older would be fined $500. The mandatory fine was paid by a party thrown to raise the funds, and the boys kept their adventure a secret. The lost cannon finally surfaced from the sand ten years later and was hauled to the De la Guerra House for public viewing. The popularity of the tale of the lost cannon is responsible for the naming of three streets in this historic area: Canon Perdido (Lost Cannon), Mason (the Colonel), and Quinientos (500).*

By the turn of the twentieth century, there were 400 Chinese residents in Santa Barbara; the south side of Canon Perdido, between State and Anacapa streets, became **Chinatown**, featuring stores, restaurants, gambling rooms, opium dens, laundries and even a few brothels. However, Santa Barbara's most noted architectural structure has to be its Spanish Moorish–inspired **Courthouse** a few blocks away in the 1100 block of Anacapa Street. Also damaged heavily in the earthquake, the functioning center for county government was rebuilt on a bigger-than-life scale. The gigantic, arched entry to the courthouse building is decorated with elaborately tiled fountains and sculptures. Moorish-peaked doorways lead to tile-implanted corridors; a variety of tiles can be seen throughout. Take the elevator to the second floor Board of Supervisors rooms to view the ornate historical murals that cover the walls and ceilings. An elevator ride to the fourth-floor tower will reward you with 360-degree panoramic views of the city. Stand on the compass painted on the floor of the observation deck and look in any direction: The views past red-tile roofs are each inspiring. You are free to wander the building on your own, as well as to explore the free-flowing garden lawns, which are noticeably lacking paved paths.

With its many Hidden Paseos, Santa Barbara's shopping district is made for pedestrians. It's just a short walk from the waterfront up State Street under Highway 101 to the vibrant center of town, with its irresistible shops, casual sidewalk cafes and superb restaurants. If you get tired of walking, hop on the electric shuttle or, in the evening, flag down a bike cab. Car-Free Santa Barbara shares the **"12 Paseos Walking Tour"** here: **https://www.santabarbaracarfree.org/wp-content/uploads/twelve-paseos-walking-tour.pdf**

LOCAL'S SECRET: DISCOVER THE HOPPING FUNK ZONE

"Santa Barbara's **Funk Zone** *has become a favorite in recent years. Over the past few decades, this district, which spans the area between the ocean and Highway 101 and is adjacent to the Amtrak station, has enjoyed an upswell of boutique tasting rooms, cafes, galleries, and shops that cater to Santa Barbara's contemporary side. Converted warehouses and buildings decorated with graffiti murals and contemporary art pieces set the tone for this hopping section of town. Surfboard shapers, winemakers and up-and-coming chefs all practice their crafts here. Visit art galleries; shop vintage and modern home goods at The Blue Door; taste at the fun, hip Municipal Winemakers (whose wine club is affectionately known as Club Awesome), and enjoy a five-star dinner at The Lark. Walk the largest part of the Urban Wine Trail — a self-guided trail of 20+ tasting rooms representing Santa Barbara County wines — and easily discover why Santa Barbara's wine country is world class. Tantalize your taste buds with an Eat This, Shoot That! food and photo tour through the neighborhood for bites of artisanal eats at Lucky Penny, glasses of craft brews from Figueroa Mountain Brewing Co., tastes of Riverbench wines, and sips from Cutler's Artisan Spirits, the city's first distillery since Prohibition."*

– Visit Santa Barbara, **https://santabarbaraca.com/**

The foothill area of Santa Barbara is drenched in charm and history. Its most famous landmark is, of course, **Mission Santa Barbara**, aptly named the "Queen of the Missions," and nearby are the city's well-known Botanical Garden and Museum of Natural History.

Stearns Wharf in Santa Barbara holds the distinction of being the oldest working wharf in California. Take a romantic stroll or sign up for a whale-watching adventure. A stroll out on the wharf on one of the city's famous sunny days is perfection. The half-mile-long boardwalk, built in 1872, is dotted with a few restaurants and shops that range from an old-fashioned confectioner's store to a palm reader's den. At the far end of the walk over the Pacific is a compass boasting artists' views in all directions: the Channel Islands ahead, the palm-lined sand, the mountain backdrop in the distance to the north and the 1929-constructed harbor in the west. A huge gray whale hangs from the ceiling of the **Sea Center on Stearns Wharf.** Owned and operated by the Santa Barbara Museum of Natural History, the center offers a marine aquarium, and docent-guided tours include a visit to the touch tank, where you may view and touch a variety of marine animals found in local waters. The center, which focuses on the understanding of the marine realm around Santa Barbara and the northern Channel Islands, is open daily. **http://stearnswharf.org/; http://stearnswharf.org/Sea-Center/**

AUTHOR'S TIP: HIDDEN BEACH

*The city is known for its gorgeous stretch of sand in this area, which can become crowded on weekends. For a sand-and-surf retreat known mainly by local residents, head for picturesque **Hendry's Beach** (also called Arroyo Burro County Park) up the coast a bit. Take Highway 101 north to the Las Positas Road off-ramp and turn west to the beach. On the left side of the road* *near a towering bluff is Hendry's Beach, its parking area studded by graceful palms. The long expanse of sparkling clean, sandy beach, protected by the scenic bluffs, hosts birds that congregate in a small ocean inlet, and some grassy areas with picnic tables. If you are traveling with your dog, this is also a popular "dog beach" in the area.*

Photo by © Ellen Clark

Just south of downtown in Montecito is **Butterfly Beach**, also a favorite of locals for sunbathing, biking and walking. Although parking can be tight, Butterfly Beach is accessible by the bike path beginning at Stearn's Wharf. Across from the upscale Four Seasons Biltmore, the west-facing beach is known to attract its share of celebrities. Remember to bring your own snacks here since there are no food services close by.

Santa Barbara's pristine beaches are well-known, but the often undiscovered or overlooked parks and gardens of the historic beach city are verdant and blooming oases hidden in plain sight. Thanks to city-planning advocate Pearl Chase, horticulturist Francesco Franceschi, wealthy plant collector Ganna Walska and many more flora-and-fauna-loving residents, Santa Barbara's special gardens offer visitors a slice of solitude while surrounded by the history and natural beauty of "The American Riviera." Some of Santa Barbara's most impressive estates have equally impressive gardens. Several of them are open to the public, offering a glimpse into another world.

Casa del Herrero is a testament to how wealth and taste can combine to create incredible beauty. Completed in 1925, the Steedman family's 11-acre Montecito estate features a main house designed by renowned local architect George Washington Smith and extensive gardens created by a trio of local legends. Pines join palms to frame mountain views, roses bloom within frameworks of geometric hedge rows, and trickling fountains await discovery in secret corners. The gardens and the exquisitely decorated antique-filled house are open to the public by reservation only. **http://casadelherrero. com/**

Also, in Montecito is the exotic 37-acre **Lotusland**, an extravagant collection of gardens comprising thousands of varieties of rare and exotic plants. Begun as a private commercial nursery in 1882, the gardens as they appear today were largely created by Polish opera singer Madame Ganna Walska, who purchased the property in 1941 and served as the "head gardener" until her death in 1984. The most famous of her 17 gardens is devoted to the cyad, a rare low-growing, cone-bearing plant with frond-like branches, which grew during the dinosaur age. Surprises include the working clock and 26 animal figures in the topiary garden, the koi pond and stone-slab steps in the Japanese Garden and the more than 400 prehistoric plants – fossilized forms found in 250-million-year-old rock strata – known as the "jewels" of Lotusland. Open to the public by reservation only. **https://www.lotusland.org/**

AUTHOR'S TIP: UNIQUE PARKS

*A park lover's paradise, Santa Barbara has more parks than any other comparably sized area in the United States. They range in style from completely natural to intricately designed; from carefully tended to appealingly wild; from big to small; from oceanside to hillside. What they all share is an invitation – to relax, recreate, rejuvenate and enjoy. Marked by a restored antique carousel at one end, 10-acre **Chase Palm Park** is a family-friendly waterfront destination. From the carousel, follow the manmade stream past a turtle and duck pond to Shipwreck Playground, named for the play-size model of the schooner Winfield Scott, which sank off the Channel Islands at the turn of the century. Santa Barbara botanist/horticulturist Francesco Franceschi, who incidentally introduced zucchini to America, planted thousands of exotic trees in Santa Barbara. The 18-acre **Franceschi Park** is a soothing refuge offering city, ocean and Channel Islands vistas. However, the single biggest botanical attraction in Santa Barbara greets guests at the Amtrak station. The impressive **Moreton Bay fig tree**, providing some 21,000-square-feet of shade, is thought to be the largest of its kind in the nation. Planted in 1877, the tree is 76 feet tall, 167 feet across and has a trunk diameter of 12.5 feet.*

Carpinteria

Going south along the coast from tony Santa Barbara and Montecito leads to the surfer-friendly town of Carpinteria, population 13,600. The casual beach town likes to boast the "world's safest beach," but it also offers a bevy of nature and walking distance recreation, from local food stops to antique shopping. The area surrounding is additionally the largest producer of cut flowers in the country, filled with wholesale nurseries--with a couple open to the public.

The 110-acre **Carpinteria Salt Marsh Nature Park**, restored in the late 1990s, is one of the last remaining healthy wetlands along Southern California's coast. More than 200 species of birds make their way to this marshland. Follow interpretive trails or take a docent-led tour. **http://www.carpinteriacoast. com/salt_marsh.html**

AUTHOR'S TIP: HARBOR SEAL PRESERVE

*One of the most interesting secrets in Carpinteria is the **Harbor Seal Preserve**. The preserve is home to nearly 100 adult seals who give birth to their pups on the shoreline here. The protected stretch of beach is closed for several hundred feet to protect the seals and their families from December through May. To reach the rookery, take the Bailard Avenue exit and travel to the Bluffs parking lot overlooking the ocean. urn towards the ocean and go into the Bluffs parking lot; a short trail leads to down to the bluff, over the railroad tracks then along the bluff top to the preserve overlook.*

White-sand **Carpinteria State Beach** is the idyllic spot for surfers, swimmers and sandcastle builders. The gradually sloping beach has earned it the "safest" title. It is also a great spot to explore tide pools at low tide, which are home to starfish, sea anemones, crabs, snails, octopi and sea urchins. Seals and sea lions can be spotted from here, as well as gray whales during their winter migration. **https://www.parks. ca.gov/?page_id=599**

AUTHOR'S TIP:
WHERE'S SANTA CLAUS?

You didn't miss it. It is long gone. For generations, Carpinteria's Santa Claus Lane got the instant attention of coastal motorists who spied the giant Santa emerging from a chimney. Unfortunately, not much remains of the roadside attraction except a few of the buildings with assorted businesses that have nothing to do with Christmas these days.

Ventura County

https://www.centralcoast-tourism.com/ventura-region/

At nighttime a glowing cross, originally established by Father Serra, "hangs" high over the city of **Ventura**, a reminder of its historic beginnings. The city has experienced a great deal of commercial growth, yet Ventura maintains a small-town feel in the charming downtown area that has been restored around the 1782 San Buenaventura Mission. In fact, a trip to explore many of Ventura's historic beginnings may be accomplished in one area—full of interesting sites, museums, quaint inns, Victorian homes and businesses, bargains and small-town color.

Mission San Buenaventura, restored in 1957, was the ninth and last mission founded by Father Junípero Serra. You can pretty much park the car in downtown Ventura and walk a few blocks in any direction around the 1782-established San Buenaventura Mission to experience the charming, restored old town area that has taken on increased pedestrian traffic and energy. In addition to some second-hand stores that already populated the area, a new emergence of art galleries, public art, shops and bistros line Main Street. Walking on down Main Street, take a close-up view of the many intriguing structures and take special note of the intricate detailing, the dates stamped in the pavement and old signs on the sides of buildings. The revived **Peirano's Market**, now café and delicatessen, at 204 East Main Street is the oldest brick building in the city and was operated for more than one hundred years by the same family, first as a general store, then as a grocery store. Notice the colorful antique murals on the side of the building advertising Ghirardelli Ground Chocolate and 20 Mule Team Borax. Twenty-eight historic gems are highlighted in the city's self-guided Historic Walking Tour, which gives visitors an opportunity to discover the rich history of Ventura at their own pace. **https://downtownventura.org/wp-content/uploads/assets/HistoricWalkingTourBrochureFINAL-2011.pdf**

LOCAL'S SECRET: DOWNTOWN SHOPPING

"After brunch, I usually take a leisurely stroll down Main Street located in the hub of Downtown Ventura. For the antique and thrift store hunter, shops abound from Goodwill Retail Store (404 E. Main) to Arc Foundation Thrift Store (265 E. Main). A stop in at the Refill Shoppe, 363 E. Main Street (open 10 am to 6:00 pm daily), is also a must. You can sniff lovely aromatic scents and mix up personalized lotions, potions, and bath, home and beauty products. BYO reusable bottle or purchase one of the many designs that suit your taste."

– Maryann Ridini Spencer, award-winning screenwriter, producer, television and print lifestyle journalist, and author of the Best Book Award Winning novel, "Lady in the Window,"
https://maryannridinispencer.com/

A European-style hostelry in downtown Ventura makes touring the area easy with its strolling to cafes and stores. The **Bella Maggiore Inn** at 67 South California Street is just a half-block south of Main Street. The small, Italian-style inn can be easily identified by its ornate carvings. The intimate lobby with fireplace, comfortable seating, piano and breakfast area lends an inviting air. Guests can also enjoy the complimentary breakfast fare in the flower-filled courtyard with fountain, reminiscent of Tuscany. The tranquil decor of the inn features antiques, Italian chandeliers and artwork. The two dozen guest rooms are furnished in a simple Mediterranean style, with Capuan beds, shuttered windows, fresh flowers, and private baths; other amenities might include bay-window seats, wet bars, refrigerators and microwaves and fireplaces. When you book your room, consider asking about (or avoiding) Room 17. It is rumored that a ghostly resident, Sylvia, who hanged herself in the room's closet many years ago, is still "enjoying" occupancy there. The playful spirit, some say, is manifested in the scent of rose perfume and the pinching of gentlemen's behinds. **https://www.facebook.com/bellamaggioreinn/**

AUTHOR'S TIP: SEE ARTISTS AT WORK

A few blocks from Main Street is Working Artists Ventura (WAV), a $57-million, state-of-the-art artist community that meshes affordable living and working space for more than 100 artists of every genre. The entire LEED-certified community was built with the highest standards of green building technology, from recycled building materials to renewable power from the sun. A gallery theater and leased gallery space are on the forefront for WAV, but, for now, catch the artists at work on the first Friday of every month in First Friday Art Walks, a self-guided tour of galleries and artist studios. The arts eco-village is located at the

corner of Ventura Avenue and Thompson Boulevard. http://
www.wavartists.com/index.html

Nearby is **Art City Gallery and Studios**, established in 1983 as
a think tank for experimental sculpture by artist Paul Lindhard.
The outdoor gallery hosts more than 20 professional sculp-
tors and amazing stone specimens for buyers. The result
of more than three decades of evolution, the amazing creations—from desktop pieces to monuments—are all works in
progress scattered around a casual outdoor garden. http://
artcitygalleryandstudios.com/ventura/

LOCAL'S SECRET: IDYLLIC PATIO DINING

*"A visit to **Café Nouveau** at 1497 E. Thompson Boulevard for brunch is a
great way to start off any day. The cozy eatery, situated inside a 1920's
Spanish bungalow, has the feel of dining at a friend's home. The inside
décor is charming and oh-so-inviting, but I prefer to dine on their outdoor patio which features a Mediterranean style garden ambiance. The
menu features a variety of breakfast delights as well as lunch salads
and fish and meat entrees made with fresh, locally sourced ingredients. The venue opens daily from 7:00 am to 2:00 pm, and for dinner
Wednesday-Saturday from 5:00 pm to 9:00 pm. Make sure to check out
their award-winning wine list."*

*– Maryann Ridini Spencer, award-winning screenwriter, producer,
television and print lifestyle journalist, and author of the Best Book
Award Winning novel, "Lady in the Window,"*
https://maryannridinispencer.com/

Not all of Ventura's rich history lies within walking distance
of downtown. Just a short drive away at 215 West Main Street
is the **Ortega Adobe**, the sole remainder of the many adobes

that once lined the thoroughfare. Just forty years after its construction in 1897, the adobe became the home base of the Pioneer Ortega Chili business, which may have been the first commercial chili manufacturing venture in California. Emilio Ortega developed the fire-roasting process for chilis and originated canned chilis, salsas, and Snap-E-Tom vegetable drink. The restored adobe is open for touring from 9:00 a.m. to 4:00 p.m.; admission is free. **https://www.cityofventura. ca.gov/640/Ortega-Adobe**

LOCAL'S SECRET: DESIGNER BOUTIQUES

"If you take a jaunt down California Street toward the ocean, you won't be able to miss award-winning Designer Deborah Yahner's Ikat and Pearls Home Décor and Accessories Boutiques (Ikat and Pearls Boutique, Ikat and Pearls Home Décor, and Ikat and Pearls Deluxe) located at 24, 48 and 40 S. California Street). The shops feature the themes of rustic farmhouse, coastal treasures, and an art gallery."

– Maryann Ridini Spencer, award-winning screenwriter, producer, television and print lifestyle journalist, and author of the Best Book Award Winning novel, "Lady in the Window,"
https://maryannridinispencer.com/

A more prominent adobe occupies a peaceful stretch of farming land not far from the Ventura Harbor. The **Olivas Adobe**, once the bustling center of Rancho Miguel's 2,500 acres of farm and ranch land, is a large, two-story residence fashioned in the Monterey style, with a second-story veranda facing a courtyard. Most of the area adjacent to the six and one-half acres surrounding the adobe is the current Olivas Links golf course. The city acquired the adobe in 1963, restoring the original structure and adding an exhibit building. The rooms are decorated in antiques, donated or on loan, and the exhibit building hosts mural displays of Ventura's history. A stroll around the tranquil gardens of the estate will reveal flower, plant and vegetable gardens; a grape arbor dates back to the 1840s. The century-old vegetation includes a pepper tree and several eucalyptus trees, as well as a fuchsia that is the oldest and largest in Ventura County. The Olivas Adobe at 4200 Olivas Park Drive is open for selected tours and events; the grounds are open daily. **https://www.cityofventura. ca.gov/648/Olivas-Adobe**

LOCAL'S SECRET: FISH TACOS & CORNHOLE

*"**Spencer Makenzie's** in Ventura makes the most delicious fish tacos, and at $5.95, it is a meal and a deal. They also make an incredible ahi burger from sushi grade tuna – it is awesome. Fast, good and cheap – it doesn't get any better than this in Ventura. There is always a line, but it moves quickly. I go every time I am town – their food is so satisfying and you don't feel guilty eating it! They have one customer – who is 90! – who drives himself down every day from Ojai – for a fish taco. I kid you not. John, the owner, on his also famous "Throw Down" cornhole tournament. It is the biggest in the country, and it is free to attend. John is very community spirited, and it is his gift to the community."* http://www.spencermakenzies.com/

– Ann Flower, President, Ann Flower Communications,
http://www.annflowerpr.com/

The Channel Islands

A dozen miles off Southern California's Pacific coastline near Ventura is a sparkling ribbon of rocks that seem to float on the horizon. **The Channel Islands**, named for the deep troughs that have isolated them from the mainland for thousands of years, are home to more than 2,000 species of animals and plants, 145 found nowhere else in the world. Today, five of the islands, including their submerged lands and the waters within a few miles around them, are protected as the **Channel Islands National Park**, granting visitors resources found nowhere else on Earth as well as a look at coastal California as it once was. The best known of the islands is Anacapa due to its proximity and popularity for day trips. The five-mile-long narrow, rocky isle hosts dramatically steep cliffs and an easy nature walk to view more than 265 species of plants and a multitude of seabirds which includes the largest brown pelican rookery on the Pacific Coast. Santa Cruz Island is a prime destination for recreation. Incredible inland hiking with ocean views, world-class kayaking and explorations of an ancient Chumash village site make this island a good choice. The outer islands are Santa Rosa, San Miguel and Santa Barbara. **https://www.nps.gov/chis/index.htm**

LOCAL'S SECRET: CALIFORNIA GOLD IN THE CHANNEL ISLANDS

"Huell Howser loved the remote Channel Islands, so we made many trips to them to film "California Gold" episodes. We traveled to the rugged Santa Barbara Island to explore its history with a ranger, but I remember traversing the narrow trails above sharp drops to the sea. It was scary. We were invited to accompany a working cattle drive on Santa Rosa Island for another episode."

--Luis Fuerte, Producer/Cameraman, "California Gold"; author "Louie, Take a Look at This," https://www.amazon.com/Louie-Take-Look-This-Howser-ebook/; *Prospect Park Books,* https://www.prospectparkbooks.com/

The best part of visiting these islands is the diversity of offerings—from day tripping to extensive exploring. There is something for everyone, including enjoying a cruise around the harbor that launches the island expeditions. To get the most from your visit to the islands, first make a stop at **The Robert J. Lagomarsino Visitor Center** at **Ventura Harbor Village**. The visitor center offers three-dimensional maps of the islands, a museum, living tide pools, a movie and exhibits on the islands and native wildlife. The center also offers great panoramic views of the islands from its tower. **https://www.nps.gov/chis/planyourvisit/visitorcenters.htm**

LOCAL'S SECRET: PEACEFUL MOTHER'S BEACH

"If you relish a day enjoying the sun, surf and sand, I highly recommend **Harbor Cove Beach** *(also known as "Mother's Beach"). The views of the coastline (ocean and mountains) are just spectacular! This quiet beach is a great place to lay down a blanket and listen to the waves while you read, sunbathe or take in nature's beauty. Protected by jetties and a breakwater, it's also a perfect beach to swim or kayak. Parking is available past Ventura Harbor Village at the end of Spinnaker Drive."*

– Maryann Ridini Spencer, award-winning screenwriter, producer, television and print lifestyle journalist, and author of the Best Book Award Winning novel, "Lady in the Window," **https://maryannridinispencer.com/**

After choosing your destination, book a tour or cruise with **Island Packers**, the official concessionaire for the islands. They are also your resource for all authorized tour companies once you arrive, from kayaking to camping. Perhaps, you would rather keep your cruising a little more local with far-off vistas of the Channel Islands while enjoying dinner or yacht-style tastings of wine or craft beer. Island Packers, your purveyor of island jaunts, has rolled out special **Ventura Harbor Cruises** on select days and evenings. **http://islandpackers. com/**

Numerous trails traverse the unspoiled islands, providing visitors with spectacular hiking opportunities from the relatively flat, signed trails of Anacapa to the unmaintained and mountainous unsigned paths of Santa Rosa. On days that the concessionaire boats run to the islands, guided hikes are usually offered by naturalists. On Anacapa, take the easy two-mile roundtrip hike to **Inspiration Point**, which affords one of the most dramatic views of the national park.

Kayaking is one of the most intimate and adventurous ways to explore the park. An authorized park guide is strongly recommended to make the most of your adventure. **Scorpion Beach** on east Santa Cruz Island is a topnotch destination for sea kayaking with easy beach access, pure ocean waters and remarkable sea caves and cliffs to explore.

The Channel Islands support a rich variety of birds, distinct in many ways from the birds of the adjacent mainland. In fact, the Santa Rosa Scrub Jay is found in no other place in the United States, and the association of northern and southern species found here is not duplicated anywhere else in the world. The islands support the only nesting population of California brown pelicans along the west coast. Boat guides will happily assist in identifying birds on your boat trip.

The park is home to more than 775 plant species, and each island is floristically unique due to a complex interplay of factors, from elevation to topography. Head to Santa Barbara, Anacapa and San Miguel islands to catch the most brilliant coreopsis flower displays that appear each spring.

AUTHOR'S TIP: HOME TO THE NIGHT LIZARD

The 1-square-mile Santa Barbara Island is the smallest of the Channel Islands and is marked by steep cliffs and distinctive twin peaks. Like San Miguel Island, explorers, hunters, ranchers and the military took its toll on the island. Today the native vegetation and wildlife are recovering, and the island is home to a rare plant and its own reptile: the "Santa Barbara Island live-forever" and the "island night lizard."

A total of 23 endemic terrestrial animals have been identified in the park, including eleven land birds that are Channel Island subspecies or races. Look for the island fox, the island deer mouse, the island spotted skunk, big-eared bats and the island night lizard as you hike the back country. Island Packers offers a popular 3 ½ -hour Channel Island Wildlife Cruise with opportunities to view California Sea Lions, Harbor Seals and ocean birds.

Crashing surf, towering sea cliffs and dazzling floral displays set against the ocean have made the Channel Islands a nature photographer's haven. The photogenic **Arch Rock** on eastern Anacapa is a must shot during sunset, but any hike or boat trip leads to photo gems, from tail-popping whales to a calcified forest.

Isolation has made the tide pools of the islands some of the best in Southern California. Anemones, sea stars, urchins, limpets, periwinkles, chitons, barnacles, mussels and many other fascinating species can be found in pristine tide pools on all the islands. The most accessible sites are at Frenchy's

Cove on Anacapa Island and Smuggler's Cove on Santa Cruz Island.

The Channel Islands are home to the most well-preserved archeological sites on the Pacific coast, with a history spanning 10,000 years of continuous human occupation. Island visitors can explore the world of the native Chumash, walk the shores where European explorers landed, discover new tales from California's ranching history and witness the remains of off-shore shipwrecks.

Oxnard

Once called the "Land of Everlasting Summers" by Spanish explorer Juan Rodriguez Cabrillo, **Oxnard** got its name from the Oxnard brothers who built a sugar beet factory there in 1898. This once-quiet little town known for its plentiful fields of produce, mainly strawberries (Oxnard still produces 20 percent of the state's crop), is emerging as a real competitor in tourism on the coast. The city still gives claim to its strawberry production, hosting the **California Strawberry Festival** each spring, but its harbor area and its recent old town revitalization are bringing more and more tourists to sample its many other delicacies.

LOCAL'S SECRET: SURPRISING OXNARD

"Oxnard is one of those cities that you could easily miss driving up Highway 101 along the Central Coast of California. I was amazed to find such a charming city with beautiful, clean uncrowded beaches and the rolling sand dunes that add to the ambience. In the distance, you can catch a glimpse of the Channel Islands National Park located just 11 miles offshore, and in the evening take in the spectacular sunsets! It's easy to access the seven beaches that stretch five miles along Oxnard's coast – simply pull up and park and there you are! A native Californian, I knew the beaches in Oxnard were special when I discovered that it's almost like having your own private beach."

– Janis Flippen, Public Relations Consultant,
https://visitoxnard.com/

Between 1986 and 1991, the city's redevelopment agency and some of the area's most notable, historically significant families joined together to preserve and bring new life to a handful of turn-of-the-last-century homes and historical structures that would have otherwise been demolished for progress' sake, as well as a few finely replicated buildings, to form a city block known as **Heritage Square**. Finely restored, the over two dozen vintage structures include a former church (now the Town Hall for meetings, weddings, and special events), the former home of a Union Oil Company president and the Justin Petit Ranch House, which is now the home of the Elite Theatre Company, an intimate, small theater group. The Victorian-designed grounds of the square hold courtyards with fountains, colorful blooms and a central gathering area that is the locale of Friday night summer concerts, weddings and other cultural events. Self-guided and docent-led tours are offered year-round. **http://heritagesquareoxnard.com/**

AUTHOR'S TIP:
HOLLYWOOD BEACH

Oxnard's beaches are not as popularized as its southern counterparts in Zuma and Malibu, but the absence of towel-touching-towel bronzing bodies and wide expanse of sandy beaches and occasional dunes make them that much more desirable. Rudolph Valentino filmed The Sheik on Oxnard's beach and later bought a vacation home there. Clark Gable became his neighbor, throwing show business–style parties that granted the sandy expanse the nickname, "Hollywood Beach." Plan your stay at the **Embassy Suites by Hilton Mandalay Beach Hotel & Resort** *right on the sand and minutes from the harbor and marina area. The Mandalay stands as the only all-suite beachfront resort in California. Spread over eight acres of lush tropical vegetation, the resort offers two- and three-room suites with two marble baths, comfortable living room, and dining areas.* **http://www.mandalayembassysuites.com/**

The **Channel Islands Harbor** in Oxnard is also a jumping off point for Channel Islands explorations offered by Island Packers. It is also the spot to add some romance to your getaway with a Venetian gondola cruise. **Gondola Paradiso**, the only place in Ventura County where such a gondola experience is offered, winds cruise-goers through the harbor as well as the canals around Coral Island. **http://gondolaparadiso.com/**

Ojai

It is probably redundant to say the word "hidden" in describing the idyllic berg of **Ojai**. The town that is found on a winding road leading inland off the 101, on the outskirts of Ventura, is fairly well secreted in general. But, within the citrus-dripping artist community, there are bountiful hidden finds awaiting the springtime visitor.

Highway 33 meanders past Casitas Springs to the entrance to Ojai, lined with peppertrees and ancient eucalyptus. The valley is backed by the dramatic Topa Topa Mountains and drenched in citrus groves that scent the air with sweet-smelling orange blossoms. To grasp an overall glimpse of the area's natural beauty, follow Ojai Avenue about two miles uphill to a stone bench lookout that captures what filmmakers aptly dubbed Shangri-La in Ronald Coleman's movie "Lost Horizon."

The idyllic berg of Ojai, known for its art, is famous for something else each April when the town celebrates **Pixie tangerine month**—that time when its crops of late season tangerines are at their sweetest height which is cause for town-wide celebration in restaurants, spas and stores— almost as celebrated as the bucolic "Pink Moment" each evening when the sun dips behind the dramatic Topa Topa Mountains that embrace the valley. Due to Ojai's unique and enviable geography, the town has the ideal microclimate for late season tangerines; the sweet, seedless and easy-to-peel orbs are exclusively grown in the valley. Frank Noyes planted the first Ojai Pixies as an experimental crop many years ago. Today, dozens of farms form the Ojai Pixie Growers Association which gathers monthly to share information about the exclusive fruit, from harvesting to selling and recipes. Thousands of trees are devoted to the sweet, seedless fruit, and fans are growing wide and strong—from baseball stadiums to restaurants that seek the sweet citrus.

Not surprisingly, Ojai has an exceptional **certified farmers' market** each Sunday from 9 a.m. to 1 p.m. Find Pixies here through May or June from Friend's Ranch, one of the original growers. Or take a **Cloud Climbers Jeep Tour** that captures a birds-eye view of the beautiful patchwork of citrus groves that forms the landscape of Ojai. **http://www.ccjeeps.com/sb/**

Much of Ojai's history and charm is centered on its natural beauty and its resident artists. It's easy to see why artists find the enchanted valley irresistible. The area is bathed in ever-changing hues of light that cast soft pink shades on the surrounding mountains. The artistic flair of the town is apparent in the charming village, lined in handicraft boutiques, art galleries and artist studios.

A stay at the **Emerald Iguana**, nestled at the top of a residential lane and hidden under a canopy of native oak, sycamore and pepper trees, places you strolling distance from the village. The tranquil grounds, designed for adults, contain just thirteen beautiful accommodations, mostly stone- and wood- constructed cottages with fully equipped kitchens, living rooms, cozy fireplaces and graceful patios. A morning continental breakfast around the pool awaits guests each morning. **https://www.emeraldiguana.com/**

Just a short stroll from the Iguana is **Bart's Books**, an Ojai "secret" since 1964. Rain or shine, seven days a week, book-lovers haunt the outdoor patios that comprise the unique book store lined in shelves jammed with used, new and rare books, numbering more than 100,000. Need a book before or after hours? No problem. Select a tome from the store's exterior shelves and drop money in a slot on the door. **http://www.bartsbooksojai.com/**

LOCAL'S SECRET: HIDDEN BOOKS, BITES & WINE

*"**Bart's Books** is one of my go-to places in Ojai (along with **Ojai Valley Inn** – love that place), but one of my favorite culinary destinations is the **Ojai Beverage Co**. From the outside it looks like nothing more than a very nice wine shop. But tucked in the back, past all the rows of local wines, is a fabulous restaurant with a great beer and wine selection (crafted cocktails, too) coupled with a great menu with lots of locally-sourced ingredients. It's nothing fancy, but it's where you'll find the locals. In fact, we learned about it only a few years ago from one of the staff members at Bart's Books. We would pass it all the time never knowing what a great culinary destination it is. I almost hate to share it – it's that great! For those who have never been to Ojai, the sidewalks roll up early – a late night at the OBC (as it's known around town) wraps up around II p.m."*

– Elizabeth Borsting, Elizabeth Borsting Public Relations, Inc.,
http://www.borstingpr.com/

Ojai's 1874 schoolhouse-turned-inn embodies south of France elegance, only much closer to home. **The Lavender Inn**, just a stroll from the heart of the village, is embraced by flowering gardens and offers romantic cottages and one-of-a-kind guest rooms with fireplaces, fresh flowers, art and private balconies. The inn, with its own mascot dogs, is dog friendly. The inn's gracious veranda makes a heavenly spot to sip wine and nibble cheese in the evening or to enjoy a chef-prepared, buffet gourmet breakfast. Both repasts are included in the stay; herbs and vegetables are picked daily from the organic garden on the grounds to accent the inn's cuisine.

The Lavender Inn, with a separate cottage spa, is also the home of **The Ojai Culinary School**, offering innovative private classes and hands-on cooking demonstrations. During the town's annual Lavender Festival, the inn offers a "Cooking with Lavender" class. **https://lavenderinn.com/**

A lazy country drive off the main road leads you past stately oaks, ranches, and the perimeters of the **Ojai Valley Inn's** acclaimed golf course. For more than seven decades, the sophisticated resort has been luring city escapees to find rich history, panoramic views of the valley and signature Spanish Colonial architecture—all on 220 tree-shaded acres. The original 1923 hacienda building features guest accommodations redecorated in Spanish Colonial style with four-poster beds, carved furniture, restored hardwood floors and 1920s decorative tile. More contemporary additions feature suites with fireplaces and Jacuzzi tubs. Recreation abounds at the inn, from golf to horseback riding, and its new 31,000-square-foot spa, Spa Ojai, is superb. Designed like a Mediterranean village, it is a blend of curving staircases, courtyards, sculpted ceilings and treatment rooms with fireplaces. **https://www. ojaivalleyinn.com/**

Leaving downtown Ojai and heading a short distance into the **Meinors Oaks** end of the valley will lead to a dining spot worth investigating. **The Ojai Ranch House**, made famous locally by stars who slip away to the secluded restaurant for a gourmet meal, is covered in vines and mature plants. The small bistro is discreetly nestled at the turn of the road on South Lomita Avenue. Guests may be seated in an intimate inside dining room, but most come to dine on the delightful outdoor garden patio; a tiny bakery on the premises produces the special desserts, such as rum trifle and fresh lime cheesecake, and sells the popular date, oatmeal, rye and soya breads served with dinner. Fresh teas come from the restaurant's herb garden; try an orange bergamot or lemon verbena cup with dessert. **http://theranchhouse.com/**

Thousand Oaks

Getting back on Highway 101 South, in the community of **Newbury Park**, you'll come to the 850-acre **Rancho Sierra Vista Park** in the Santa Monica Mountains National Recreation Area, home to the Satwiwa Native American Cultural Center and Loop Trail. Park near the ranch and check the information board for a posted schedule of events. The map here will guide you through trails to waterfalls, a pond, a view of Boney Mountain and the frame of a Chumash Indian home. The Loop Trail markers identify plants and wildlife found in this Native American wilderness for more than 10,000 years. The trail leads hikers from the high-tech Conejo community to the Chumash "community" of nature. Regular events include talks on traditional Native American survival tools and skills, bird walks, tracking and animal signs and nature walks. https://www.nps.gov/samo/planyourvisit/rsvsatwiwa.htm

Thousand Oaks, a community submerged in oaks and rolling green hills, has experienced a bounty of development in the last several decades but remains an excellent jumping-off point for a side trip into an area frequented by makers of television commercials and movies. Follow Westlake Boulevard (State Highway 33) to Lake Sherwood and adjacent Hidden Valley for a leisurely country drive. The winding road looks over the lake with its small island, which was once a public recreational area, although rural, with boating, fishing, and picnicking facilities. The lake, flanked by rocky hills and an interesting mixture of residences, is now private.

The road levels out shortly, depositing you on a country road lined by miles of white picket fences, Arabian horse ranches, deep green pastures, and massive estates. You have probably seen this area a hundred times in car commercials or as the setting for popular television ranches; watch for a line of trucks and vehicles crowding the tranquil roadway, signaling filming in progress. **Hidden Valley**, a secluded home to many celebrities through the years, offers many side roads for exploration and an opportunity to see horse jumping and an occasional horse-pulled buggy. The main road through the valley turns into Potrero Road, ultimately leading to Newbury Park.

AUTHOR'S TIP: HOLLYWOOD HISTORY

*I grew up in Thousand Oaks, spending most of my school years there. When I first moved there in the early 1960s, it was a small, rural burg with open, rolling hills and one claim to fame: Jungleland. **Jungleland** was the training ground for Hollywood's famous wild animals. It was located on the main stretch of town, and roars could be heard in the early-morning hours around feeding time without a second notice from local residents. The public could wander through this unlikely "zoo." The animal compound made major headlines when Jayne Mansfield's son, Zoltan, was mauled by one of the lions. Reportedly, he was in the wrong place when photographers were taking publicity photos of his mother. Not long after the well-publicized lawsuit, Jungleland closed its doors. Clark Gable and Claudette Colbert filmed a scene in "It Happened One Night" at a lodge that no longer exists along the same main byway; Spartacus was partially filmed at California Lutheran University; and Chuck Connors rode the hills around Wildwood Park.*

Agoura

Just south of Thousand Oaks/Westlake Village is the suburban community of **Agoura**, not too long ago an open area of grassy, oak-studded hills. A portion of this open space is preserved today as a part of the **Santa Monica Mountains**

National Recreation Area; located within this national pre-serve is the interesting **Paramount Ranch**, once a bustling cowboy movie set. It seems nearby San Fernando Valley res-idents tired of horses galloping through their yards and gun-fighters romping in their gardens, so early filmmaker Jesse Laskey found 4,000 acres of ranch land full of every type of scenery needed to film the popular Westerns of the day—roll-ing meadows, oak groves, canyons, mountains and streams—and Paramount Pictures purchased the property. In the 1950s, the constructed western town and surrounding countryside became popular for the filming of television Westerns like Bat Masterson, Have Gun Will Travel and The Cisco Kid. The ranch's many moods have been captured in recent commer-cials and past television episodes of Dr. Quinn, Medicine Woman. It was also the locale for some of the filming of Helter Skelter and Reds, and, recently, Westworld.

Today, the fate of Paramount Ranch consisting of 326 acres (Paramount sold the property in 1946) is unknown due to recent fires that ravaged the Western sets. Check for the opening of the ranch for walking, horseback riding and pic-nicking as the area recovers. A self-guided nature trail leads up Coyote Canyon behind the western town, and the National Park Service offers a variety of programs at the ranch, including a historical slide show of films, filming action and Paramount from 1920 to the present. To reach the Paramount Ranch, take the 101 Freeway to the Kanan Road exit and drive 3/4 mile to Cornell Road; turn left onto Cornell. The ranch is 2 1/2 miles south. **https://www.nps.gov/samo/planyourvisit/paramountranch.htm**

AUTHOR'S TIP: EXPLORE MALIBU CANYON

*For a special dining experience, take an off –the- beaten path trip through scenic Malibu Canyon to a secret gem, **Saddle Peak Lodge** restaurant. Twist through the winding canyon roads via the 101 Las Virgenes Road exit a few miles south of Westlake Village until you reach tucked away Cold Canyon Road. A short way up the rural passage is this former 1970's roadhouse turned exclusive bistro. It is a real case of rustic ambience meets sophisticated palate, making it a popular celebrity hideaway. An amazing and extensive wine list has a perfect match for any delicacy on the menu from New Zealand elk or Nebraska buffalo to mesquite-grilled antelope. Not into wild game? Then, settle for the frontier ambience granted by antlers on the walls and a cozy rock fireplace while you enjoy traditional gourmet fare, from striped bass to filet mignon. A lighter menu prevails as well, with vegetarian entrees and house specialties that include the bistro's own cured salmon and special carrot soup.* **https:// www.saddlepeaklodge.com/**

Simi Valley

Thousand Oaks is linked to a handful of slightly more inland communities via Highway 23. **Simi Valley**, population 100,000, is a once sleepy town that has grown into a sprawling residential and commercial community. But its past is well represented in a tucked away historical park. The **R. P. Strathearn Historical Park**, located at 137 Strathearn Place, is a small "village" situated on six and a half acres of land donated by the Strathearn family. The Strathearn House, a ranch home composed of an early adobe and a Victorian addition with gables and bay windows, is fully furnished in period decor and open to the public. Also, in the park, with graceful peppertrees and dirt paths, are an unusual monument, the original tin ranch garages, an assortment of antique farm equipment, an old general store and the Colony House. The attractive gray Victorian with white gingerbread trim Colony House is representative of twelve such houses that once formed the little town of Simi. **https://www.simihistory.com/**

More well-known but nonetheless unique, is the ninth, and largest, in a series of presidential libraries maintained and operated as a part of the National Archives system, the **Ronald Reagan Presidential Library and Museum.** Situated on a mountain- and ocean-view site nestled in the foothills between Thousand Oaks and Simi Valley, the hundred-acre estate hosts the 153,000-square-foot Library and Center for Public Affairs, as well as National Archives and foundation offices. The Spanish Mission–style buildings, with central courtyard and fountain, are surrounded by native California plants and trees.

The library houses a complete collection of official records from the White House, personal papers donated by the Reagans, photographs, videotapes, motion picture films, audiotapes and even the White House gift collection. A 22,000-square-foot exhibit area contains visual and audio displays on the life of President Reagan. The library is located at 40 Presidential Drive, Simi Valley; operating hours are 10:00 a.m. to 5:00 p.m. daily. The library is closed on major holidays. **https://www.reaganfoundation.org/**

AUTHOR'S TIP: BE A REAGAN VIP IN WESTLAKE VILLAGE

Westlake Village, an off-shoot berg of horse ranch-friendly Thousand Oaks next door, is nestled between oak-studded Thousand Oaks and tony Lake Sherwood and just 12 miles from Malibu. The six-mile-square city, dubbed "the city in the country," was developed about 50 years ago as an idyllic master-planned community centered around an attractive manmade lake with shopping, golf, tourist attractions and beautiful lake-front housing. The village has become a popular zip code for many celebrities, but, for a weekend escape, it is a perfect nesting spot for enjoying attractions in any direction.

*The ideal spot to "nest" is the **Westlake Village Inn**, built by the visionaries of Westlake Village. Over the years, it has undergone a series of reincarnations, shining even brighter today after a multi-million- dollar renovation as an upscale European-style inn and a well-kept secret. The inn hosts spacious rooms and suites, all scattered privately on 17 acres filled with romantic Tuscan wedding gardens, a swimming pool, fountains and waterfalls, all adjacent to the public golf course. If you plan to experience the Ronald Reagan Presidential Library and Museum in Simi Valley, a pleasant 20-minute ride through the hills away, then consider the total experience with the **Air Force One package**, which includes a stay in the official Ronald Reagan Suite that contains memorabilia from the Reagan era, including limited edition presidential plates, photos of the President and First Lady in the White House and on their ranch, as well as an official jar of Presidential Jelly Bellies. The stay also includes lemonade upon arrival; two tickets to the Ronald Reagan Presidential Library, home of Air Force One; and a copy of The Reagan Diaries.* **https://www.westlakevillage-inn.com/packages/air-force-one/**

If you have ever seen a Western pre-1965, then you have already seen **Corriganville**. The original 2,000-acre movie ranch in Simi Valley has a long history of stars and location shooting. After many changes and closures, it is once again open to give the public a close-up glimpse of Old West movie locales. The ranch was originally purchased by stuntman Ray "Crash" Corrigan in 1935 for just $15,000. The ranch was a Western-movie location dream, with stark rocky outcroppings, a small lake, oak-shaded trails and rolling meadows. And in the middle of all this rustic beauty stood a 1937-built western town, with post office, saloon, church, bank and shops. The public got to tour the working movie ranch on weekends beginning in 1949, an arrangement that attracted some big crowds. In 1965 Corrigan sold the ranch to Bob Hope, who renamed it Hopetown. It closed the following year, and fires destroyed most of the structures in the ensuing few years. Hope put the land up for sale. Today, the park is home to five different trails that wind around the 246- acre property owned by the Rancho Simi Recreation and Park District. Choose from the Loop Trail, the Wildlife Corridor Trail, the Stagecoach Trail, the Hummingbird Connector Trail and the Interpretive Trail. **http://www.rsrpd.org/simi_valley/trails/ cooriganville_movie_ghost_town.php**

Fillmore

Highway 23 from Simi and Moorpark to the small community of **Fillmore** takes you through the heart of citrus country on a picturesque, rural back road dotted by occasional ranches, a variety of groves and eucalyptus and olive trees. Highway 126 links Fillmore to Santa Paula; the roadway is lined with citrus groves and fruit stands. At Toland Road is a charming red schoolhouse, built in 1896. The **Santa Clara Schoolhouse**, with bell tower, weathervane, turnstile entry and white gingerbread trim, is still in use. The school was the third one built to fill the needs of the farmers' families in the area and cost, without indoor plumbing, $2,634.35.

Sleepy, historic Fillmore was awakened by the devastating 1994 Northridge earthquake, and the downtown area was heavily damaged. Today downtown has been proudly restored, and the quaint charm has been recaptured. Take a walk through downtown and stop for a bite at **La Fondita Mexican Restaurant and Bakery,** which has been serving authentic fare since 1870. The **Fillmore Fish Hatchery**, run by the state and specializing in trout, offers self-guided tours daily. Just down the road from the hatchery is **Cornejo's Produce Stand**; wet your throat with freshly squeezed orange juice from the fragrant orchards that caress the town.

Walking the streets of downtown, you are transported to the early 1900s. The neo classical-designed city hall, adjacent to the Central Park Plaza, is home to fragrant rose gardens, fountains and the railway stop for the **Fillmore & Western**, a fully operational vintage train. The antique 1920's- style Pullman and restored dining, sleepers, commuter and baggage cars are all staffed by workers in vintage costume. Even if you have never been to Fillmore, you have probably seen the train. The railway has been used in more than 200 movies and countless television programs and ads. Special tours offered by the railway range from "North Pole" visits during the holidays to murder mystery dinner trips to antiques hunting in nearby Santa Paula. **http://www.fwry.com/**

Santa Paula

Santa Paula is a product of a remarkable era of growth and invention at the turn of the last century. When railroads opened up the west, a new populace arrived in the small town just as oil was discovered with the town's first gusher in 1888. The railroad, oil and citrus industries, and later airplanes and movie making, have granted the city a rich heritage. Enjoy its tree-lined streets, parks, Victorian homes and views of foothills across orange, lemon, avocado and walnut groves. A little surprisingly, Santa Paula reigned as the pre-Hollywood movie capital between 1911 and 1916, when Gaston Melies brought in early film personalities to star in his productions; today movie crews are a familiar sight in this picturesque community.

A stroll through downtown Santa Paula reveals why it was selected by the National Main Street Center to be the first "main street city" in California as a showcase for its historic, promotional and economic revitalization programs in the West. Begin a self-guided tour at the red railway station depot, which also houses an art gallery. **The Depot**, built in 1886 by the Southern Pacific Railroad Company, is the only depot in the county on its original site. The historic structure was used for the filming of the 1983 television miniseries "The Thorn Birds." Directly across the street is an impressive Moreton Bay Fig Tree, one of the few trees that survived an original shipment of Australian figs planted in the 1880s.

A walk down Main Street past its small shops takes you to the **California Oil Museum** at the corner of Main and Tenth. The corner Victorian structure boasts ornate carvings and decorations, and it served as the 1890s headquarters of the Union Oil Company. The company continues to own the structure, built in 1888, but has transformed the first-floor offices into a public museum hosting early oil-drilling equipment, tools and machinery. **https://www.caoilmuseum.org/**

Located at the tiny and historic **Santa Paula Airport** is another museum worth visiting: **Aviation Museum of Santa Paula**. The museum is composed of a chain of hangars, each one offering a different phase in the airport's history. Throughout the years, the tiny airport has been widely recognized around the world for its antique, classic and experimental aircraft, and the many famous pilots who have flown in and out---including

Charles Lindbergh and Chuck Yeager. **https://www.aviation-museumofsantapaula.org/**

Piru

Nearby **Piru** is a part of the original 14,000-acre Piru Fruit Rancho, situated near the base of the mountains where the Piru Creek and the Santa Clara River meet. However, most visitors come to Piru for the bountiful recreation of **Lake Piru**. The foothill lake recreational area is located in the Los Padres National Forest, next to a condor sanctuary and offers fishing, boating, water skiing, swimming, hiking, camping and picnicking.

Another attraction near Piru is the **Rancho Camulos Museum**, which captures the history, myth and romance of the early California ranchos. The setting for the 1884 novel by Helen Hunt Jackson, "Ramona," the 40-acre, National Historic Landmark is situated within an 1800-acre working ranch. The historic buildings include two old adobe haciendas, a chapel and a winery. Worth the visit, the museum stands as one of the best surviving examples of an early California rancho in its original rural environment. **http://ranchocamulos.org/**

INLAND VALLEYS & SOUTHERN SIERRA NEVADA

Inland Valleys

The central inland valley of Southern California, when combined with its northern valley area, ranks as the single most productive agricultural region in the world, providing more than half the fruit, nuts and vegetables grown in the United States. Bounded by mountains to the east and west, the mostly flat area hosts an abundance of early California history and natural beauty.

Tulare & King's Counties

Hanford

If you happen to visit **Hanford** on a Thursday evening, May through October, you'll encounter the tiny downtown resembling a movie set. Wander the stalls of the **Thursday Night Market Place** with valley produce aplenty, plus a beer garden, live entertainment, vendors, a petty zoo and more. The charmingly restored 1877 downtown is draped in hundreds of twinkling lights; its milling crowd of all ages visiting and munching on baked goods while entertainers work on informal stages; and, a few yards away, the quaint town square with old-fashioned carousel awhirl.

Even in the bright midday sun, Hanford stands as the epitome of small-town America and one of California's hidden treasures. As a certified California Main Street community, hundreds of volunteers work to bring the town center alive with activities. Most of the area worth savoring is within walking distance of the town square, at the heart of which is the vintage former courthouse, which now houses shops and restaurants and is surrounded by flowing lawns, called **Courthouse Square**. The hand-carved carousel on the lawn (moved from Mooney Grove Park in Visalia) was completely renovated.

Across the street at 325 North Douty is the **Superior Dairy**, a spot for hanging out for a giant-size, whipped cream-topped sundae or malted, whether you're six or sixty. Faithful customers come from all over the county to enjoy the homemade ice cream and the ambience, which is virtually unchanged since the dairy's beginnings in 1929.

If you're lucky, you'll be savoring those old-fashioned sundaes after a movie or special performance at the **Hanford Fox Theatre**, across the way at 326 North Irwin. Probably the best-kept secret in the Inland Valley is this "fantasy palace" built in 1929 by William Fox. From the street, the theater looks like any small-town movie house from the 1930s, but one step inside and you've entered another era, when a movie premiere was a front-page event and everyone gathered for the festivities. Restored to its 1929 elegance, the Hanford Fox Theatre is one of only thirty-three remaining "atmospheric" theaters in the nation. The 1,000-seat theater transports its patrons to a romantic Spanish courtyard, surrounded by tile-covered buildings with lighted windows, balconies and turrets, and the original oil-painted mural screen creates a backdrop of a Spanish village with a church bell tower, cypress trees and terra-cotta-roofed buildings in the distance. The ceiling twinkles with "stars," a crescent moon lights the European "sky," and you can almost hear a fountain gurgle placidly a few feet away. **http://www.foxhanford.com/**

Not all the history in Hanford is centered on its historic downtown area. A short drive away on the east edge of the city is **China Alley,** containing several interesting buildings established by the Chinese immigrants who moved to the San Joaquin Valley in the late 1800s. **https://www.chinaalley.com/**

The **Taoist Temple** is one of the oldest Chinese temples in the United States, built in 1893; it provided free room and board to any Chinese person traveling through the area seeking employment in the vineyards, in the orchards or on the railroad. At one time the temple also housed a school. The first floor of the building now holds a gift shop and a small museum displaying artifacts from early-twentieth-century Hanford's Chinese history. Tours of the brick building, with its original teakwood and marble chairs, altars, embroideries, and more, are handled by the Taoist Temple Preservation Society by appointment only. **https://www.chinaalley.com/taoist-temple/**

AUTHOR'S TIP: BEWARE OF THE TULE

If you travel to the Central Valley during the winter months, be prepared for a unique weather phenomenon that can mean dangerous driving conditions. The "tule fog" that sweeps the valley has caused massive car pileups. Named for the Native American Tule tribe, the thick, low-lying cloud cover makes morning travel especially difficult.

Visalia

A twenty-minute ride from Hanford takes you to **Visalia**, a charming valley town that is growing by leaps and bounds; along with this growth is a blooming tourism business. The city is known as the "Gateway to Sequoia National Park" because of its location as the only major city before the park, 46 miles away. But Visalia has many other things to offer, as well.

The area's fertile farming heritage is celebrated with festivals, tastings and farm-to-fork culinary experiences. Visit in early spring to see the hills vibrant with blossoming fruit trees and smell the sweet aroma of citrus across the valley floor. In the fall, look for pumpkin patches and fields of yellow corn. And, many locally owned restaurants build their menus around the fresh taste of fruits and veggies—straight from the farm to their kitchens.

The agricultural town offers a dose of historical charm as well with several neighborhoods boasting superior early twentieth-century architecture. Take a **self-guided tour** and read about the homes and businesses that first set-tled modern-day Visalia. **https://www.visitvisalia.com/visalia-historic-walking-tour**

All this meandering may fire up your appetite for a special meal, and Visalia is famous in the valley for such a restau-rant. Don't rush your meal at **The Southern Pacific Depot**; you won't miss your "train" here. You'll just feel like you're in between stops. The restored 1890s Southern Pacific depot at 207 East Oak Street (near the train tracks, of course) has been transformed into a unique dining spot. Step through the massive doors; note the stained glass fashioned for the depot from church ruins, and enter the lounge with loco-motive engine light. The Dome Room, with multiple works of stained glass, train memorabilia and tables decorated in old train stock shares, is the main dining area, where the popular luncheon fare of sandwiches, salads, and specialties is served, as are steak and seafood dinners. **http://depotvisa-lia.com/about.html**

A visit to **Mooney Grove Park** is a step back in time in the city, when residents spent their leisure time on paddleboats and picnicking under massive oaks. Established in 1909, Mooney Grove Park hosts the remainder of the great oak forest that once existed in that area. At the entrance to the park is a bronze replica of the famed statue End of the Trail. The original statue actually resided in the park for many years. Ancient oaks still caress the landscape of the expansive parkland that is looking forward to needed renovation, which also boasts a lake with fishing, arbored picnic areas and the Tulare County Museum. The museum offers a small pioneer "town" grouping of buildings and machinery with interesting items from valley history. **https://tularecountyparks.org/park-cards/mooney-grove-park/**

Nine miles off Highway 99 on the way from Porterville to Bakersfield is **Allensworth,** one of the most interesting ghost towns in California. Allensworth is located about forty-five minutes northwest of Bakersfield. Unlike most of California's other ghost towns, this community was not established during the search for gold or silver, nor was it abandoned due to the depletion of the precious minerals or to natural destruction. Born into slavery, Allen Allensworth escaped during the Civil War, retiring in 1906 with the rank of lieutenant colonel as the highest-ranking black officer of his time. Hoping to create a place where blacks could own property and avoid discrimination, Colonel Allensworth established this town in 1908, on a site boasting several artesian wells. The diversion of water to the other agricultural areas in the valley gradually dried the flowing wells, and, by the thirties and forties, the inhabitants of the once bustling town were forced to seek work elsewhere. The town is now a state historic park, the **Colonel Allensworth State Historic Park**. The California Department of Parks and Recreation is now in charge of restoring the town's appearance to what it was when the courageous black pioneers first settled.

The visitor center is open from 10:00 a.m. to 4:00 p.m. daily and is a good starting point for viewing the seven restored historical buildings of the town, thanks to a thirty-minute film on its history. Nearby is the restored Allensworth School and the home of Colonel and Mrs. Allensworth. Walking or driving through the streets of the town reveals several remaining structures, a few restored with push-button "personal" accounts of the life and people who worked and resided there. Several signs with the original floor plans, photographs, and information on original town structures sit on lots awaiting reconstruction in this worthwhile project. The wide-open grounds of the state park offer covered picnic areas and quiet, peaceful countryside. **http://www.parks. ca.gov/?page_id=583**

Kern County

Bakersfield

California's country music capital is located in the southern San Joaquin Valley town of **Bakersfield**, also important for its oil, cattle and agricultural production. The city is the Kern County seat and is growing vigorously.

A visit to Bakersfield is not complete without celebrating its country music heritage, which gets its roots from Dust Bowl migration days. Now visitors and locals alike have the opportunity to celebrate in style at **Buck Owens' Crystal Palace**. What has been referred to as "hillbilly deluxe," this emporium contains musical showcases and a museum. The 550-seat frontier-style theater with circular-tiered seating is impressive, with not a single country music ornament overlooked.

Legendary country star Buck Owens, who spent a fortune building the palace, began his career in Bakersfield playing in honky-tonks. He returned to his roots to play again in his own palace with his Buckaroos until spring 2006. On March 24, 2006 he told the Buckaroos to play without him; he was heading home. Walking to his car, he encountered a couple from Bend, Oregon who told him they'd driven 700 miles just to see Buck perform. He changed his mind and played his usual 90-minute set and shared the story of the encounter with the audience. When the performance ended, he drove to his ranch, went to bed and died in his sleep in the early morning.

His family and Foundation continue to honor his legacy, celebrating his life by carrying on the operation of the Crystal Palace the way they know he would have wanted. His music has become something transcendent and timeless, still fresh and influential over half a century later. Those who have followed the career of Owens and his Buckeroos will especially delight in the museum displays here: his embroidered jackets, the official Hee Haw lunchbox and one of his original Fender guitars. The food is good beef fare. Buck Owens' Crystal Palace is located at 2800 Buck Owens Boulevard. **https:// www.buckowens.com/**

Hitch your buggy to a post and step back a hundred years in time to walk through California's largest outdoor historical museum. A sixteen-acre assemblage of buildings from Kern County's pioneer days makes up Bakersfield's **Kern County Museum** with its own "pioneer village" at 3801 Chester Avenue. Considered by local educators to be one of the most valuable study assets in the county, this "living museum," which demonstrates the manner in which the people lived, worked and enjoyed themselves, offers fifty-eight reconstructed or renovated homes, stores, offices and more to investigate. The tree-lined streets of the village lack all but the real mid-1850s inhabitants to be authentic. Special events throughout the year, such as "Safe Halloween," when children may trick-or-treat from house to house in the tiny town and enjoy a Victorian haunted mansion; and Christmas, when the streets and buildings are decorated in early-twentieth-century glitter and a holiday gala is presented, help support the ever-growing museum. The Kern County Museum connects to the **Lori Brock Discovery Center**, where children of "all ages" can have adventures through Kid City or discover the world of science in the Gadgets and Gizmos exhibit. This participatory museum also features changing exhibits so that every visit can be a new hands-on experience. Admission to the Kern County Museum also includes entrance to the children's museum. **https://kerncountymuseum.org/**

AUTHOR'S TIP:
BASQUE CUISINE CAPITAL

Bakersfield may be known as the country music capital of the state, but it is also known for its Basque cuisine. The city's more than 3,500 Basque residents are represented by an array of restaurants offering family-style, multicourse feasts. The 1893 Noriega Hotel is the oldest and most famous of the city's Basque eateries, but you'll discover more of the hearty feasts in the Old Town Kern neighborhood—also known as the Basque Block, which offers the largest concentration of Basque restaurants in the country.

A local teacher in Bakersfield was responsible for starting a unique museum dedicated to the animals and plants of California. The **California Living Museum (CALM)** is a one-of-a-kind experience in the area between Los Angeles and Fresno. The nonprofit museum, funded mainly through community donations, now offers several animal exhibits (all the animals are non-releasable and on loan from the Department of Fish and Game or the U.S. Fish and Wildlife Service), including a children's petting zoo area and a waterfowl grotto with wild ducks and geese in a natural setting. Make sure you check out the bear cub exhibit. The riparian area is an artificial stretch of river simulating the Kern River flow from the high mountain areas to the valley floor; the plants are identified, and the area provides a refreshingly pleasant stroll. The recently added California Coast Room, located just off CALM's education center and gift shop, features a 10-foot aquatic touch tank, housing numerous sea creatures such as snails, crabs, urchins, sea slugs and sea stars. CALM's Education Center is located in a 6,000-square-foot ranch guest house that was donated and moved to the site in 1983. The building houses administrative offices, a gift shop, a library, classroom and laboratory areas, and fascinating natural history exhibits. **http://calmzoo.org/**

AUTHOR'S TIP: DUST BOWL ROOTS

Thousands of farmers left their drought-depleted, wind-ravished farms in Oklahoma during the Depression to find new farmland out west. Many of these immigrants found their way to the rich farm areas of the San Joaquin Valley. Although they left poverty behind them, many were exploited by large California landowners. John Steinbeck described the Dust Bowl immigrants' plight in his Pulitzer Prize–winning novel The Grapes of Wrath. The Okie capital of California is Bakersfield, which was founded by Thomas Baker, who planned a canal that would link Kern Lake with the San Francisco Bay. The Okie influence is still alive in Bakersfield and surrounding farming communities. Country singer Merle Haggard, who is known for his hit "I'm Proud to Be an Okie from Muskogee," hails from the Bakersfield suburb of Oildale.

Tehachapi

Historians can't quite agree about the origin of the name **Tehachapi**. Either it is derived from an Indian word meaning "sweet water and many acorns," or it means "windy place." Both appear to be accurate descriptions for this town on Highway 58 about 40 miles from Bakersfield. If Tehachapi meant "land of the miraculous railroad climb," that, too, would be fitting, for what is known as the **Tehachapi Loop** is definitely noteworthy in this area.

To get a good view of the loop, both close-up and from a spectacular vista point, take a side trip off Highway 58 to Keene. The winding road through and beyond Keene takes you next to and above a series of railroad tunnels and track to California Historical Landmark 508, which oversees the intricate railroad network from 1,000 feet up. The historical monument reads in part: "From this spot may be seen a portion of the world-renowned 'loop.' It was completed in 1876. . . . In gaining elevation around the central hill of the loop, a 4,000-foot train will cross 77 feet above its rear cars in the tunnel below."

AUTHOR'S TIP:
CAMEL HEADQUARTERS

At the summit of the Tejon Pass in the Tehachapi Mountains south of Bakersfield is the tiny town of **Lebec** (population 400). The town's claim to fame is its beginnings as the headquarters of the U.S. Camel Corps. From 1854 to 1864 the army used the camels to carry supplies from Texas to the heart of Apache country. Living history presentations and Civil War reenactments are held in Lebec at the restored fort.

You don't have to be a railroad buff to be interested in Tehachapi. The fresh, clean air of this 4,000-foot-elevation town is reason enough, and together with the area's other lure, apples, it is a combination hard to beat for a city-worn traveler. Several apple orchards open each September for picking and buying the fruit, and the annual **Tehachapi Apple Festival** held in October is a highlight. Be warned that apples are often in short supply by festival time. Check with Pulford Appletree Orchard, one of the most notable in the area, to gauge the best time to visit. **http://www.pulfordapple-treeorchard.com/**

AUTHOR'S TIP:
THE 'OTHER' ROSE PARADE

Acres and acres of roses and rose trees in brilliant rainbow colors paint your path on the back road to Bakersfield along Highway 43 on the way to Delano. Going this route, you will reach **Wasco**, *a small agricultural town that boasts its own Rose Festival and Rose Parade the first weekend after Labor Day. The event is less elaborate than the Pasadena version but nonetheless authentic, with rose-covered floats and a queen pageant.*

Hidden in the mountains near Tehachapi is a special family-owned cattle ranch that offers overnight hospitality and good, plentiful food to visitors a portion of the year. The **Quarter Circle U Rankin Ranch** in Walker's Basin was founded in 1863 and stands as one of the largest and oldest privately-owned cattle ranches in the state. History abounds at the 31,000-acre ranch, established by Walker Rankin Sr., who arrived from Pennsylvania in the early 1860s and was responsible for first bringing the white-faced Hereford cattle to this part of the West. The ranch is a member of the California 100 Year Club, open to ranches with one-family owners for one hundred years or more, and the Rankin Ranch is well into its second century. Staying at the Quarter Circle U Rankin Ranch has been compared to living a part in television's The Big Valley show. Guests may ride on horseback over meadows and mountains, fish for rainbow trout from little Julia Lake (and have them fried up for breakfast), play horseshoes and enjoy old-fashioned cookouts. More modern pastimes include tennis, swimming, volleyball and shuffleboard. The family establishment offers a wonderful children's program with picnics, crafts, rides and parties during school vacations. The intimate group of guests, limited to forty, enjoys the ambience of the main ranch house, furnished with family antiques, historic mementos and books. Be sure to reserve early for this family-run ranch that has a loyal following. **https://www.rankinranch.com/**

Southern Sierra Nevada

The Sierra Nevada that gently hug the Inland Valley are dramatic rises marked by the towering giants of sequoia, crystal lakes and waterfalls, wildflower fields, austere wilderness and small foothill and mountain towns that offer peaceful surroundings and hospitality. It is not difficult to find oneself off the beaten path in any of these areas, but the following information might give you some ideas for exploring, a base for venturing out and discovering some of California's nearly untouched natural beauty.

Three Rivers

A scenic way to reach Sequoia and Kings Canyon National Parks takes you through the Inland Valley town of Visalia to the petite town of **Three Rivers**. The artists' haven of Three

Rivers is nestled along the Kaweah River; the small town boasts some distinctive artwork and remnants of what was to be utopia for a group of idealists in the 1880s. The colony no longer exists, but the tiny vintage post office still does, and the residents pick up their mail from the boxes there just as they did in 1890.

History aside, current-day Three Rivers has a stop worthy of a side trip—**Reimer's**. The almost edible-looking, ginger-bread-bedecked building in red and white looks a lot like its contents: homemade candies and ice cream and year-round Christmas delights. Reimers uses only Guittard and Nestlé chocolates and has a following of loyal mail-order chocolate buyers who claim his candy is the best. Reimer's also offers a large cream store that features their own homemade creations. Around Christmas Reimers also makes a heavenly stollen, which can also be sent around the world. **http://www.reimerscandies.com/**

For a moderately priced and cozy overnight stay in Three Rivers, try an intimate cottage overlooking mountains, meadows and fruit orchards or a bed-and-breakfast stay in a contemporary redwood home that includes a gourmet breakfast. The **Cort Cottage**, just four miles from the entrance to Sequoia National Park, offers a very private stay in a contemporary wooden cottage with a large deck and panoramic views, a kitchen with coffee and tea and a morning breakfast to go with the eggs supplied in the cottage's full kitchen. **http://www.cortcottage.com/**

The giant sequoias of **Sequoia National Park** have endured for thousands of years in the face of natural disasters and man's indifference—they can make your troubles seem small. Join in one of the campfire programs and hear the story of their survival under the starlit sky. Sequoia and Kings Canyon National Parks together make up more than 800,000 acres of wilderness with a minimum of roads. The opportunity to create your own wilderness adventure among these 200-foot giants awaits, if that is what you choose, or the parks will provide you with films, displays, ranger-led or pamphlet-led explorations and more. Probably the best place to begin is in the Giant Forest at the main Lodgepole Tourist Center.

AUTHOR'S TIP: EXPLORE MINERAL KING'S WILDERNESS

*If Sequoia and Kings Canyon National Parks still seem too populated to warrant a real wilderness escape, then take the winding road 25 miles southeast of Three Rivers to **Mineral King**. This untouched area contains some of the most exquisite natural beauty the Sierra Nevada has to offer. You may know the name from past publicized lawsuits involving a proposed ski development by the Walt Disney Corporation in this otherwise untouched area. The ski development was opposed, and Congress has since transferred the area to Sequoia National Park for management. Mineral King, so named for the silver and ore strikes that men dreamed were there but that never materialized, offers open subalpine meadows and towering timber-lined peaks. Hikers can view the rustic area by reaching one of the lake basins that surround the valley floors; trails from the valley floor are all quite steep. Note: Facilities at Mineral King are limited.*

The list of natural wonders to take in is quite long at these parks, but one visit that more than hints at uniqueness is the ranger-led tour of **Crystal Cave**, just below the Giant Forest. Discovered by two fishermen in 1918, the cave is now open to the public from late May through the end of September. Cave visitors hike along scenic Cascade Creek on a nature trail lined with evergreen woodland and waterfall views. Inside, visitors are treated to a fifty-minute tour of exciting crystalline marble formations, dramatic stalactites and stalagmites and gurgling rivers. Take along a sweater since the air is chilly, and keep your hands to your sides to preserve the precious mineral makeup of the cave. Children are welcome on the tour, but be warned that the return hike is uphill and takes some endurance. Resting spots are nicely placed, and sturdy shoes help. Tours run on the hour or half-hour depending on the dates. **https://www.nps.gov/seki/index.htm**

Lone Pine

The **Lone Pine area** is not far from Death Valley on Highway 395, tempting visitors with its own brand of mountain beauty. You may not know the **Alabama Hills** by name, but when you see the weather-beaten rock formations of the heavily mined hills, you may recognize them from numerous movies (more than 250) and commercials. The hills are located just northwest of the small town of Lone Pine. Each fall, Lone Pine celebrates its moviemaking history with the **Lone Pine Film Festival**. This unique event, begun in 1990, features almost continuous movies (of films made in the Alabama Hills), discussion panels, "in-person" guest stars from the featured films and hour-long, guided bus tours to all the movie locations throughout the hills. Other festival happenings include barbecues and arts and crafts shows, but none of these can compete with seeing the location where Cary Grant started across that suspension bridge (with an elephant following) in Gunga Din! If you can't time your visit for the film festival, be sure to stop at the **Museum of Western Film History** at the south end of Main Street. Tour the fascinating collections and exhibits that celebrate the area's film heritage. **https://www. museumofwesternfilmhistory.org/**

AUTHOR'S TIP: HOW THE WEST WAS FORMED

*A horizonless sea of golden-colored granite boulders that rise up dramatically from the desert floor make up the Alabama Hills of Lone Pine. The rounded mounds and twisted rock formations came about by the current of thawing Ice Age snow that first sharply chiseled the igneous stone. The pursuant winds shaped the rough edges into smoothed-over hills with east-west-looking archways. Only nature could create such a perfect movie set ripe for gunfights, bad-guy hideaways and long, dusty trail rides. Just three miles west of Lone Pine, follow the path taken by your western movie favorites up Movie Road until it intersects with Whitney Portal Road. Take the 8-mile jaunt up to **The Store at Whitney Portal** for the best giant pancakes in the west, backed by exquisite mountain scenery. Located at the trailhead to Mount Whitney, it is the perfect way to feed a hiker's appetite.*

Bishop

Farther north in the Owens River Valley is **Bishop**, a popular recreation starting point and destination. Bishop is nestled between the state's two highest mountain ranges. Bishop Creek Canyon just west of Bishop on Bishop Creek Highway offers dramatic 1,000-foot cliffs on each side and a series of dams that generate power for the Los Angeles area. Each Memorial Day weekend Bishop puts on a big show featuring, of all animals, the mule! **Mule Days** attracts more than 40,000 people annually and almost 600 mules in ninety-four events, ranging from steer roping and jumping to chariot races. The raucous mule party also includes chuck-wagon races, the world's largest "nonmotorized" parade, dances, barbecues and arts and crafts.

Bread-lovers will want to stock up at the **Erick Schat's Bakkery**, home of the Original Sheepherder Bread. The bread was introduced to the Owens Valley during the California Gold Rush by immigrant Basque sheepherders who missed the bread of their homeland. They shaped loaves of their traditional bread by hand, used stone ovens for baking and produced the first sheepherder bread. Schat's still forms the loaves by hand that are baked in European stone hearth ovens. All of Schat's bakery goodies are made of quality ingredients such as well water from the Sierras, stone ground unbleached flour and never any chemicals. **http://schatsbakery.com/**

AUTHOR'S TIP: HISTORY NOT FORGOTTEN

*An old stone sentry station off a dirt road leads to **Manzanar**. This historical camp is one of ten that held a total of 120,000 people of Japanese ancestry after the bombing of Pearl Harbor. The 800-acre **Manzanar National Historic Site** is now under the control of the National Park Service, which has opened the grounds for touring. Manzanar has been designated to represent all the camps because of its high degree of preservation. Watch the 22- minute film Remembering Manzanar; plan on spending about an hour to see the exhibits and artifacts. Adjacent to the Visitor Center is Block 14 where you will find two reconstructed barracks and a mess hall with exhibits. Take the 3.2- mile self-guided driving tour around the site to experience the Manzanar landscape that includes Japanese gardens and ponds that have been excavated, foundations, historic orchards and other remnants of the camp await you if you explore on foot beyond the tour road. To reach Manzanar, take Highway 395; the site is* *located halfway between Independence and Lone Pine.* **https://www.nps.gov/manz/index.htm**

_____

About 5 miles northeast on Route 6 is the **Laws Railroad Museum and Historical Site**. The eleven-acre restored former railroad community of Laws was once an important outfitting center for the farming and livestock industry as well as a mining center during the early twentieth century. At that time the narrow-gauge railroad was the only means of transportation for the eastern Sierra region; the Laws–Keeler branch of the Southern Pacific was the last operating narrow-gauge public carrier west of the Rocky Mountains. The "Slim Princess" arrived at Laws for the last time in 1960, but the site has been preserved for future generations to enjoy by donations given to the Bishop Museum and Historical Society. Among the thirty-plus sights, visitors can view the Laws railroad station depot and its artifacts, the agent's house (with antique local furnishings), the post office, the 1880 print shop, the antique fire station, the bottle house, a restored 1900 ranch house and the Wells Fargo building. Donations are accepted. **http://www.lawsmuseum.org/**

Keeler, located along the eastern shores of Owens Lake (a dry lakebed) along State Route 136, became home to about 300 miners in the early 1870s, but with the coming of the railroad in 1883---with its terminus near Keeler—large marble quarries opened in the area. The town also became a popular layover stop for stagecoach riders on the way to Mojave. Today, it is populated once again, serving as a sort of "living" ghost town with a population of less than 70 people. Unfortunately, not much remains of the area's other ghost towns, Darwin and Swansea, except interesting histories and sparse remnants of original structures.

INLAND EMPIRE

The Inland Empire is nestled between Southern California's high and low deserts and is near the greater Los Angeles area. Other than the absence of ocean coasts, this wide-open country represents, in miniature, Southern California's varied scenery. You'll eye proliferous groves of oranges, cherries and apples; stagecoach trails and small country towns; cities encircled by rocky foothills and snow-frosted mountain hideaways; and restored vintage neighborhoods as well as Indian mud baths. The Inland Empire boasts bright blue skies filled with skydivers and ultralight aircraft, and unique museums that capture yesteryear in fossilized findings or old-fashioned trolley rides. Here you are guaranteed to find an abundance of off-the-beaten-path roads for exploring in all directions.

San Bernardino County

Ontario, known best for its fast-moving speedway and international airport, is also a region dripping in California's citrus and agricultural heritage. You just have to know where to look. You'll find a lot of it in the city's **Museum of History and Art**—but it is really all around you, from the vintage cottages to century-old family businesses.

Extolling the virtues of visiting **Graber Olive House**, the oldest existing business in Ontario, is appropriate any time of the year. However, the olive house which has been family owned and run since its beginnings in 1894 is also haunted—making a tour of Graber's an ideal Halloween experience for those who believe. The Franciscan missionaries from Spain planted the first olive trees, a flourishing crop that would populate early California ranches, at the Mission San Diego de Alcala in 1769. C.C. Graber purchased land in Ontario in 1892 and discovered olives which he considered one of the finest delicacies in the state. After lots of research, Graber cured several barrels and found his "perfect" method of olive making two years later and began Graber Olive House.

Graber's method has made the olive house stand-out throughout generations of Grabers. The olives are allowed to mature on the trees to a cherry-red color and are tenderly handpicked and cured in covered vats without being oxidized. The remainder of the process is all by hand as well—including the sorting, canning and labeling. Even in the gift shop where olives may be purchased and sampled, along with olive oil from the Graber trees and other gift items, there is no computer. The motto here is "if it was good enough for C.C., it's good enough for us." Guests are invited to a guided tour of the process from vats to labeling. However, they are apt to get more from the tour than the olive process—they might meet who the ghost of founder C.C. Graber. **https://www. graberolives.com/Default.asp**

AUTHOR'S TIP:
THOSE GOLDEN ARCHES

Show business wasn't their entry into riches for Hollywood-bound New Hampshire-ites Maurice and Richard McDonald, so they opened a drive-in restaurant near San Bernardino in 1937. It did well, so they opened another a few years later. The brothers conceived the fast-food concept in the late 1940s and began selling hamburgers for 15 cents, French fries for 10 cents, and milk shakes for 20 cents. The "golden arches" (a large M) *signaled their eateries, and their slogan became "If you want fancy, go someplace else. If you want a simple good meal and you want it fast, come to us." Ray Kroc, a malted-milk-machine salesman, offered the McDonalds a percentage of the profits if they would give him franchise rights to their restaurants. Kroc, a high school dropout, made more than $8 billion in sales in 1984, the year before his death.*

If Frank Cuccia's uncle hadn't eaten a bowl of spaghetti in front of customers at his grandmother's French dip and orange juice stand, then **Vince's Spaghetti** might not have been born in 1945. Other customers wanted the pasta creation (from a secret family recipe) and Vince's began. Today, the restaurant is still owned and operated by the original Cuccia family in its original restaurant on Holt. Vince's, which can easily serve more than 9,000 meals a week, translating into more than 15,000 miles of spaghetti a year, does not take reservations and is closed on Wednesdays, but its casual environs are packed with families consistently. The winning formula might be a collaboration of a winning recipe paired with monumental servings. Hardly anyone gets out the door without a doggie bag. The cost is a factor too, says Frank Cuccia, especially in times when it is difficult for families to dine out together. In 1946, the menu offered a plate of real spaghetti and meatballs for 65 cents or 40 cents for a smaller plate. Today, the generous portions are still hard-to-believe bargain priced. **https://www.vincesspaghettirestaurant.com/**

AUTHOR'S TIP:
WIGWAM STAY ON ROUTE 66

*A journey along California's Route 66 is not complete without a stop at the **Wigwam Motel** in San Bernardino that has been welcoming travel-weary friends since 1949. The Patel family took over the iconic motel a dozen years ago and restored the 19 "wigwams," also adding a pool, grill and upgrades such as flat screen televisions and refrigerators. Beyond the novel façade, the motel offers standard rooms that are sprinkled privately around the grounds. The Patel's call their motel "the last historic stop" on the road before heading back to reality.* **https://www.wigwammotel.com/**

Along the Mother Road in San Bernardino County is Victorville, home to another Route 66 museum. About 10,000 visitors make the **California Route 66 Museum** a must-see stop. Surprisingly, nearly 60% of visitors are international travelers who have seen the "Grapes of Wrath," and, more recently, Disney's "Cars." The museum has three rooms dedicated to the history of the Mother Road and several hands-on exhibits that make unique photo ops, from an old VW hippie van to a classic 40's aluminum trailer set for a picnic. **http://califrt66museum.org/**

Mountain Resorts

State Route 18 leads to the high mountain resorts of the Inland Empire and becomes the aptly named Rim of the World Drive Highway that twists high above the valley floor, granting unparalleled vistas of all below. The four-lane rim drive becomes a two-lane thoroughfare at around 4,000 feet, as the "whole world" begins to unfold in this section of the San Bernardino National Forest. Connecting Highway 38 leads to the north shore **Big Bear ranger station**, a perfect stop for gathering hiking and trail information in the Big Bear area. Of the many hiking and touring trails in the forest area, history aficionados will especially enjoy the historic **Gold Fever Trail** auto tour, with panoramic views of the natural terrain. The self-guided tour through San Bernardino National Forest's gold country takes you through the Holcomb Valley, where the saga of early miners can be traced through the area of Southern California's richest gold mining per square mile. The nearly 20-mile round-trip begins on a dirt road and terminates on the state highway; plan on about three hours to view these sites, where prospector Bill Holcomb ate boot soup to survive and where the miners reached pay dirt that, by 1860, averaged three pounds of gold a day. The actual "mother lode" of the Last Chance Placer has reportedly never been found! The tour also includes a look at the remains of the log Two Gun Bills Saloon, a stately juniper Hangman's Tree, a cabin from the gold-rush town of Belleville and the incredibly rich Gold Mountain Lucky Baldwin Mine.

Big Bear Lake, boasting recreation year-round, is home to an old-fashioned, sprawling mountain village. To experience the wild of the surrounding woods in a tame environment, follow Moonridge Road in town as it climbs up through residentially settled slopes. The **Big Bear Alpine Zoo at Moonridge** is tucked away in the mountains here, not far from town, and offers an authentic wilderness zoo in a picturesque natural setting. The small zoo is occupied by North American wildlife that are non-releasable because of injury or handicap. Dirt paths among the pines and over a stream lead to roaming deer, timber wolves, bobcats, coyotes, eagles, hawks, raccoons, mountain lions, snowy owls, ringtails and forest bears. **http://bigbearzoo.org/**

Winter in SoCal isn't only about the glistening beaches. Find the "other" glistening stuff just a short drive from Los Angeles in **Big Bear Mountain Resorts**. Snow play is fresh and plentiful all winter, with a new mountain thrill ride that is found no other place in the state: **Soaring Eagle.** The family-friendly, dual-seated zipline ride, designed for all ages, gives guests the sensation of flying high above Big Bear's snow-covered forest floor. Skiers and snowboarders at Big Bear Mountain Resorts, Snow Summit and Bear Mountain enjoy the $12 million investment in snowmaking equipment a few years ago that guarantees snow buffs non-stop powdery fun all winter. **http://www.bigbearguide.com/**

A perfect spot for settling in and absorbing the ambience of the surrounding Big Bear area is a 1920s lodge once used by wealthy gold miners and later frequented by the movie greats of the thirties. **Gold Mountain Manor Historic B&B**, located in a wooded residential area of Big Bear City, was the private mansion of the Peter Pan Woodland Club, a magnificent log-and-stone lodge equipped with the luxuries of the Roaring Twenties: a full movie theater, a ballroom, a banquet room, five oversize fireplaces and beautifully appointed guest accommodations. The demand from the wealthy and famous to belong to the club was so great that owner Harry Kiener built a private mansion for the lodge. The 7,000-square-foot mansion, now the Gold Mountain Manor, was three stories high and featured bird's-eye maple floors, beamed ceilings, ten bedrooms, seven fireplaces, a wine cellar, a billiard room, chauffeur's quarters and stables. The Peter Pan Woodland Club was destroyed by time and fire, but the gracious mansion still stands to host overnight guests in luxury. The mansion has been restored to the grandeur it had when Clark Gable brought his bride, Carole Lombard, to Big Bear for their honeymoon. The seven guest accommodations, which all have fireplaces, include the Clark Gable Room, with an antique French walnut bed and the fireplace enjoyed by honeymooners Gable and Lombard. **https://www.goldmountainmanor.com/**

Another lake resort area off the highway, **Lake Arrowhead**, offers a sparkling, man-made lake and multileveled Village surrounded by tall pines and the best of nature for hiking, water activities, dining, boutique shopping and automatic decompressing. One of the best times to visit the resort area is in the fall when the liquid ambers, oaks and maple trees take on a vivid palette of oranges and rusts—a brilliant display set against the dark-green pines. It is also time to get in on an old-fashioned **Oktoberfest** celebration. Flowing steins of beer, German sausages and oompah players fill the Village stage and environs. The free family event, held outside in Lake Arrowhead Village, draws locals and visitors alike for apple bobbing and beer chugging contests and added fall ambience while dining or shopping in the Village.

LOCAL'S SECRET: DISCOVERING TUNNELS UNDER LAKE ARROWHEAD

"Following Huell Howser with camera gear in hand was always an adventure as he looked for the unusual wherever we explored for his television show "California Gold." In 2000, we traveled up into the San Bernardino Mountains to Lake Arrowhead. Instead of marveling at the beautiful lake, Huell went down a 100-foot shaft to explore the tunnels under the lake that were once slated to be used as part of an irrigation project that didn't come to pass."

– Luis Fuerte, Producer/Cameraman, "California Gold"; author "Louie, Take a Look at This," **https://www.amazon.com/Louie-Take-Look-This-Howser-ebook/**; Prospect Park Books, **https://www.prospectparkbooks.com/**

While wandering the shops in the Village, take an hour to tour the lake itself on the **Arrowhead Queen**. Board and buy tickets right on the waterfront in the Village for the one-hour, narrated tour. The old-fashioned paddlewheel-looking vessel glides slowly around the 14-mile shoreline of the lake, granting unobstructed views of the estates that grace the private lakefront. The impressive homes, some with heated driveways that melt winter snows and many with gondolas that carry homeowners up and down to their boat docks, also have (or have had) some illustrious owners. Mark Harmon and Pam Dawber, Mike Connors and the Beach Boys' Brian Wilson (look for his boat named appropriately California Girls) all have or have had homes along that famous shore. Former owners include Heather Locklear, Charlie Chaplin, Patrick Swayze, Liberace and Priscilla Presley—to name just a few. More than 120 movies have been filmed in the area, and your host points out those mansions that have been used as settings for some of your favorites, including The American President and Parent Trap 2. Shopping and eating in the Village is a great way to pass the day. Shopping is a surprising blend of one-of-a-kind boutiques, art galleries, and national outlets. In the summer, the Village is host to free concerts. **http://www.lakearrowhead.com/village.htm**

Redlands

Snowcapped mountaintops in the distance guide the way to the nearby sunshine-filled community of **Redlands**. Lots of us simply buzz by the outskirts of Redlands on the I-10—a city nicely taken for granted with all the usual modern-day comforts from fast food to neat motels and multiplex the-aters. Suburbia and progress have taken hold of this, one of Southern California's oldest towns, however, when you take the correct turn off the 10, you'll enter a lost world brimming over in late 1800's California architecture at every turn. The Downtown exit into Redlands delivers you to a nostalgic time dominated by hand-cut stone curbs, elegant tree-lined streets and homes and storefronts that speak of gentler times when the city was a newly found haven of winter-time warmth and health for cold Midwesterners and Easterners.

Through time, Redlands has earned several deserved nick-names, including the "City of Millionaires" and the "City of Beautiful Homes." Founded in 1888 and named for the color of the soil underfoot, the city may be one of the few towns in California that can honestly boast more than 1,500 remaining period homes and structures constructed at the beginning of the twentieth century. Ranging from Victorians to Mission and California Bungalow homes and multi-storied brick-front stores, a large percentage of the abodes are still occupied by descendants of the original owners, while others have become part of the public heritage in the form of museums or public facilities.

AUTHOR'S TIP: TOUR THE NEIGHBORHOODS

You can discover the wonders and history of the old town area and vintage neighborhoods by taking a self-guided tour that should include:

*The **Burrage Mansion** at 1205 West Crescent Avenue is a 28-room estate, originally situated on 22 acres, and built in 1901. "Monte Vista" was inspired by the Santa Barbara Mission. The house, owned by the founding president of the American Orchid Society, was used primarily for entertainment only two months a year. The family was known for hosting elaborate parties which were highlighted by the area's only glass-enclosed swimming pool that was often covered by a wooden dance floor.*

*The **William F. Holt House** at 405 West Olive Avenue at Alvarado Street was built in 1903. The 3,000- square- foot house* in Moorish style was designed for St. Louis capitalist and developer William Holt, who has been called the "emperor of the Imperial Valley" because of his influence in El Centro, Brawley and Holtville. The house's most unique feature is a one-lane bowling alley in the basement.

The **Morey Mansion** at 190 Terracina Boulevard has been referred to as "America's favorite Victorian home." The Victorian gem, built as the dream home of Sarah and David Morey in 1890, has been a bed and breakfast inn in recent years, but is now a private residence. The specimen structure features a Saracenian dome, a French Mansard tower and an abundance of Queen Anne and Stick-style elements.

The **A.K. Smiley Public Library** at 125 West Vine Street was designed in the Moorish style as well. The completed structure was dedicated on April 29, 1898, but additional wings were added throughout the years to meet the growing needs of the community. In fact, the signature tower was reconstructed not too long ago. The amazing interiors of the library are alive with gargoyles, griffins, stained and leaded glass and rich oak carvings and book cases. The interiors have such a pristine and glorious feel that the most common question the staff hears is whether this building was a church at one time. But the library has always been just that, only more celebrated with age. The library is open seven days a week.

The **Lincoln Shrine**, located directly behind the library in Smiley Park, is the only shrine, library, and museum dedicated to Abraham Lincoln and the Civil War west of the Mississippi. The unique octagon-shaped building was built and donated to the city of Redlands in 1932 by philanthropists Robert and Alma Watchorn, as a tribute to Lincoln and as a tribute to their son who died in World War I. The shrine houses an impressive collection of books, documents, artifacts and art works about Lincoln and the Civil War.

Highland Avenue, another beautiful residential lane lined with palms, flowing estates, and Victorian mansions, leads you to yet another spectacular estate—**Kimberly Crest House & Gardens**, at 1325 Prospect Drive. This fairy-tale–like French chateau overlooking the San Bernardino Valley was built in 1897. Mr. and Mrs. J. A. Kimberly of the Kimberly-Clark Paper Manufacturing Company became the new owners in 1905, adding terraces, fish ponds and a stairway and balustrades with planters to the already elaborate grounds covered by arbors and gardens and surrounded by orange groves. The home was deeded to a nonprofit organization to preserve it for the people of Redlands in 1979; the house and grounds are open to the public for tours and events. At the foot of the estate is Prospect Park. The park, a 39-acre botanical garden, was given to the city as an 80th birthday present and is, today, a popular spot for events with its vintage Carriage House. The oldest and largest park in Redlands, the site once held the city's first hotel. Cut-stone walls and curbs, rare trees and plants still fill the park. However, thirty-one acres are dedicated to citrus orchards. Take a few minutes to meander the grounds—the intoxicating blend of orange blossom and rose petal scents will underscore your visit and remind you of days gone by in historic Redlands. **http://kimberlycrest.org/**

The historic **Redlands Bowl**, an outdoor venue surrounded by stately palms and a century of history, offers a summer music festival unlike others. It is your chance to enjoy world-class music—for free. Entirely donor supported, the concerts run from late June through August on assorted evenings. **https://redlandsbowl.org/**

AUTHOR'S TIP: MUSEUM FOR ALL

*Directly down Orange Tree Lane in Redlands, off Interstate 10, is a museum worth the better part of a day. The **San Bernardino County Museum** offers three floors of exhibits, art galleries, and a separate Discovery Hall filled with hands-on science and history exhibits for children of all ages. Unique outside displays include one centering on artifact digging, a 1908 Southern Pacific engine, and an air force jet fighter. But what may be the best part of the museum are its changing displays and its clever handling of exhibits. The museum is located at 2024 Orange Tree Lane.* **http://www.sbcounty.gov/museum/**

Riverside County

The nearby community of **Banning** is closely linked with neighboring **Beaumont**. Picturesque Mount San Gorgonio, rising to the north of the city, and Mount San Jacinto formed the necessary passageway for westbound travelers and traders in the 1800s. Banning was named after daredevil stagecoach driver General Phineas Banning, who led a seventeen-mule train through the San Gorgonio Pass; his impressive Southern California historical legacy can also be traced in Wilmington and on Catalina Island.

AUTHOR'S TIP: GLIMPSE THE WESTERN FRONTIER

Surrounded by cottonwoods and watered by three natural springs, the Gilman Ranch in Banning was home to the Cahuilla Indians, and later served as a portion of a large cattle ranching operation under the rule of the Spanish government. Today the **Gilman Historic Ranch and Wagon Museum** *offers visitors a unique peek into early California history. Visitors are invited inside the homestead ranch of James Marshall Gilman and into the museum that hosts artifacts of the mid-1800s era. Plan to picnic on the spacious and scenic grounds. The ranch and museum are located in Banning at Sixteenth and Wilson Streets.* **https://www.rivcoparks.org/ gilman-historic-ranch-and-wagon-museum/**

Travel 5 miles north of Beaumont on Beaumont Avenue, lined with pine trees and open fields, to verdant **Cherry Valley** in the foothills of the San Bernardino Mountains, which is home to the Cherry Blossom Festival each summer. Although there were a lot of orchards at one time, many have given way to development. But, still, the celebration goes on bringing around 40,000 cherry enthusiasts to the small city and pretty much everyone in town, cherries or not. If you miss the Cherry Festival, think about the Lavender Festival at the 2,400-acre historic **Highland Springs Resort** for a touch of Provence. The family-friendly fest invites visitors to stroll through the winding paths of organic lavender at the resort's 123 Farm, take guided tours in horse-drawn hay wagons and taste lavender-inspired dishes. The organic marketplace showcases specialty items made with the farm's lavender, from honey and balsamic vinegar to essential oils and fresh bouquets. Guests may explore the historic grounds, attend a demonstration on the growing, harvesting and processing of lavender or just relax and listen to music. Food is plentiful and includes such delicacies as lavender lattes and ice cream. You'll discover an area devoted to kids' activities, including a petting zoo, croquet and craft activities.

Follow the signs on Oak Glen Road in Cherry Valley to the **Edward-Dean Museum & Gardens**, a Riverside County art and cultural center. Nestled among cherry orchards and ranches is this tile-roofed, Classical-style structure with a "cherry-blossom pink" cast. The tranquil country surroundings are an ideal setting for this unusual art museum and its meticulously landscaped gardens. Inside, view a homelike exhibit of eighteenth-century furniture and art, including paintings by the masters, ceramics, crystal, Persian carpets, Oriental treasures and one of the finest collections of Far Eastern bronzes in the United States. **https://www.edward-deanmuseum.org/**

Oak Glen

Follow Oak Glen Road as it climbs through the foothills of the snow-topped San Gorgonio Mountains. The roadside hills feature oaks, occasional ranches and brilliant springtime apple blooms in varying shades of pink and white. A dangling red apple sign welcomes you to **Oak Glen**, where crisp, juicy apples are grown in mile-high orchards fed by pure mountain streams. The largest apple-growing region in the southland, Oak Glen sells all of its produce directly to the public and is the largest operation of its kind in the United States. A scenic drive through Oak Glen, be it for apple buying, apple-blossom viewing or a slice of homemade apple pie with fresh cider, is a worthwhile side trip. September through December marks the harvest period of the ranches in the area, which are painted in autumn shades of crimson red, burnt orange and amber; visitors may stop by the plentiful roadside stands and barns for the more than forty varieties of apples sold by the pound or by the bushel, as well as baked in pies and pressed for cider. Visitors are also invited to watch the presses in operation.

You won't get lost on this day's meanderings—everything circles back to its beginnings on what has been named the "Scenic Loop." The five-mile circle leads you past u-pick farms, apple stands and ranches filled with rural pleasures— from horseback riding, apple tasting and scenic trails to shopping and home-style dining. With all the apples that line your drive, it is difficult to believe that the area's first crop was actually potatoes!

On your journey, you will discover several ranching operations in Oak Glen that are owned and operated by different members of the Riley family, including two main destinations: **Riley's Farm** and **Rileys at Los Rios Rancho.** Even though the ranches are nestled among historic orchards, the Riley clan first moved to Oak Glen in 1978, when Dennis Riley moved his wife and three sons to the area to get out of the city, purchasing acreage from the son of an Oak Glen pioneer who first settled in the area in 1871. Decades later marked more land acquisitions and grown children to take over and expand the creative visions of the ranches.

Los Rios Rancho, which began as an apple farm in 1900, is also headquarters of the Wildlands Conservancy which has preserved this site as a "living history" lesson and developed nature trails past ponds and forests, as well as plentiful picnic areas. Rileys at Los Rios Rancho is a working apple orchard and living history farm featuring pick-your-own fruit and vegetables, a petting zoo and play area and tours of the old apple Packing House. Besides picnics and hiking, peruse the country gift store or stop in the bakery and savor a giant apple fritter. **https://losriosrancho.com/**

Riley's Farm (not to be confused with Riley's at Los Rios Rancho) is a step back in time to early America, from its 18th-century colonial tavern and bakery, The Hawk's Head, to special programs that are packed with living history ambience. There are plenty of u-pick opportunities as well, from apples to berries and pears, in addition to some intriguing shows and tours. From March through December, the Riley's Farm Theater Company presents unique, family-friendly dinner theater in the quaint, candle-lit pub, as well as in the historic Packing Shed Theater. One of the most popular is the autumnal dinner theatre event, The Harvest Feast, in November. Held in the Hawk's Head Public House, the production features a farm-fresh feast, tomahawk throwing, live music and 18th century dancing, a toast contest and interactive historical drama. **https://rileysfarm.com/**

Sign up for the Old Joe Homestead Tour to glean Oak Glen history. Tour-goers have a look back at the simple home arts of 19th-century farm life as they learn what has transpired since 1871 when Joe E. Wilshire ("Old Joe") purchased hundreds of acres of Oak Glen farmland for a saddle, a jug of whiskey and a chicken. **https://rileysfarm.com/index.php/living-history/old-joe-homestead-tour/**

The oldest farm in the area, **Parrish Pioneer Ranch**, is the site of the first apple tree planted here in the late 1860s. Fall brings apple sales in the barn as well as an assortment of pumpkins. The ranch pasture across from the apple shed hosts farm animals for the kids. Also, on the ranch grounds is the Parrish House, founder Enoch Parrish's 1876 home, now antique store. Look for the giant 1905 sequoia tree near the ranch. **https://parrishranch.com/**

For more than five decades, **Oak Tree Village** along your Scenic Loop has been a stop for shoppers and families, as well as those wanting to indulge in a mile-high slice of apple pie or giant chicken pot pie meal. The weekends bring pony rides for the kids, and a handful of locally-owned and operated shops selling everything from caramel apples to leather goods. Stop for lunch at Apple Annie's, a tradition around here. The restaurant has a unique guarantee to satisfy the hungriest apple picker—if you are still hungry when your plate is clean, they will serve you another meal for free. Sorry, no doggie bags with the encore meal!

AUTHOR'S TIP: PICNIC AT SCHOOL HOUSE

*While you are touring, make a stop at the **Oak Glen School House Museum**—a great spot if you have packed a picnic. Although the first school days happened in the living rooms of local ranchers, a wooden school house was eventually built on the Wilshire farm. In 1927, the school district built the one-room stone school house that exists today as a museum and park with playground equipment and nature trails.*

Riverside

Interstate 215 leads into the city of **Riverside**, birthplace of North America's navel orange industry, a city that boasts of some unique firsts. Riverside was the first community in the nation to hold an outdoor Easter sunrise service and the first to have an electrically lighted outdoor Christmas tree, and it is the home of the oldest air force base on the West Coast. Traveling down the interstate through the city, you can still see the rocky hills and tall palms that hint of the city's more rural beginnings.

It may be hard to believe that two little orange trees from Brazil could pave the way for an entire city that would be a favorite of presidents, movie stars, movie debuts and wealthy vacationers and entrepreneurs. Riverside is much more than the County seat—it was built more than 130 years ago on a

California 'Gold Rush' of a different kind. Today, the remnants of the city's beginnings can be discovered and savored—just as delicious and tangy as the citrus that gave it life.

The mission padres may have planted the first Mediterranean varieties of citrus on the grounds of Mission San Gabriel around 1803, but it was emigrant William Wolfskill who had a "crazy" vision that citrus could flourish as an industry in Southern California. He developed acres and acres of lemon, lime and orange trees in what is now downtown Los Angeles. Around the same time in the late 1800s, Mrs. Eliza Tibbets of Riverside was gifted two young Washington navel orange trees, a Brazilian native orange known for its sweetness. Today, nearly all of the Washington navel orange trees grown in the state are descended from these two trees. And, one of the original trees, the **Parent Navel Orange Tree**, still grows at the intersection of Riverside's Arlington and Magnolia avenues.

About the same time Wolfskill's crops were beginning to flourish, gold was discovered at Sutter's Mill, bringing a flood of fortune-crazed prospectors out West. Gold not only brought opportunity to California, so did the birth of the lucrative citrus industry. Lured by land promoters promising endless sunshine and a new industry, Riverside became one of the state's pioneer agricultural settlements in 1870. The California Fruit Growers Exchange (Sunkist) and the Southern Pacific Railroad began to advertise the romantic allure of the destination to wealthy Midwesterners. And, it worked. They arrived in droves to share in the "riches" that the warm, citrus-filled environs offered, as well as the romance and prosperity this newest gold rush promised.

Exit off Van Buren Boulevard and you'll land in the historic Arlington district of the city filled with Victorian mansions and its citrus growing beginnings. Follow it past the Van Buren Drive-In Theater, nearly a historic monument itself as one of only about 400 drive-in theaters still operating in America.

When you reach Dufferin Avenue, you will be greeted by an old-fashioned "orange stand" that signals the **California Citrus State Historic Park**, a step back into the early 1900s with Craftsman-style structures, grassy tree-shaded areas and picnic areas, palm-lined trails and leafy green groves.

Opened in August 1993 as a living historical museum, visitors discover 186 acres of lush citrus groves with navel and Valencia oranges, grapefruit and lemons. Besides the groves, visitors will discover a fascinating visitor's center/museum and gift shop. Within the center, catch a short movie that explains it all and tour exhibits that trace the evolution of the citrus industry. Be sure to take a "Tour and Taste" tour, offering a guided walk through the sweet-smelling citrus groves along with tidbits of history and delicious fruit samplings straight from the trees. Tours are generally offered Fridays, Saturdays and Sundays at various times. **http://www.parks. ca.gov/?page_id=649**

It is the old downtown section of Riverside that bespeaks the splendor and history of its roots. **The Mission Inn Hotel & Spa**, a historic treasure that has provided lodging to presidents, movie stars and royalty, is the city's most famous period offering. After an extensive renovation to preserve its antiquity, the palatial hotel reopened to guests in 1992. It is a major draw to the city, and the castle-like turrets and majestic towers of the inn can be spied from far away, as the city, county, state and national historic landmark hotel holds court over the city. Located at 3649 Mission Inn Avenue, the inn was converted from a twelve-room adobe (known as the Glenwood Cottage) to one of America's most unusual hotels, covering a modern city block. The transformation began in 1876 and took sixty-five years to complete. The Mission Inn's original owner, visionary Frank Miller, transformed the small cottage into an overnight hostelry, adding wings in Mission Revival–style architecture, Cloister and Spanish wings, and an International Rotunda wing, which includes the renowned

St. Francis Chapel with a gold-layered, centuries-old Rayas altar and also includes the Galeria. The fascinating hotel holds thousand-year-old antiques and priceless international art pieces. Today the hotel offers 235 elegant guest rooms and suites, each individually decorated, as well as eleven meeting rooms, two restaurants, an Olympic-size pool with Jacuzzi and a spa. The Mission Inn Foundation maintains a museum adjacent to the hotel with some of the hotel's original furnishings and an extensive collection of artifacts from all over the world. Time a visit for the Christmas holidays, and you'll be treated to the **Festival of Lights**, when the historic inn and grounds are illuminated with over five million lights. As a part of the festivities, the inn offers a variety of room packages and holiday dining and events such as lighting ceremonies and carolers. **https://www.missioninn.com/**

Photo by © Ellen Clark

AUTHOR'S TIP:
EXPLORE THE INN'S SECRETS

You won't experience the whole Mission Inn mystique until you indulge in the docent-led history tour that gives you access to the areas and the stories of the hostelry that most visitors would otherwise never see or hear. Before you begin your journey, you might be surprised to know the four main misconceptions that docents counter every day: The Mission Inn was never a mission; ghosts have never been spotted at the resort (as far as they know); there are no underground tunnels or catacombs; and you will not find a consecrated church at The Mission Inn—just a wedding chapel—although the historic hotel has been the setting of countless weddings through the years, including ceremonies for Bette Davis twice, Humphrey Bogart and President Richard and Pat Nixon. The daily tours, that are open to both guests and nonguests, are conducted by the non-profit Mission Inn Foundation and guide visitors through the decades and personalities that comprise the resort's history, from its beginnings as a 12-room adobe boarding house to a prestigious resort. The tour begins in the Mission-Revival decorated lobby with 94-foot-long carpet depicting the 21 California Missions. Portraits of U.S. Presidents line the lobby walls, celebrating the ten U.S. Presidents who have visited here. Residing in the lobby is a unique chair made expressively for President Taft's visit. Tour-goers go on to explore the four great wings of the inn: the Mission Wing, the Cloister Wing, the Rotunda Wing and the Spanish Wing. Details of art collections, stories of the inn's birth and rebirth and owners' passions to make the inn an icon, from the beginning to present-day owners Duane and Kelly Roberts, keep the tour moving rapidly. Not-to-miss highlights include the two-story Anton Clock Tower with revolving figures, the collection of 400 bells that grace the grounds, the Court of the Orient with eight-foot-high Buddha, the gold-leafed 18th-century altar and Tiffany art glass windows in the St. Francis of Assisi Chapel, the Spanish Art Gallery and priceless treasures too numerous to name.

The Mission Inn Hotel & Spa stands at the heart of downtown history with numerous historic structures within a short walk—some occupied by quaint cafes or boutiques. The surrounding streets hold an abundance of historical points of interest, from the Riverside County Courthouse to the Metropolitan Museum. Get a walking guide to history online at **http://www.riversidedowntown.org/visitor-information/** or pick one up at The Mission Inn Museum.

The nearby **Fox Performing Arts Center** in downtown offers a rich past and, like The Mission Inn, provides a popular present-day venue for entertainment. Built in 1929, the Spanish Colonial Revival style corner structure has become a centerpiece of the city's art and culture scene since its careful renovation in 2009. The theater, part of the Fox theater empire in its early years, was a popular venue for previewing future Hollywood releases. Riverside's Fox is best known for being the first theater to screen the 1939 film "Gone with the Wind." **http://www.riversidelive.com/**

The **Riverside Art Museum** at 3425 Mission Inn Avenue, the former YWCA, was designed by one of America's most famous architects, Julia Morgan of Hearst Castle fame, and was built in 1929; the building boasts a Spanish influence with a graceful second-story veranda, black wrought-iron touches and a red-tile roof. Inside, guests may view regional and national exhibits and fine art collections. **http://www.riversideartmuseum.org/**

About a block from the Mission Inn at 3824 Main Street is another noteworthy museum, the **California Museum of Photography**. This University of California at Riverside facility opened in 1990 in this downtown renovated dime store. The museum explores the relationship of photography to politics, the arts, and society and features an Ansel Adams exhibit, examples of cameras from 1839 to the present, and an impressive collection of stereoscopic cards. Shows at the museum change periodically. **https://artsblock.ucr.edu/**

Not all Riverside's rich past is found in the downtown section of the city. A drive out Magnolia Avenue, where the road widens and is lined by tall palms, leads to **Heritage House**, a restored Victorian mansion turned living museum. The pale green Queen Anne residence, with dome and shingle siding, was built in 1891 for Mrs. James Bettner, widow of a civil engineer and orange grower. Since 1969 volunteers and museum staff have worked to restore the house and its grounds to an accurate representation of Victorian-era Riverside. The home, listed on the National Register of Historic Places, boasts a dramatic staircase, tiled fireplaces, gas-lamp fixtures, Oriental rugs, artwork and period decor. Guided tours of the mansion are offered. It is surrounded by lawns, mature trees, citrus trees, rosebushes, a carriage house and a picturesque white gazebo. Tours are conducted on certain days. Admission to the city-owned museum, located at 8193 Magnolia Avenue, is free, but donations are appreciated. **https://www.riversideca.gov/museum/heritagehouse/default.asp**

The **Jensen-Alvarado Ranch Historic Park** at 4307 Briggs Street is a thirty-acre historic park that features the replanting of historic orchards and vineyards. Captain Don Cornelio Jensen—a pioneer merchant, banker, ranchero and county supervisor—married Doña Mercedes Alvarado in 1854; in 1865 the couple purchased this portion of the Rubidoux Rancho to begin an orchard, vineyard and home, where they would raise their ten children. Between 1868 and 1870 their brick mansion-like ranch house with a Danish flair, different from any other in the state, was constructed using bricks made by Chinese, Mexican and Indian laborers. The ranch house, the county's oldest standing home, as well as a little brick milk house, a small brick building used as a winery and later a livery stable, and a large winery building close to the main house, may be viewed at the historic park. The Riverside

County Parks Department plans an ongoing restoration program of California's first full-time working historic agricultural museum, but visitors are able to view many of the original furnishings of the ranch, which remained in the family until its recent purchase by the county. The historic park also contains an interesting gift shop. **https://www.rivcoparks.org/ jensen-alvarado-historic-ranch-and-museum/**

Just outside Riverside on Highway 60 is the community of **Jurupa.** Let the realistic-looking dinosaurs perched on the hillsides be your guide to the area's most unusual offering, the **Jurupa Mountains Discovery Center**. Originators and prime movers of the center, Sam and Ruth Kirkby, began the center on forty-five acres of land. Today the center encompasses more than 100 acres and includes a seasonal natural spring, botanical gardens, and an earth science museum with outstanding displays of minerals, fossils, rocks (including meteorites and a piece of moon rock) and mining implements, along with eight displays of Native American tools and artifacts. The center is also a registered archaeological site. **https://jmdc.org/**

Corona

Interstate 15, beyond the urban center of **Corona,** takes you past the fringes of suburbia, with views of orange groves and towering foothills. A turnoff on rural Temescal Canyon Road traces the historic route used by Indians, gold miners, and stagecoaches in earlier days and leads to **Tom's Farms**. This popular fruit-and-produce roadside stand has expanded through the years to include a few attractive farm-like structures connected by cobblestones, as well as a newer, 24,000-square-foot structure filled with antiques and antique reproductions. The family destination has cafes and a family fun zone with mini train and mining. The expanded roadside stand is located at 23900 Temescal Canyon Road in Corona. **https://www.tomsfarms.com/**

Not far down the road from Tom's is the entrance lane to **Glen Ivy Hot Springs**, affectionately known as Club Mud. Statuesque palms, orange groves and peppertrees grace the road, which winds back to the historic mineral springs first used by a semi-permanent village of around 500 Indians. The Indians who camped here built sweat lodges for ceremonies of purification and renewal, giving the valley its name, Temescal—the Aztec word for "sweat lodge." After the Spanish arrived to evangelize the Indians, the property became a cattle ranch for Mission San Luis Rey, and the Indians stayed on to tan hides for the mission. When the state took over the mission land, a Captain Sayward built the first adobe on the site as a retreat for his ailing wife; they adopted seven children. Around 1890 the adobe opened as a commercial bathhouse, or plunge, and hotel and was called Glen Ivy because of the profusion of ivy that grew in the remote canyon. The popularity of the retreat has ebbed and peaked, but the resort has been in continual use since the 1920s, hosting the likes of presidents, sports figures, and movie stars.

Today Glen Ivy's popularity is not in jeopardy, as evidenced by the hearty weekend crowd that comes to enjoy the fresh country air, numerous mineral pools, red clay mud baths, saunas, massages and surrounding botanical beauty. Totally upgraded and beautifully landscaped with flowering gardens featuring its logo bird-of-paradise and manicured shrubs, Glen Ivy still retains some historical charm, though no longer an overnight resort. Glen Ivy retains on-site mineral water wells that vary in temperature from 80 to 110 degrees, together forming an ideal temperature of about 104 degrees. Glen Ivy is nicknamed "Club Mud" due to the resort's unique red clay mineral bath—just one of many mineral treatment options on the grounds. The communal bath is filled with fresh mineral water daily but browns to a rich terra cotta as the clay dissolves in it. Indigenous to Southern California and mined in the canyon, the red clay has a purifying effect on the skin, cleansing the pores and tightening the skin.

Besides the clay bath, the day-rate entrance entitles springs goers to a wide selection of pools and relaxation areas on the five-acre retreat. Dotted about the grounds is a water aerobics pool, individual deep soaking baths, champagne pools with extra bubbles, a lounge pool, terrace "quiet" pools and two saltwater pools. Massage and spa treatment buildings abound, as does a simple but reasonable café and modern, fully stocked locker and shower areas for men and women. But the highlight of the resort is its unique **Grotto**, an underground moisturizing treatment area which is available at an additional charge. The underground Grotto is an inexpensive treatment with rich results. Guests are escorted underground via elevator and emerge in a cave-like area. Attendants with super-sized paint brushes apply a sea kelp moisturizing mask to all parts of the body not covered by a bathing suit. Guests then enter a relaxing hydrating chamber for at least 30 minutes allowing the mask to penetrate. A mineral shower area removes the green gooey mixture and is followed by a cooling down room where hot tea is served. Guests emerge totally relaxed and very soft. **https://www.glenivy.com/**

Perris

Temescal Canyon Road intersects with I–15 once again down a country path. An 8-mile trip south on the highway leads to Lake Elsinore. Highway 74 from Lake Elsinore leads to **Perris**, a town that doesn't begin to resemble the one in France. But for lake enthusiasts **Lake Perris** offers 9 miles of shoreline for boating, fishing, sailing and swimming. Lake Perris is the terminal reservoir for irrigation water from the Colorado River. Just southeast of downtown, look to the skies for a daring, spectacular free show of flying or parachuting. Amid the open pastures of the area are located two specialty flight fields next to each other: the **Perris Valley Skydiving Center** and a balloon launch field. Weekends are active times for groups of skydivers, who fill the sky repeatedly with colorful jumps over the surrounding fields. Balloon lovers will have to arrive at the park area predawn to catch a glimpse of these brightly adorned crafts ascending from the earth.

The small community of Perris is also home to one of southern California's most unusual and interesting museums. The **Orange Empire Railway Museum**, located on twelve acres of country land off A Street, marks the preservation of an era gone by in Southern California. Judy Garland immortalized the trolley in 1944 when she sang "Clang clang, clang went the trolley," but around that same time, Southern California lost its popular "red car" trolleys when new bus transit systems bought up and scrapped the electric-powered cars. The tracks were yanked up, and the electric mass-transit system that linked Los Angeles to ocean resort towns was gone. Many of the red cars were junked, but a few have been saved and restored for new generations to enjoy. The Orange Empire Railway Museum was founded in 1956 and has grown to one of the largest displays of its kind in the nation, all accomplished by volunteers and donations. The outdoor museum is open daily, but visit on the weekend or a holiday, if possible, to be able to actually ride up to four of these restored trolleys and trains on tracks that run out to pastures of trolleys and trains in various stages of restoration. The conductor onboard will give you the history of the car you are riding, as well as point out other sites on the rural, parklike premises. You may ride in one of the red cars, in a 1921-built narrow-gauge California Car, in a 1938 Green Car, or in a 1950s vintage San Francisco Muni Car, to name just a sampling. **https://www.oerm.org/**

Hemet

The roots of the nation's longest running outdoor play, **"Ramona,"** has been the hallmark of the small city of **Hemet**. Reminiscent of a 1940's "Andy Hardy" movie—the part when

Mickey Rooney gathers the kids in town to put on a play—the cast is almost completely composed of town folk. This town effort began in Hemet in 1923 and is still garnering its cast of hundreds, made up almost entirely of town residents, each spring to put on the big-as-real-life production based on early California life and its struggles. Celebrities have graced the outdoor stage many years, from Raquel Welch, who played the title role when she was 18, to Cloris Leachman. Although the love story and struggles of Native Americans during California's transition from Mexican rule to American during the 1850s is compelling, it is the outdoor setting that immerses the audience in the play. Often called "magical," the 160-acre canyon amphitheater was especially designed for this production. Boulders, dirt trails, craggy hills and an authentic-looking rancho set the "stage" for the production that includes more than 480 local volunteers, including the 100 children who play Native Americans positioned around the hilltops. Add to this, a dozen horses and a handful of mules that dramatically transport their riders through the setting's canyon territory. **http://ramonabowl.com/**

Temecula

It is easy to see that **Temecula** and its rich valley is bursting at the seams with new housing developments and shopping centers, but it's the city's rural and historic sides that lure those in search of new offerings that are found in its beginnings, from its vintage town to its rolling hills lined in vineyard plantings. Those who explore, will discover new wineries, new tastings, new restaurants, new inns and even southern California's very first wave cave.

Gently rolling hills that were once home to the Pechanga Indians caress the Victorian western town of **Old Town Temecula**. Temecula's Old Town, found near the I-15 and straddling Front Street, was established in 1859 and offers an old west experience from its wooden sidewalks to preserved historic sites turned businesses. Wander quaint shops and bistros and get in the cowboy mode by taking a horse-drawn carriage ride down the main thoroughfare to hear about the town's days of gun fights and bank robberies. If your visit includes a Saturday morning, the weekly **Farmers' Market** takes place in the heart of Old Town. Grab some locally grown, organic produce, flowers, olive oils and hand-crafted items in the impressive venue as you wander the frontier streets or head straight to the vineyards for a picnic.

LOCAL'S SECRET: LAVENDER IN JUNE

Temecula Lavender Company offers tours during the short window of harvest time, usually during the month of June. Walking tours through the gardens include demonstration of extracting oils as well as a tasting of delicious lavender lemonade and lavender cookies. Reservations can be made by calling their store in Old Town Temecula, (951) 676-1931.

– Annette Brown, Director of Public Relations, Visit Temecula Valley,
www.visittemeculavalley.com

The Bank, a Mexican-food restaurant on the corner of Front and Main Streets, was the 1912-built First National Bank. The locally owned bank was known as the "pawn shop" by its rancher directors. After the bank was robbed in 1930, the townspeople captured the robber themselves and recovered the loot; the bank notably stayed open during the Depression. For many years the second story of the building served as a dance hall and community center, but today's visitors may enjoy lunch or dinner in the spacious green structure that boasts huge, black, wrought-iron chandeliers that hang from the heavy-beamed high ceilings. **http://www.bankofmexicanfood.com/**

Thursday nights in Old Town means **Jazz at the Merc** in Old Town. The intimate theater experience is like a trip to New York's SoHo. Located in one of Temecula's original, restored buildings—the Mercantile—a different jazz group performs each week. **https://tickets.temeculatheater.org/**

LOCAL'S SECRET: SPRING ROSES

"Spring is a beautiful time to visit Temecula Valley's Rose Haven Heritage Garden. Home to more than 1600 roses, including hybrid teas, floribundas, climbers and mini roses, the garden is picture perfect (and especially fragrant) when the blooms begin to arrive. Special events take place on weekends during the bloom season for families and discerning travelers. The rose garden is free to visit, open daily and picnic tables are available. The garden is located at 30592 Jedediah Smith Road, Temecula, just a few minutes south of Old Town Temecula."
http://temeculavalleyrosesociety.org/rosehaven.shtml

– Annette Brown, Director of Public Relations, Visit Temecula Valley,
www.visittemeculavalley.com

Across the street from the Mercantile Store is the **Hotel Temecula**, a nicely restored two-story Victorian with upper and lower verandas and flowering trees. Recently opened, the hotel was built in 1891 and still speaks of earlier days. All the hotel's historic guest rooms are located on the second floor, where there also is one shared Gentleman's Room with 2 showers, and one shared Ladies Room with 2 showers. Next door to the hotel is the tiny frontier-style Emigrant Office. **http://thehoteltemecula.com/**

If you don't have time to venture to Temecula's wine country as well as Old Town, take heart. Over the last few years, winery tasting rooms and wine tasting bars have opened in Old Town Temecula to bring a taste of wine country to historic Old Town. You will find everything from quaint tasting rooms where local wineries offer wine tasting to upscale wine bars that offer local wines by the glass as well as flights from around the world. However, Temecula harvests more than wine. The **Temecula Olive Oil Company** grows, produces and sells top-quality California extra virgin olive oils, as well as wine and handmade olive soaps. Make a stop to sample the farm-fresh harvest. **https://www.temeculaoliveoil.com/**

AUTHOR'S TIP:
TOUR AN OLIVE GROVE

Blessed with climate similar to the Mediterranean olive grow-ing regions, Temecula proved a perfect locale for olive grow-ing for couple Thomas and Nancy Curry, who had spent over 20 years in the sales and marketing side of the wine business. Their Temecula Olive Oil Company not only hosts several tast-ing rooms in San Diego County, the ranch offers regular tours. Enjoy a 90-minute guided walk through the olive groves, learn-ing about sustainable agriculture, growing olives, harvest tech-niques, milling and pressing along with a tasting of our extra virgin olive oils and balsamic vinegars. Tours of the Temecula area ranch are offered on the second and fourth Saturdays of each month. **https://www.temeculaoliveoil.com/book-a-tour**

After some Old West wandering, head to the hills of Temecula for samples of one of the valley's finest products—**wine.** A leisurely day's outing through rolling hills, vineyards and orange groves will take you to more the wineries of the region. Temecula has demonstrated through the years that it is a perfect locale for growing over twenty-eight varietals of wine grapes, hosting an enviable balance of geography, microclimate and well-drained soil. Even the neighboring community of Fallbrook is trading in much of its avocado crops for grapes.

After all, over 200 years ago winemaking made its debut in California at Mission San Juan Capistrano, just 18 miles west of Temecula; mission vineyards were first planted in the area of Temecula in 1820. The winemaking tradition flourishes today with over two dozen wineries and more on the way. All of the seasons bring a new reason to visit, but fall is the best time to sample the newest harvests here and experience some unforgettable winemaker dinners and events.

The first modern commercial vineyard was planted in 1968 by the late Vincenzo Cilurzo and his wife Audrey. Temecula Valley received formal recognition as an American Viticultural Area in 1984, first as "Temecula AVA" with a subsequent name change to "Temecula Valley AVA" in 2004.

Temecula Valley now boasts more than 50 licensed wineries, producing over 500,000 cases annually. Temecula Valley wines regularly receive scores of 90 and above by wine media, and the region has received thousands of domestic and international wine awards. **https://www.temeculawines.org/**

Photo courtesy of Visit Temecula Valley

AUTHOR'S TIP: TOUR THE VINEYARDS BY HORSEBACK

*With equestrian outfitters and guides, picturesque riding trails and an equestrian center with exciting events, Temecula Valley is becoming as popular with visiting equestrians as its wine country. After all, the ranch life is part of Temecula's heritage. From the 1800s until as recently as the 1960s, the area was pre-dominantly grazing land for cattle. The Vail Ranch spanned more than 87,500 acres, and Temecula's Old West lifestyle flour-ished. When the Vails sold their ranch, the valley transitioned to a pastoral, master planned community that would incorporate equestrian ranches and agriculture, including wine grapes. The valley has expanded, but it is nice to know that its agrarian roots are intact. A bounty of horseback riding tours and opportunities exist, several designed to combine the area's wine-tasting pop-ularity with the equestrian experience. **Saddle Up Wine Tours** provides gentle horses and guides for rides alongside vineyards, ranches and wineries that line the De Portola Wine Trail. Along the route to wine tastings, riders hear historical wine country anecdotes. Wine-tasting destinations include wineries such as Oak Mountain with wine tasting in the mountaintop veranda with valley views.* **https://saddleupwinetours1.godaddysites. com/wine-tasting-tours**

You might call it the state's "grape movement" that has taken the rustic barn-type tasting room that began the movement here to mega-tasting rooms with sweeping vistas, restau-rants and state-of-the-art technology. One such new winery is **Fazeli Cellars Winery**. The 20,000 square feet of buildings that span 11 acres were carefully situated to catch the best of both sunrise and sunset from the winery's hillside perch, granting spectacular 180-degree views of surrounding wine country. **http://www.fazelicellars.com/**

AUTHOR'S TIP: SOCAL'S FIRST WINE CAVE

*Oak Mountain Winery is certainly not new, but the first Southern California wine cave, located at the hilltop winery, is. The **Wine Cave at Oak Mountain Winery** has recently opened after two years in the making and some monumental engineering challenges that made owners Valerie and Steve Andrews question their mammoth undertaking along the way. During the eight-month digging process, the owners unearthed some interesting local history in the layers of soil; in fact, a geologist is penning a book on the discoveries. The 11,500-square-foot cave was worth the angst, and the vision to have vineyards growing on top of the cave while, inside and below, wine temperatures and humidity stay in the ideal range has been realized. Not just ideal for barrel aging, the high-tech attractive cave space is a new alternative for special events, from private parties and weddings to unique seated Cave Club Member tastings.* **http://www.oak-mountainwinery.com/**

Owner and vintner Jim Carter, the creator of award-winning **South Coast Winery**, wanted to do something a little more exclusive and intimate with the recently opened **Carter Estate Vineyard & Winery**. As soon as you arrive, you feel the difference. The 42 Mediterranean-fashioned villas sit behind a private gate and are positioned on the edge of the young vines here. Positioned before the gates to the villas is the estate's upscale tasting room that features relaxing sit-down tastings accompanied by a knowledgeable host and a platter of edibles that pair with each tasting sip. The 109-acre estate that sits kitty-corner from its sister South Coast Resort is best known for its Methode Champenoise sparkling wine. You can even accompany your tasting with a tour of the vines and the making process just outside the tasting room door. Mr. Carter's Reserves here are among the best in the valley. The Carter Estate tasting experience is not your party bus variety; plan on a subdued and delightful hour spent with a variety of great wines and equally fine conversation. **https://www.carterestatewinery.com/**

LOCAL'S SECRET: THE GREAT OAK

"Visitors to Pechanga Resort & Casino in Temecula hover around gaming tables and slot machines unaware of (limited) tours offered by the Pechanga Band of Lisueño Indians to their Great Oak on adjacent land. Estimated to be 1,800 years old and standing 88 feet tall (with roots reaching down more than 10 feet), the tree's immense canopy once created a social venue for guests at the ranch of Perry Mason creator/writer Erle Stanley Gardner."

– Janice Kleinschmidt, author/editor

GREATER
LOS ANGELES

https://www.discoverlosangeles.com/

Los Angeles and the wide metropolitan expanses that surround make up the Greater Los Angeles area, known for celebrity haunts, major tourist attractions, famous beach cities, moviemaking history and posh designer boutiques. But the area also possesses a surprising amount of natural beauty and open space—even in the midst of city life! You will discover historical landmarks, multiacre gardens and parks, a variety of fascinating bistros, gracious vintage neighborhoods, hideaway lodgings and some behind-the-scenes looks at the stars and the movies.

San Fernando Valley

The San Fernando Valley was a rural farming area for many years after its neighboring Los Angeles County communities had developed sophisticated city structures and housing. Today there is no denying the dramatic spurt of suburban growth that the once agricultural area has experienced over the past fifty years. But a curious visitor to the area will glean more than shopping-mall escapades from the valley, as hints of its early farming days still exist.

Begin your exploration of the area's hidden treasures in **Calabasas**. Take the Mulholland Drive exit off Highway 101 and turn right on Calabasas Road. The road leads shortly into the historic village of the town, which boasts a handful of quaint Victorian, frontier-style shops and a small creek park. Blooming flowers and eucalyptus trees, oaks and graceful peppers signal the historic **Leonis Adobe** and **Plummer House** at 23537 Calabasas Road. Nestled between the freeway and suburbia, the vintage duo is surrounded by arbor-entwined vineyards and hollyhock-filled gardens. The two-story Leonis Adobe was built in 1844; the restored farmhouse with ginger-bread-decorated veranda and shutters was the home of Miguel Leonis, a colorful personality in early Los Angeles history, and is a nicely preserved Monterey-style adobe. Stockyard pens hosting longhorn cattle, horses, and sheep are adjacent to the ranch house. The petite Plummer House, situated on the other side of the Leonis, was originally located in Plummer Park in West Hollywood. Moved to this site to avoid demo-lition, the restored Victorian cottage now serves as a visitor center for the adobe. The cottage, known as the oldest house in West Hollywood, offers displays, period costumes, and a gift shop and bookstore. Tours are offered weekly on selected days. **http://www.leonisadobemuseum.org/**

AUTHOR'S TIP:
GRANDPA WALTON'S
FOREST THEATER

It is difficult to tell the difference between audience, stage and forest at the **Will Geer Theatricum Botanicum***, deep in the heart of Topanga Canyon. The stage sits at the base of a low slope under a canopy of oaks. For several decades, crowds have flocked to this enchanting theater, which the late Geer (for-merly of TV's The Waltons) reopened with his family in 1973. Summer evening performances are almost magical—get there early and have a picnic and take a hike in Topanga State Park.* **https://theatricum.com/**

Hidden away in the midwestern end of the valley is another gem rich in the history of the valley's early settlement days. The **Orcutt Ranch Horticulture Center** is located at 23600 Roscoe Boulevard in Canoga Park. Cut across the valley, and a few blocks past the intersection of Fallbrook and Roscoe is this secluded garden paradise with rose gardens and ancient oaks. Established in 1917, the Orcutt Ranch was the vacation residence of William and Mary Orcutt, who lived in Los Angeles and came to retreat here in their cabin under the oaks. William worked for Union Oil and is often referred to as the "father of modern geology." He is credited with discovering the skeleton of an extinct giant ground sloth in the La Brea Tar Pits; he later became a vice president of Union Oil. The beautiful Spanish-style home, dubbed Rancho Sambra del Robles, or Ranch of the Shade of Oaks, was built in 1920 on 200 acres of what was then called Owensmouth, and although many additions have been made through the years, the original home boasted more than 3,000 square feet. The home, a centerpiece for the impressive gardens, also boasts 16-inch-thick walls, Mexican-tile floors, and mahogany and walnut hand-carved fireplace mantels from the Philippines. Around the house were planted miles of citrus and walnut groves over the surrounding hills, and palms were used to line the estate border. Many of the valley oaks and coastal live oaks were already on the property; the oldest oak is located on the Justice Street side of the park and is said to be 700 years old. In 1966 the Los Angeles City Park and Recreation Department purchased the designated historical monument estate and gardens for the public to enjoy. Follow the path to the gravel nature trails that traverse the estate past lush, marked vegetation and shady picnic areas. A maze of pathways leads to a small creek with a bridge; a rose garden past sculpted hedges is the site of weddings. The grounds of Orcutt Ranch are open every day; free tours of the house are conducted on selected days. **https://www.laparks.org/ horticulture/orcutt-ranch**

Back on Interstate 5, continuing on to Newhall, take the Pico Canyon exit for a visit to a movie cowboy's home turned park. The **William S. Hart Park**, nestled in wild hillside country, was the ranch of film star and author William S. Hart who made about seventy silent films, his last being Tumbleweeds in 1925. Hart, known to his public as Two Gun Bill, purchased the 265-acre old Horseshoe Ranch in 1921 and, along with his sister, Mary, designed the spectacular hilltop mansion. The mansion's construction took three years to be completed and cost $90,000. The home, furnished with Russell, Remington and Flagg paintings and sculptures as well as Indian relics and a gun collection, was used quite often to entertain celebrities of the time. Mr. Hart lived at the ranch until his death in 1946; he willed the estate to the County of Los Angeles to be used by the public without charge, having stated not long before his death, "While I was making pictures, the people gave me their nickels, dimes and quarters. When I am gone, I want them to have my home."

Take an afternoon to explore Two Gun Bill's home, which includes 110 acres of wilderness area. When you enter the park, you first see the site of the original ranch house constructed in 1910; the present ranch house was built in 1926 after a fire destroyed the bunkhouse. It contains some interesting memorabilia, such as western gear from Hart's movies and photographs. A pleasant picnic area sits next to the house, which is flanked by two roads up the hill to the mansion. Take the dirt path up if you are in the mood for a moderate hike past the native oaks and pines. At the top of the hill the Spanish-Mexican–style mansion, named La Loma de los Vientos, reigns majestically over the estate, with panoramic views in all directions. The rambling twenty-two-room hacienda, with a cowboy weather vane silhouetted against the blue sky, balconies covered in striped awnings and patios, is framed by giant stands of cactus and pine. Tours of the mansion are offered on selected days. **http://hartmuseum.org/**

With thanks to the oil industry, Southern California has an untouched piece of woodlands that has recently opened up to the public. The oil industry created this "preserve" more than one hundred years ago as the former Chevron Oil Co. Newhall Oil Field. The 4,000-acre **Santa Clarita Woodlands Park** is nestled near Santa Clarita and Newhall off Interstate 5. Within the park is **Mentryville**, once the center of life for the oil workers and a mere Victorian ghost town today. You'll see the old schoolhouse that was once lit with natural gas from the fields and Alex Mentry's early-twentieth-century home that was "moved" to this locale, about 18 inches, during the 1994 Northridge earthquake. An old diner sign shaped like a cowboy hat stands alone. There are several good hiking trails at the woodland, offering outstanding mountain and canyon views and year-round streams and meadows. A few miles northwest of the park is Rice Canyon. The Rice Canyon Trail within the park is a moderate 3-mile loop; the Townsley Canyon Loop is a more challenging 7-mile hike, with unsurpassed views of the San Gabriel Mountains. **https://mrca. ca.gov/parks/park-listing/santa-clarita-woodlands-park/**

In tiny **Acton**, big roars can be heard at the **Shambala Preserve**. Shambala is home to more than 40 big cats, from lions and tigers to leopards and bobcats, who have found forever homes here thanks to actress/animal advocate Tippi Hedren—its Roar Foundation's president and founder. The preserve for exotic felines has given sanctuary to more than 235 felines after being confiscated by various authorities. As a true sanctuary, Shambala does not buy, breed, sell, trade or subject animals to commercial use. The sanctuary's only purpose is to allow the magnificent animals to live out their lives with love and dignity. Hedren's passion has ensured that each "wild one" has the best human, nutritional, medical, emotional and mental care possible. One special weekend each month (and on other days for private groups or parties) the Shambala Preserve opens its gates to the public for a series of exciting and informative "safaris" through the world of the big cats, all of whom are endangered or threatened species. Meet African lions, Bengal and Siberian tigers, and black and spotted leopards, servals and mountain lions, up close. The afternoon Safari consists of a 3-hour planned program, including a I-hour guided walking tour. The tour culminates at Shambala Lake, a great spot to picnic. **http://www.shambala. org/about.htm**

After an absence of nearly one hundred years, the lost art of winemaking returned to Los Angeles County in the fall of 2001 in **Agua Dulce**, a pleasant rural area past the Vasquez Rocks Natural Area Park off Highway 14. **Agua Dulce Vineyards** is the largest grower of premium wine grapes in the county on its 100-acre spread with a country-style tasting room. Wine tasting is conducted daily that includes tasting up to five of the winery's award-winning wines. Pack a picnic, grab a bottle of wine and head over to the gazebo to enjoy horseshoes or bocce ball. Sign up for the special barrel tasting tour and picnic lunch for an up-close look at the working vineyard. Agua Dulce Vineyards now offers a stay in the middle of the vineyard in the former vintner's house. The 4-bedroom, 5,000-square-foot home is a perfect place to recharge, go horseback riding on the Pacific Crest Trail or spend the day winetasting. **https://www.aguadulcewinery.com/wp/**

AUTHOR'S TIP: THE BIRTH OF FAST FOOD

It seems that Southern California has been the inspiration for many now-popular fast-food chains. Here are a few of those you are sure to recognize:

Big Boy, founded in 1936 in Glendale

Del Taco, founded in 1964 in Barstow

Fatburger, founded in 1952 in Los Angeles

In-N-Out Burger, founded in 1948 in Baldwin Park

Marie Callender's, founded in 1947 in Long Beach

Taco Bell, founded in 1962 in Downey

Wienerschnitzel, founded in 1961 in Wilmington

Carl's Jr., founded in 1941 in Anaheim

Denny's, founded in 1953 in Lakewood

IHOP, founded in 1958 in Toluca Lake

Jack in the Box, founded in 1951 in San Diego

McDonald's, founded in 1940 in San Bernardino

Tommy's, founded in 1946 in Los Angeles

Winchell's, founded in 1948 in Temple City

The San Fernando Valley is also the center of television filming, from talk shows to your favorite comedies and dramas. Although **Universal Studios** is well known for its theme park fame, many productions are currently filming on the famed **Warner Bros. Studios** lot. And you can get an insider's glimpse of "working Hollywood" on **Warner Bros. Studio's VIP Tour**. Because nothing is staged on this VIP back- lot excursion, there is no telling what or whom you might encounter. In the early days of Warner Bros., James Dean could be seen speeding through the lot on his motorcycle and, on one special tour, Tom Cruise boarded a cart filled with tour guests to listen to the tour guide's history of New York Street and its transformation into ancient Tokyo for the movie "The Last Samurai."

The studio, founded in 1923, began with such legendary films as "Casablanca" and "Rebel Without a Cause" and television classics like "Maverick" and "The Waltons." The studio itself sits on 110 acres in the heart of **Burbank** and features 29 working soundstages on the front lot and numerous back-lot outdoor sets you are bound to recognize. Every day at the busy studios is different, so no two tours are the same. Since your group includes just 12 people, the tours are often tailored to the group's interests. Tour guides stay in communication with production so that, when possible, guests are escorted to active soundstages and back-lot film sets for a personal look at filming in action—sometimes within inches of the what's going on. On occasion, VIP tour guests have been cast as extras in film and television productions. At the end of the 2 ¼-hour tour via electric carts, guests may explore the studio museum at leisure. The museum contains a rich collection of the studio's history—from costumes and props to sets. If you have the time, the Deluxe VIP Tour offers a 5-hour, in-depth look at the craft of movie making. The highlight of the tour may very well be your lunch in the studio commissary, sitting next to one of your favorite celebrities. **https://www.wbstudiotour.com/**

LOCAL'S SECRET: TIKI STEAKHOUSE

"Damon's Steak House in Glendale has been around since 1937. While it's called a steak house, everyone loves it for its totally tiki ambiance! Polynesian murals on the walls, a huge fish tank, an outrigger canoe (with dusty monkeys) hanging from the ceiling, mai tais (Mai Tai Monday specials) and fun Hawaiian-shirt decked-out wait staff who have been there forever. The food is good, but go for the ambiance. Be sure to order the house salad --classic chopped salad ala the 1960s; the twice baked potatoes; and, at lunch, the steak sandwich." http://www.damonsglendale.com/

– Barbara Beckley, travel writer, journalist/editor,
www.facebook.com/BarbaraBeckley.9

In the southeastern portion of the San Fernando Valley, in **Valley Glen**, you'll discover one of the longest murals in the world. At 2,754 feet, **The Great Wall of Los Angeles**, located on Coldwater Canyon between Burbank Boulevard and Oxnard Street, is regarded as one of the city's most successful depictions of ethnic and cultural cooperation. Part of a beautification project in the area, the project began in 1974 and was completed five summers later. The wall employed 400 youth and their families from diverse socio-economic backgrounds, as well as artists, oral historians, ethnologists, scholars and community members. Each year was dedicated to depicting a different decade in California history from the viewpoint of different ethnic minorities. http://sparcinla.org/

In 2007, a large part of Van Nuys was renamed **Lake Balboa** and the 80-acre **Anthony C. Beilenson Park**, formerly Balboa Park, received a million-dollar redo with a maritime-themed playground and interactive drum play area. Lifeguards are on-site at Lake Balboa, which is located in the park, making it an attractive place for boating and fishing. But a spring visit, might reward with cherry blossom trees in full bloom. But at all times, don't forget to enjoy the miles of trails that line the park, which branch off from the trail around the lake. **https://www.laparks.org/aquatic/balboa**

AUTHOR'S TIP: IT'S THE BRADY BUNCH HOUSE!

If you're cruising around Studio City, you are apt to eye one of the most famous houses in television history, the Brady Bunch house. Located at 11217 Dilling Street, exterior shots of the house were used for more than 100 episodes, as well as a few sequels. The house actually sold recently for $3.5 million—which was $1.6 million more than the asking price. A bidding war between singer Lance Bass and HGTV, saw the food network as the winner. So, we may be seeing more of the famous home on the television screen.

Encino, across the valley, offers a five-acre historical park maintained by the state of California on all that remains of an original 4,460-acre ranch called the Encino. The **Los Encinos State Historical Park**, in a secluded location at 16756 Moorpark Street in a residential part of the city near Balboa Boulevard, contains the living and working center of the 1849-established ranch and is open to the public on selected days. The gracious grounds, dotted by giant cacti, graceful peppertrees, citrus groves and a lake that dates from 1872, make for a pleasant stroll. On the grounds you will observe the 1870's limestone blacksmith shop, which was later used as a bakery for ranch bread. The Garnier Building, also constructed of limestone in 1873, is a copy of the ranch-owning

Garnier family's home in the south of France. The ground floor of the French farmhouse held the kitchen and dining room of the ranch, and the upstairs housed ranch hands. **http://losencinos.org**

More than 4,00 acres of both natural chaparral-covered terrain and landscaped parkland and picnic areas make up **Griffith Park**, one of the largest municipal parks with urban wilderness areas in the country. Even with many world-known attractions, from a zoo and theater to an observatory and museum, a large portion of the park remains virtually unchanged from the days when Native American villages occupied the area's lower slopes. Discovering the lesser known attractions in the park is worth the exploration, such as the **Bronson Caves**. More than one hundred years ago, a rock quarry existed in a part of the park. Although the quarry closed in the 1920s, some caves remained. The Bronson Caves have now become a popular filming location for dozens of films and television shows, including the original Batman series, where the cave was the mysterious entrance to the Batcave. To visit the Bronson Caves, just park in the free public parking spaces at the Bronson Canyon entrance to Griffith Park and follow the Bronson Ridge Trail. **Travel Town** in Griffith Park is a lesser known attraction that reminds visitors of L.A.'s rich railroad history. In fact, the museum has been educating the public about trains and railroad travel through tours and miniature train rides since 1948. The miniature railroads carry almost 600,000 passengers each year, mostly locals for birthday parties, on the one-mile-long route that crosses over several bridges and goes through an 800-foot tunnel. **https://www.laparks.org/griffithpark#attractions**

LOCAL'S SECRET: ABANDONED ZOO

When visiting LA you could, of course, visit the famous Los Angeles Zoo and that would be loads of fun! But what if I told you there is actually a forgotten, well-hidden zoo behind the Los Angeles Zoo? Sounds way cooler right, that's what our Spotters thought as well. The Griffith Park Zoo was built in 1912 and later closed when the animals held there were transferred to their current location. You can find the zoo behind a long hiking trail, with all the caves, bars and other enclosures used for the 15 animals that were held there. It's a spooky looking place, as if the ghosts of the animals still linger...One of the best things about the old zoo is its hidden nature. Most people do not know there is another zoo. The zoo is not well marked and you'll need some directions from locals.

– James Hsiao, spotter, Spotted By Locals, https://www.spottedbylocals.com/blog/12-hidden-los-angeles-gems/

Pasadena

Less than 10 freeway miles from downtown Los Angeles is the city of **Pasadena**, abundant in art, theater, history and scientific offerings. Pasadena is best known for its famed **Rose Parade** each January 1, as well as the Rose Bowl game held the same day. Pasadena, cradled in the foothills of the San Gabriel Mountains, was established in the early 1900s as an exclusive winter getaway for the wealthy. The city's rich history and genteel hospitality pervade today with nearly 10 percent of Pasadena's 22 square miles historically designated. Its gracious mansions on tree-lined streets, impressive list of 1,000 structures on the National Register of Historic Places, acres of botanic gardens, world-class art and distinct neighborhoods for exploring, make Pasadena a great day or weekend trip.

When you reach the intersection of Colorado and Raymond Avenue, you've entered Pasadena's original downtown and its historic past. **Old Town** is always in a state of revitalization, with many of the stucco exteriors stripped away and interior layers of paint lifted to expose the Craftsman-style brickwork and beautiful woodwork and frozen glass of an era gone by. Many of these buildings, most no taller than two stories, are already on the National Register of Historic Places. Examples include the 1906 Braley Building at the corner of Raymond and Colorado. Boutiques with antiques and clothing fill the century-old structures, as do intimate restaurants and art galleries. Enjoying Old Town Pasadena on foot and close-up is the way to go, treasuring all of the renovation as it unfolds in this area. **Pasadena Heritage Tours** makes this discovery much more interesting through its variety of scheduled, docent-led walks. **https://pasadenaheritage.org/**

AUTHOR'S TIP:
SMELL THE ROSES CLOSE UP

*More than one million people line the streets of Pasadena and approximately 500 million watch on television each New Year's Day to view the **Tournament of Roses Parade**. Die-hard fans camp in sleeping bags overnight for a prime viewing spot, and still others wait until after the parade to get a close-up view the few days following as the floats are lined up in nearby **Victory Park**. The first parade was held January 1, 1890, and was begun at the insistence of a zoologist named Charles Frederick Holder, who loved roses and found Pasadena's climate to be a perfect spot for raising the buds.The Rose Bowl is world famous for its namesake **Tournament of Roses football game**, home of the UCLA Bruins football team, and its huge, monthly flea market. However, now you can see hidden gems throughout "America's Stadium" with the **Rose Bowl Stadium Tours**. Explore the Rose*

Bowl Stadium, from the field to the press box, and learn every-thing about the historical site of Super Bowls. For those want-ing a very exclusive behind-the-scenes tour, sign up for the VIP experience. **https://www.rosebowlstadium.com/tours**

If you are in the mood for pâté rather than french-fried pota-toes or mahimahi instead of meat loaf but want to dine in an era gone by, then reserve an intimate table at the **Raymond Restaurant**. The Raymond, a short distance out of downtown at 1250 South Fair Oaks in Pasadena, hosts a notable heritage and enchanting ambience. The bistro's history begins with the Raymond Hotel, the first great resort hotel of Pasadena, built in 1886. Perched on Bacon Hill, the Royal Raymond had 201 guest rooms plus libraries, parlors, reception rooms, bil-liard rooms and a grand ballroom. On Easter Sunday in 1895, the wood-framed hotel burned to the ground; just six years later the Raymond was rebuilt, but because of the passing of Pasadena's heyday as a resort location, it succumbed to indebtedness. The Raymond was razed in 1934, the same year its founder, Walter Raymond, died. The award-winning restaurant is located in the 1930's caretaker's cottage of the grand hotel and is tucked away from the busy roadway among bright blooming gardens and vine-covered arbors. The meticulously restored cottage, boasting a bevy of inti-mate, garden-surrounded patios, is difficult to spot from the main road, so look closely for the intersection of South Fair Oaks and Raymond Hill Road. And, be sure to experience its "hidden" bar, **1886**, a locals' favorite with a bevy of changing cocktails and bar bites. **http://theraymond.com/**

Although Pasadena's many tourist attractions are fairly well-known, the locale voted the "best unknown tourist attrac-tion" by Pasadena Weekly is the **Pacific Asia Museum**. The curling green roofline of the magnificent Asian structure at

46 North Los Robles Avenue hints at its interior but leaves much for the curious visitor to discover within. The museum claims to be the only institution in Southern California specializing in the arts of Asia and the Pacific Basin. The Chinese Imperial–style palace that houses the exhibits is the historic Grace Nicholson Building; walk through the entry to a serene, central Chinese courtyard garden, whose pools are stocked with giant koi. Inside, visitors can wander the rooms of red-tinted walls hung with delicate paintings of far-off lands and view Asian and Pacific exhibitions, as well as changing displays, a contemporary Asian arts gallery, a children's gallery and a research library. Interesting programs, including guided tours, lectures and demonstrations, films and performances, are offered. **https://pacificasiamuseum.usc.edu/**

It very well could be that Pasadena's greatest treasures are its grand estates, reminiscent of the city's wealthy beginnings and gracious present. The mansions and their flowing lawns and manicured gardens, sometimes secured behind iron gates, occupy several older neighborhoods within the city and spread into the adjacent community of exclusive **San Marino**. A great deal of history can be unearthed while touring these estates of Pasadena's wealthy settlers from the East.

The **Fenyes Mansion** at 470 West Walnut Street was built in 1905 for Dr. and Mrs. Adalbert Fenyes. The magnificent white-columned mansion, located behind a tropical garden of tall palms, birds-of-paradise, ferns and bamboo, was a popular gathering place for the art community of the times due to its owner, artist and patron, Mrs. Eva Fenyes. Douglas Fairbanks and Tom Mix were just a few of the movie greats who starred in movies made at the mansion. Occasionally the photogenic mansion is still used for filmmaking, but family members turned the house over to the Pasadena Historical Society in the mid-1960s to be used as a museum and headquarters for the society. Docent-led tours are offered

Friday through Sunday. **https://pasadenahistory.org/tours/ fenyes-mansion-tours/**

Another mansion of note in the same neighborhood is the **Gamble House** at 4 Westmoreland Place. The showplace home is fronted by expansive lawns, and brown shingles and vines cover the venerable house's outside walls. The Gamble House was designed by renowned Pasadena architects Greene and Greene and is internationally recognized as a masterpiece of the early-twentieth-century Arts and Crafts movement. The National Historic Landmark mansion was built in 1908 for David and Mary Gamble and is complete today with the home's original furniture, lighting, landscaping and accessories, all designed by Greene and Greene for the house; visitors will note that the spectacular woodwork has been hand-rubbed to a glass-like finish. Guided tours of the Gamble House are offered on various days. **https://gamble-house.org/**

The centerpiece of historical lodging in Pasadena is **The Langham Huntington Hotel**, which in every way captures the splendor of days gone by. A Pasadena hotel legend since 1907, the restored and elegant property still reigns supreme as a hideaway for "those in the know." Located at the base of the San Gabriels, the grand hotel offers 379 guest rooms and suites, a legendary restaurant, afternoon tea on Wedgwood, a spa, lush gardens, tennis and an Olympic-size pool. **http:// www.langhamhotels.com/en/the-langham/pasadena/**

Fashionable **San Marino**, home of the renowned Huntington Library, adjoins Pasadena amid the ivy-covered estates of Pasadena's first social elite. Nestled in one such neighborhood is a historical reminder of even earlier days, **El Molino Viejo**. El Molino Viejo, whose name means "the old mill," was the first water-powered gristmill in Southern California. The rather primitive mill, built around 1816 by Indian labor under the supervision of Mission San Gabriel padres, replaced the previous method of grinding grain by hand. After the mission's secularization in 1833, El Molino Viejo was used primarily as a residence for such colorful residents as the first Los Angeles newspaper editor, James S. Waite. For a short while, the mill served as the golf course clubhouse for the nearby Huntington Hotel. The mill house was restored in the late 1920s and is now owned by the city of San Marino and serves as headquarters of the California Historical Society. The historic landmark is open to the public several days a week; walk inside to view the mill's Grinding Room and its thick walls and tall wooden shutters, as well as changing exhibits relating to state history. Take the staircase downstairs to see the model exhibit of the mill as it was in the former wheel chamber. http://www.old-mill.org/

LOCAL'S SECRET: CAFÉ TIME WARP

"The **Colonial Kitchen** *on Huntington Drive in San Marino is a time warp return to a 1960s café with big booths and classic American diner comfort food. Sit at the counter or in a big booth and be surrounded by the locals who have been coming forever. A true slice of Americana (even though it's now owned by a local San Marino couple originally from Hong Kong). They smartly haven't changed it. And, it's been used as a backdrop for several movies."* https://www.facebook.com/Colonial-Kitchen

– Barbara Beckley, travel writer, journalist/editor,
www.facebook.com/BarbaraBeckley.9

Located at the base of the foothills adjacent to Pasadena is a destination known for rocket research and space exploration. The **Jet Propulsion Laboratory** (JPL) is the operating division of the California Institute of Technology (Caltech), a leading research and development center for NASA. Nestled on 177 acres and employing more than 5,000 people, JPL is leading the way into the twenty-first century for the study of Earth and its neighbors and the exploration of space. Prearranged guided tours are available at JPL at no charge. **https://www. jpl.nasa.gov/events/tours/views/**

Nestled in the San Gabriel Mountain foothills is the wooded, tranquil community of **La Canada**, which is home to the **Descanso Gardens**. Part of what was once the 30,000-acre Spanish Rancho San Rafael, the gardens began being developed in 1939 and now consist of 165 acres of native chaparral-covered slopes, maintained as an environmental study area by the Los Angeles County Department of Arboreta and Botanic Gardens. A forest of California live oak trees is the setting for year-round blooms at the gardens: one of the world's largest displays of camellias (more than 600 varieties), outdoor orchids, lilacs, roses and much more. The gardens also contain a spectacular four-acre rose garden, featuring modern roses and the roses of "yesterday." Near the lilac grove is the Oriental Pavilion, a charming teahouse surrounded by a Japanese garden with pools and waterfalls. **https://www. descansogardens.org/**

AUTHOR'S TIP: A MILE OF LIGHTS IN ALTADENA

*For nearly a century, people have been strolling down **Altadena's Christmas Tree Lane**, one of the oldest large-scale Christmas lighting spectacles in the nation and designated National Historic Landmark #990. The stately Italian deodar trees came to this area near Pasadena in 1883, introduced by city founder John P. Woodbury. Proclaiming them the most beautiful trees he had ever seen, Woodbury brought the imported seeds to his brother's ranch, and two years later the prospering trees were* *transplanted along Santa Rosa Avenue. In 1920, the idea of lighting the trees for the holidays first took hold and expanded over the next few years to all 135 trees, today strung with more than 14,000 lights—all screwed in by hand by community volunteers. The street, located between Woodbury Avenue and Altadena Drive, is closed for the evening to cars during Christmas Tree Lane so that visitors may walk the mile; flashlights are suggested.* **http://www.seecalifornia.com/christmas/trees/alta-dena-christmas-tree-lane.html**

The Los Angeles County Department of Arboreta and Botanic Gardens offers more than another stroll through nature's beauty just east of Pasadena and southeast of La Canada. Step into deepest, darkest Africa or escape to a lush, tropical isle at the **Los Angeles County Arboretum and Botanic Garden** in **Arcadia**, which delivers a vast array of scenery within its peaceful 127 acres of gardens. The gardens' rich history spans from the time the Gabrielino Indians camped by the spring-fed lagoon to the mission days through movie filming in the late 1930s to the present. During the Mission period and the years that followed, the arboretum land was known as the Rancho Santa Anita. Elias Jackson Baldwin, rich from his share in the Comstock Lode, purchased nearly 80,000 acres of Southern California property—part of this holding was the rancho. The colorful, late-1800s owner of Rancho Santa Anita built the Victorian cottage on his working ranch (livestock, racehorses, fruit and nut trees, grapevines and grain) for the sole purpose of entertaining his friends in style. "Lucky" Baldwin himself always stayed in the original ranch house, a sparse adobe built by Hugo Reid. **https://www.arboretum.org/**

AUTHOR'S TIP: TOUR THE FILMING SITES

Visitors to the Arboretum may follow the one-way trail through the Prehistoric and Jungle Garden for a look at Baldwin's cottage and adobe up close. Follow the trail as it edges the lagoon lined with tall palms and filled with a wide array of migratory bird life, and you walk along the same path as did Dorothy Lamour, Bob Hope and Bing Crosby in the Road to Singapore. Duck under the wandering vines that cross the jungle route lit by soft sunlight filtered through the dense bamboo and tropical foliage. Any second, Tarzan may swing through the trees ahead of you, just as Johnny Weissmuller did with Maureen O'Sullivan when he filmed his Hollywood classics in this very spot. The site is best known to television viewers as Ricardo Montalban's Fantasy Island, complete with tropical lagoon, bell tower and gingerbread-decorated Queen Anne cottage. (In 1978 the studio constructed its own replica of the Queen Anne cottage.)

Hollywood Area

Hollywood isn't just a place. It has often been called a state of mind. Capturing the glamor and legend of Hollywood's glory days—the days of Clark Gable, Marilyn Monroe and Charlie Chaplin—is the goal of many film enthusiasts. One of Hollywood's greatest landmarks, the **Egyptian Theatre** at 6712 Hollywood Boulevard, has returned with all of its classic glamor intact. Although the 1922-built theater was the prestigious site of Hollywood's first premiere, by the 1990s it was relegated to third-rate movie house status, offering $1.50 seats. It is now the home of the film institution's **American Cinematheque** and has made a dramatic transformation.

Restoration details on the grand theater include its dramatic sunburst ceiling "shining" once again and the acquisition of a 1922 Wurlitzer pipe organ. A total of $14 million has been invested in the theater, much of that spent to ensure not only its restoration but also its improvement for generations to come. **http://www.americancinemathequecalendar.com/ egyptian_theatre_events**

Paramount Studios is the last major studio remaining in Hollywood, and its history of moviemaking makes for a great guided tour of its back lots. It was originally home to the Peralta Studios, which moved across the street on Marathon in 1917. It was then Brunton Studios, and then United Studios, before becoming the Paramount made great by Jesse Lasky when he took over in 1926. Paramount was home to such stars as Mary Pickford, Claudette Colbert, Mae West, Bob Hope, Bing Crosby and Dorothy Lamour. One of the 1919-built stages remains, as does the original and distinctive gate, even though it sits in a new location these days. Touring the studios, whether on the regular or VIP tour, always includes unplanned surprises, from filming in action to spying celebrities. **http://www.paramount-studiotour.com/studio-tours.htm**

When former "Truth or Consequences" television show writer Milt Larsen stared out of his office window in Hollywood in the early 1960s, he routinely fastened his gaze on a 1909 "castle" perched on the hill above—complete with swirling turrets, colorful stained-glass windows and lots of peeling paint. The stately home had gone from prestigious estate to boarding house decay over the decades, but Larsen, from a family of magicians, saw only magical possibilities for the structure. Larsen and his brother charmed the owners of the property into letting them transform the mansion into their vision of what would become the world's most famous club for magicians and magic enthusiasts, as well as the home of The Academy of Magical Arts. On Jan. 2, 1963, **The Magic Castle** opened its doors with 150-member magicians. Today, the former Lane family mansion stands as one of Hollywood's most popular backdrops for movie and television filming. Multiple theaters and bars exist within the walls of The Magic Castle, including the Houdini séance room and the Close-Up Gallery, its most intimate venue. But every room in the mansion has its supernatural touches, from the ghost piano player in the lounge to the question-answering owl to the bar stool that unexpectedly moves its occupant up and down. It's no secret that The Magic Castle's dining room for members only is one of the most sought-after dinner destinations in Los Angeles. The members-only club is technically open just to those who are a part of The Academy of Magical Arts or guests of members, but there are ways to see it all. http://www.magiccastle.com/

AUTHOR'S TIP: HOW TO EXPERIENCE THE CASTLE

Although The Magic Castle is a private club, it is possible to be a part of the mystical fun. One way is to be a guest of a member; another is to attend a rare public performance. But short of having a member friend, you can visit by staying with a "member" overnight—that is, the adjacent **Magic Castle Hotel**. *Guests of the hotel (not a part of the Castle) will find the doors of the legendary magic club next door hospitably open to them for an unforgettable day or evening. Not to say that your stay itself at the hotel won't be magical. Formerly living quarters to stars and starlets, the hillside hotel offers a half-century of its own interesting history. Today, it offers overnight guests totally redone suites (most the size of full apartments) and an enormous amount of customized personal service and flexibility to meet the guests' needs. Admittance to The Magic Castle is not guaranteed, but you have a good chance of getting in on the magic!* **http://magiccastlehotel.com/**

Your imagination, as well as your camera, will get a work out at **The Museum of Illusions**. The unique museum's one-of-a-kind interactive unique 3D paintings just call out for selfies. And you are invited to take as many photos as you want in front of a wide range of exhibits, from climbing the highest mountain tops in the world to playing Jack & Rose as the Titanic sinks. **https://laillusions.com/**

A stop that guarantees "celebrity spotting" is the **Hollywood Forever Cemetery** on Santa Monica Boulevard. It is the final resting place for hundreds of celebrities, from Judy Garland to George Harrison. The full-service funeral home is more than one of Los Angeles' oldest cemeteries, established in 1899, it is filled with towering monuments and unusual headstones. **https://hollywoodforever.com/**

It's nice to know that "going Hollywood" still applies to Hollywood "the place." The community, which interestingly has never become a city, regally reigns as the historic "keeper" of early Hollywood and a present-day escape into the world of movie-star magic. Park your car near Hollywood and Highland, grab your camera and spend the day following the "stars." Don't let anyone tell you that you can't attend an "A-list party." **Madame Tussauds Hollywood** opened its doors in 2009, and the wait was well worth it. Nestled between the Kodak Theatre, home of the Academy Awards, and the world-famous TCL Chinese Theatre, the collection of realistic wax celebrity figures is nothing short of amazing. From early Silver Screen icons to present-day blockbuster stars and athletes, the figures seem alive. Several interactive exhibits allow guests to have a shoot-out with John Wayne and even share a chocolate with Forrest Gump. **https://www.madametussauds.com/hollywood/en/**

A little bit hidden and less known is the four-story **Hollywood Museum** which contains the largest collection of Hollywood memorabilia you'll find anywhere. Located in the former Max Factor building, it is the ideal setting for the museum's 10,000-piece collection and mesmerizing exhibits. You'll discover such treasures as Marilyn Monroe's million-dollar dress, Rocky's boxing gloves and Hannibal Lecter's jail cell. **http://thehollywoodmuseum.com/**

The **Dolby Theatre**, situated where the historic Hollywood Hotel once stood, is now the home of the Oscars. But many other televised events happen there, including the American Idol Finals and Daytime Emmys and the AFI Awards. Daily guided tours of the theater will take you well beyond the red carpet to a close-up view of the famous statue itself, the location of where your favorite celebrities sit, a visit to the exclusive George Eastman VIP Room and an insider's view of the "Winners Walk." **https://dolbytheatre.com/tours/tour-information/**

AUTHOR'S TIP: BE A PART OF TELEVISION FILMING

You're invited to join the fun in a studio audience for a unique and free "behind the scenes" Hollywood experience by Audience Unlimited, the company that provides live audiences for myriad television productions. Shows are produced at various studios in the Los Angeles area, and tickets are released for most shows starting 30 days prior to show date so plan ahead. **http://www.tvtickets.com/**

To feel a real part of Hollywood's heritage, plan to stay at the legendary **Château Marmont**, a French-Normandy–style hotel built in 1927—the same year Graumann's Chinese Theater opened. Surrounded by lush gardens and nestled on a hillside right above Hollywood's Sunset Strip, the grand hotel, with its cathedral-arched entry, has spanned the eras of movieland virtually unchanged. Guests at the Marmont might wonder if they are checking into a room where Marilyn Monroe slept or the bungalow in which John Belushi died (cottage 3). Other famous residents include Jean Harlow, who lived for a year in suite 33 with her third husband, Hal Rosson, and Boris Karloff, who lived at the château for seven years. Howard Hughes favored the penthouse; Garbo checked in using the name Harriet Brown; and current frequent guests include Diane Keaton, Richard Gere and Dustin Hoffman. Tony Randall and his wife were guests (in the bungalow next door to the one made infamous by Belushi) for five years during the filming of television's The Odd Couple. **http://www.chateaumarmont. com/**

AUTHOR'S TIP:
SECRET STAIRCASES

Before car travel and highways became synonymous with Los Angeles, the area was connected by a series of more than 400 staircases. For those looking for urban climbs, it's interesting to know that many of those staircases remain intact and are open for the public. You'll discover an easy to reach series of stairs off Highland in back of the Hollywood Bowl. Enjoy dramatic overlooks of the city from here; also, nearby are the Beachwood Canyon Stairs, which include views of the Hollywood Sign and Lake Hollywood.

Grab inspiring city views from the **Baldwin Hills Scenic Overlook**. Its 500-foot peak, accessed via hiking trails or a set of steep concrete stairs, reveals spectacular views of the Los Angeles Basin, Pacific Ocean and surrounding mountains once you reach the summit. Take time at the visitor center to peruse exhibits of the area's early oil production history and learn about conservation measures happening today. **http:// www.parks.ca.gov/?page_id=22790**

The Hollywood Reservoir, also known as Lake Hollywood, is a reservoir that was created by the 1924-built Mulholland Dam. The reservoir is located in the Hollywood Hills and overlooks the Hollywood Sign. The Hollywood Reservoir has appeared in films such as Chinatown, where Hollis Mulwray is discovered dead along the shores, as well as Earthquake. The reservoir and surrounding neighborhood overlook the Hollywood Sign. The newly repaired trail around the **Lake Hollywood Reservoir** is a great way to enjoy a walk, jog or bike with Hollywood views. It starts on the northwest side with available parking on Lake Hollywood Dr. Along the way, you'll encounter ducks, views of the Hollywood Sign and a beautiful Mulholland Dam.

Anyone arriving in Hollywood for the first time will feel they have really "arrived" when they eye the sign that is positioned in large letters on a hillside reigning high above Hollywood. Better look from afar, however. It is now illegal to hike or get near the **Hollywood Sign**. Here is one great way to get close and see other Hollywood landmarks along the way!

Photo by Roberto Nickson, unsplash.com

LOCAL'S SECRET:
TAKE JOSH'S HIKE TO THE HOLLYWOOD
SIGN PAST THE WISDOM TREE

"Hiking to the Hollywood Sign is something that most visitors want to do when they come to Los Angeles. While there are many ways to get there, one of the shortest (but steepest) is the hike to the Wisdom Tree on Burbank Peak and over the Getty Ridge Trail To the back of the Hollywood Sign. This 3.5-mile trail provides a good leg burning work out and at the same time some fantastic views of Los Angeles in the distance...Parking for the hike is located north of Lake Hollywood Reservoir along the street on Lake Hollywood Drive...The trail starts on Wonder View Drive, but you can't park there so you will need to walk up to it. From Lake Hollywood Drive, head up Wonder View Drive, by walking along the cement road for about a tenth of a mile. Eventually, the road will end at the base of the hill, which is where the official trail for this hike begins. From here it is about a half mile up to Burbank Peak and the Wisdom Tree...The trail quickly gains elevation and gives impressive views of downtown LA and the Griffith Observatory in the distance. As the trail continues to bend along switchbacks, the Wisdom Tree will come into view, which is the first point of interest. The Wisdom Tree can be seen from all over Los Angeles, and it is an unofficial point of interest in the city. This tree was one of the only trees to survive the 2007 fires, and people now make the hike to it to look out over the city and to write dreams and ideas in the journals that sit in the trunk below the tree. From here the trail goes back along the Aileen Getty Ridge Trail over to Mt. Lee with a decent amount of uphill and downhill along the way. There are great views along this portion of the trail, and eventually, you will reach the second point of interest Cahuenga Peak. This peak is a small dirt patch with a 360-degree view of the surrounding area and a small plaque marking the summit. From here the trail heads back down the hill, and it is pretty steep as well before making one last final ascent

> to an overlook that allows you to see the Hollywood Sign. There are two plaques in this area, one for Hugh Hefner and another for Aileen Getty. They both were influential in purchasing the land and donating it for public use instead of development, which is why you can hike here today. The trail then heads down to the cement road, and you will walk up it to the summit of Mt Lee. There is a small hill in the back you can get the best view looking down on the sign, and there is a bench to relax at on the hill as well. This is the best viewpoint for the sign and Downtown Los Angeles in the distance."
>
> – Josh, California Through My Lens, https://californiathroughmylens.com/hiking-hollywood-sign-wisdom-tree

Culver City

Not as well-known as Hollywood for the business of "show business," **Culver City** has a very rich history of motion picture and television production. Iconic films such as "The Wizard of Oz," "Gone with the Wind," a portion of "Grease" and the Tarzan series were all filmed in Culver City. From its incorporation by Harry Culver in the early 1900s to the renovation and revitalization of its downtown that began in the 90s, Culver City has been known for its studios. Metro Goldwyn Mayer built their studios there in the 1920s; the facility later became Sony Pictures Studios, which is the city's largest employer today. Howard Hughes opened his Hughes Aircraft plant in 1941 in Culver City, but by the early 2000s, parts of the Hughes empire had been purchased by or merged with General Motors, Boeing, NewsCorp and Raytheon.

AUTHOR'S TIP:
CUTS AND COCKTAILS
IN CULVER CITY

Only in this celebrity Mecca will you find a barber shop that doubles as a cocktail bar. You just have to continue the pampering in the rear portion of Blind Barber. Not only do you get a cocktail with your cut, you can go "between" trims and just enjoy Blind Barber's cocktail menu and grilled cheese delights **https://blindbarber.com/**

Beverly Hills

At the beginning of the twentieth century, **Beverly Hills**, or what was then called Rodeo de las Aguas, was mainly known for its lima bean fields. It wasn't until the 1920s that the "gold-paved" town began to gain its prestige—when movie star royalty such as Douglas Fairbanks and Mary Pickford established mansions in the intimate village. At that time Rodeo Drive had a bridle path down the center of the street so celebrities could ride their horses into town.

Beverly Hills, the capital of glamor and affluence, is still in part that same 1920s village, which is evident when visiting some of the city's glorious early estates. One famous Beverly Hills estate is now open to the public as a picturesque, tranquil park. The **Virginia Robinson Gardens** was once the site of lavish Hollywood parties. Mrs. Robinson was known as the "first lady of Beverly Hills," hosting royalty and stars; her neighbors were Glenn Ford, Lillian Disney and Elvis Presley. In 1974 Mrs. Virginia Robinson bequeathed her impressive six-acre hillside estate to the county for preservation and to be used as a public botanical garden, a lushly landscaped botanical show-piece laden with flowers, shrubs and fruit trees. Visitors traverse a series of patio gardens on terraced hillsides and take footpaths and brick stairways past palm groves filled with tropical specimens, a rose garden and sixty-year-old trees. Tours are by reservation only. **https://www.robinsongardens.org/visit/**

Another one of Beverly Hills' hidden gems is the **Greystone Mansion & Gardens**. The former Doheny Estate, tucked away in the hills, offers park grounds for visitors to enjoy, as well as special programs. Completed in 1928 for the son of oil tycoon Edward L. Doheny, the estate was purchased by the city in 1965, and in 1971, the entire 18-acre site was formally dedicated as a public park. Greystone was listed in the National Register of Historic Places in 1976 and in 2013 was designated Beverly Hills Local Historic Landmark No. 4. Long an iconic location for motion picture and television shoots, Greystone has been featured in dozens of films, including The Big Lebowski, Spider-Man, The Social Network and There Will Be Blood. **http://www.beverlyhills.org/exploring/greystonemansiongardens/**

If you want to go from "memory lane to the fast lane," then this newly renovated museum nestled on Los Angeles's museum row is for you. The **Petersen Automotive Museum** was begun in June 1994 by Hot Rod magazine publisher Robert Petersen but is operated by the Natural History Museum. Petersen's tribute to cars in Los Angeles includes interesting car dioramas—you'll even see a full-scale replica of a 1929 Richfield gas station. Exhibits change constantly, but can include some rare antique autos as well as cars of some of the area's greatest stars. **https://www.petersen.org/**

AUTHOR'S TIP:
DRIVES FOR LOVERS

Los Angelinos are in love with their cars, so it follows that there are some spectacular drives to experience—and love. Try one of these:

Follow Sunset Boulevard all the way from Hollywood to the coastal bluffs of Pacific Palisades. The trip will take you less than an hour; it's about 20 miles.

You can do more than "park" on romantic Mulholland Drive. Take it from the Santa Monica Mountains all the way to Hollywood for a half-hour trip; it's about a 15-mile drive.

Jump on historic Route 66 all the way from Los Angeles to Pasadena. It's just a 7-mile trip and will take about fifteen minutes, depending on traffic.

The **La Brea Tar Pits** in Los Angeles, just a few miles from Beverly Hills, were discovered in 1901 by Bill Orcutt, a Union Oil geologist. Orcutt secretly told John Merriam of the University of California at Berkeley about his find of bones of extinct animals so finely preserved in the tar (brea means "tar" in Spanish). Merriam confirmed the discovery a few years later, and then wide-scale digging began. Remarkably, almost all of the bones for each preserved animal were uncovered. An extinct coyote species, called Canis orcutti, was named in honor of Orcutt. In 1915 the tar pits were deeded to the county of Los Angeles as a park. Today museum-goers can peer into the dark black pits, imagining the mastodons and imperial mammoths captured by their sticky goo, and then wander the museum filled with the re-created skeletons of the prehistoric animals that once roamed Los Angeles. Some trivia: The oldest fossil from the La Brea Tar Pits is a wood fragment dated at around 40,000 years. Wolves are the most common mammal in the tar pits; the second most common is the saber-toothed cat, which today is the state fossil. **https://tarpits.org/**

Touring Beverly Hills can be rather distracting: designer shops, celebrities milling down the streets and cell-phone-chatting drivers. Make the trip easy. The city offers free trolley service between Civic Center and Rodeo Drive on Saturdays and Sundays from II a.m. to 5 p.m., excluding holidays. Additional trolley service days are added during the summer and winter seasons. **http://beverlyhills.org/exploring/trolley/?NFR=I**

AUTHOR'S TIP:
SUMMER CONCERTS ON CANON

Locals make their way to Beverly Canon Gardens on Thursdays in the summer for the free **Concerts on Canon***. Presented by the City of Beverly Hills, the concerts are held in the beautiful Beverly Canon Gardens, nestled between Montage Beverly Hills hotel and Sweet Beverly. Seating is first-come, first-serve with space both on grass and café tables. The live music performances take place every Thursday night, from the beginning of June through August.* **http://lovebeverlyhills.com/articles/view/concerts-on-canon**

Farmers market events have become a sought-after phenomenon in Southern California—an in-city experience for stocking up on fruit and vegetables fresh from the fields, as well as the Pacific's latest catches, herbs, flowers, baked goods, culinary delights and more that are locally produced. But let's not forget the granddaddy of them all, the innovator of the concept: the famous Farmers' Market in Los Angeles. The **Original Farmers' Market**, a Los Angeles institution for decades, was really an "accident" of the Depression. In 1934 farmers in the San Fernando Valley were invited to park their pickup trucks filled with vegetables to sell in the city. The village square idea came about with local developers, who convinced landowner Arthur Fremont Gilmore to let his large tract of land be leased for 50 cents per day for the use of a wooden stall. The Farmers' Market of today, often referred to as the "best grocery store" in Los Angeles, may not look the same as it did when once surrounded by vast parking spaces, but within its confines it is totally authentic and actually serves up even more of the same. The iconic Farmers' Market Clock Tower at the entrance has welcomed visitors for half a century, but when the adjacent Grove at Farmers Market entertainment complex was constructed several years ago, the clock tower was carefully moved and erected in its new location. The trolley that shuttles between the Market and the Grove is a replica of the original Red Car system that served Los Angeles in its early days. But what makes the destination the most appealing is the atmosphere: from the scent of giant donuts frying to the convergence of people who linger, eat, talk and meet—from nearby CBS executives to teens on break from school. Another thing distinguishes the Farmers' Market: the store owners and workers, many representing family dynasties along with old-fashioned business practices, such as making candy by hand. **https://www.farmersmarketla.com/**

AUTHOR'S TIP: FARMERS' MARKET ROYALTY

James Dean reportedly ate his last breakfast here, and Walt Disney is said to have designed Disneyland while sitting on one of the patios.

Los Angeles is blessed with many museums, but probably the most notable in recent years is the **Getty Center**, with its dramatic hilltop setting overlooking the city. The Getty isn't particularly "off the beaten path," but it is unique in many ways. It contains not only a world-respected art museum but also five institutes and an arts grant program that is both admirable and enviable. Despite the incredible art on view on the inside, from van Gogh to Rembrandt, touring outside the museum may bring you just as much beauty. From the time you step aboard the driverless, computer-operated tram that climbs silently 3/4 of a mile up Getty Center Drive to the arrival plaza, you are mesmerized by the views unfolding below you and the brilliance of the travertine buildings and gardens that await you. Travertine stone, resembling marble and dating back over 80,000 years, was brought in from Italy for this project. Used everywhere as wall cladding and pavement, it is a spectacular sight that is only enhanced by the elaborate fountains, water features and gardens of the center. Waterfalls, pools with arcing jets and even a "floating bridge" of square stones interact with the Central Garden, which is a work of art all by itself. Commissioned by the Getty Trust, the 134,000-square-foot Central Garden offers visitors constantly changing experiences conditioned by the weather, the hour of the day, the time of year and the use of seasonal plants. Bougainvillea arbors, pools adorned with azalea mazes and intimate reflection areas abound. Cafes surround the gardens, and box lunches are available for picnicking. **http://www.getty.edu/**

AUTHOR'S TIP: GET A 'ROTEL' VIEW OF LA

*When we think of iconic buildings in the Los Angeles area, the Capitol Records Building in Hollywood is definitely one of the most notable. Built in 1956 to resemble a stack of vinyl 45 records, the 13-story circular building remains a highly photographed landmark. However, not far away there is another round building—this one 17 stories high—that everyone recognizes, even though it may not be quite as iconic. The former Holiday Inn, perched over the 405 freeway at Sunset Boulevard, has greeted mobs of motorists heading in several directions since the 1970s. However, just a few years ago, the aging Holiday Inn in Brentwood became the nation's first "rotel." Now the **Hotel Angeleno**, guests can wake up to a choice of views: Hollywood, Santa Monica or Downtown Los Angeles. **https:// www.hotelangeleno.com/**

Downtown Los Angeles

Downtown Los Angeles and its surrounding neighborhoods represent a mingling of ethnic communities—a colorful blending of cultures, foods and customs. A drive from one area to another reveals vintage edifices nestled between shiny skyscrapers, as well as attempts to preserve Los Angeles's heritage in spite of the spirit of growth that followed westbound pioneers heading for the city of "angels" and opportunity.

Downtown Los Angeles is a colorful melding of food and fragrances. One quick way to absorb the city's cultural mix is a visit to the **Grand Central Market** at 317 South Broadway. A Latin flavor dominates the spacious market, which hosts dozens of food-vending stalls. Hard-to-find spices, live poultry, homemade dulces, or sweets and mounds of fresh vegetables and fruit fill the spacious market, while carnival-like activity whirls all around. The iconic establishment that sees about 2 million patrons a year was sold to an investor in late 2017 who vows to maintain the historic feel of the market. **http://www.grandcentralsquare.com/**

Across the street from Grand Central is the **Bradbury Building**, whose unprepossessing exterior hides one of the most unusual interior spaces ever designed. Built in 1893 by ailing millionaire Louis Bradbury, the building was designed by science-fiction devotee George H. Wyman after he supposedly consulted his faithful Ouija board for guidance. His ultimate interior design of the unique building was inspired by a sci-fi novel that described a typical commercial building in the year 2000 as a "vast hall of light." A profusion of French iron balustrades decorates throughout, as do tiles from Mexico and pink marble staircases from Belgium. The open-cage elevators were originally powered by steam. One of the most unusual buildings in Los Angeles and used as a location for many films, the Bradbury, at 304 South Broadway, is open to the public. **https://www.laconservancy.org/locations/bradbury-building**

Heritage Square, three miles from Civic Center, is a parklike assemblage of splendid Victorian structures, all rescued from demolition in and around Los Angeles. The seven structures include a vintage mustard-yellow train station, as well as an ebony early-twentieth-century mansion with elaborate scroll- and brickwork and bay windows. The outdoor museum of original buildings from the period 1865 to 1914 is a living reminder of Los Angeles's architectural heritage. Weekend tours of the square are offered. **http://heritagesquare.org/visit**

To wander authentic neighborhoods that have survived progress, head for Carroll and Kellam Avenues, offering the largest concentration of Victorian homes in Los Angeles. To reach the Angelino Heights neighborhood overlooking downtown, you will pass by the protected lake of Echo Park, a weekend mecca for family city-goers. Step back in time on **Carroll Avenue**, located in one of the oldest neighborhoods in Los Angeles, Angelino Heights. This historic street is lined with Victorian manors that date to the 19th century. Many of these private homes can be seen in films, TV shows and music videos such as Michael Jackson's "Thriller." Note the Victorian architectural features as you stroll down Carroll Avenue, including the distinctive lamp posts as well as hitching posts that secured horses back in the day. The entire 1300 block of Carroll Avenue was added to the National Register of Historic Places in 1976, and several homes have been named Los Angeles Historic-Cultural Monuments. One of the best ways to tour the neighborhood is with a walking tour of Angelino Heights offered by the Los Angeles Conservancy. **https://www.laconservancy.org/events/angelino-heights-walking-tour**

The **South Bonnie Brae Historic District** overlooking MacArthur Park is not as well-known as its Carroll Avenue counterparts, but its stately occupants boast an interesting array of scrollwork, spindle work, fish scaling, towers and gables. The area was a part of one of Los Angeles's earliest suburbs and is home to a unique museum home. The **Grier-Musser Museum** is located at 403 South Bonnie Brae Street; the apple-green and raspberry 1898 Queen Anne–Greek Revival Victorian is filled with an amazing collection of fine antiques. The mansion was meticulously restored by owner Dr. Anne Krieger and her daughters, Susan and Nancy, in honor of Krieger's mother, Anne Grier Musser. Many of Musser's heirlooms, such as her watercolor paintings, Haviland Wedding Band pattern china and wedding dress from the late nineteenth century, can be found in the house. **http://www.griermussermuseum.org/**

AUTHOR'S TIP: VISIT LA'S UNDERGROUND ART

Construction of Los Angeles's Metro Rail subway stands as one of the nation's largest public works projects to date. Beginning in 1986, miners removed enough dirt to fill the Rose Bowl three and one-half times, poured enough concrete in the tunnels to pave a 5-foot-wide sidewalk from Los Angeles to Boston, and used enough steel to build 90,000 cars. Traffic jams, accidents and perilous weather may be creating havoc on the freeways above, but under the earth's surface, L.A. subway users experience a different world, one that often reflects the history and culture "above." From themes of flight to neon to cinema, as well as to early California history, the subway stops in L.A. provide art-goers a fascinating "moving" gallery. For example, the Civic Center Station was created by artist Jonathan Borofsky; the station's theme of "I Dreamed I Could Fly" is an interpretation of the artist's dreams of soaring above the ground. Six fiberglass figures (resembling the artist) hover, casting shadows high above the station. The playful creation includes audio as well—listen for the occasional trill of a bird.

Even if you aren't visiting Los Angeles by train, plan on a stop at **Union Station** to fill your senses with history, beauty and a bounty of nostalgia. The fifth busiest station in Amtrak's network, the 1939-built Art Deco enclave has undergone a continuing renewal process—carefully overseen as the "art masterpiece" it is for Los Angeles. It stands as the last great railway station built in the United States and everything you eye is authentic or replaced as originally built. Millions have been gone into the restoration thus far, and another $24 million will be invested in coming years. In other words, this is not the same sad station you may have experienced a decade ago. Movie and television filming is a regular occurrence at the station. You've seen it as the backdrop recently in the George Clooney movie "Hail Caesar." You might remember the Judy Garland classic, "The Harvey Girls." The Harvey House in Union Station has been beautifully restored, giving you an authentic look at the glamorous days of rail travel when travelers were served meals in luxurious banquettes as they stopped on their travels. Free architecture and history tours are offered twice a month. **https://www.unionstationla.com/**

AUTHOR'S TIP: BE A PART OF THE GRAMMYS

Before you nestle down in front of the television screen to watch the GRAMMY ® Awards, consider a jaunt to Los Angeles' **GRAMMY Museum** *to learn in-depth about the annual awards and winners, the history of music and how music is made. The 3,000-square-foot GRAMMY Museum is located within the L.A. LIVE complex, adjacent to the Staples Center. The four floors of the one-of-a-kind museum are dedicated to two dozen interactive, multimedia permanent and traveling exhibits and features nearly 30 original and unique films from a dozen filmmakers and more than 300 compelling artifacts, among them Elvis' guitar and Pavarotti's tuxedo. Don't miss a look at the 200-seat Grammy Sound Stage, which is also home to many of the museum's public programs. Catch the rotating program, "Great GRAMMY ® Performances" here which showcases some of the most unforgettable GRAMMY footage.* **https://www.grammymuseum.org/**

While in the city, take an early-morning stroll past exotic flowering plants and bright bouquets of mums, baby roses, and carnations. The 3-block-long **Los Angeles Flower District**, at 742 Maple Avenue, holds the prestigious distinction of being the largest single flower district in the United States and features virtually every type and variety of cut flower, potted plant and exotic flower that is commercially available. In addition to flowers and plants, the market offers the largest selection of floral supplies on the West Coast and conducts a design school. Claiming to be America's flower garden, the Flower District is open to both wholesale and private customers, with the exception of a few stalls that are well marked for wholesale buyers only. Things get going early at the Flower Mart, around 2:00 a.m., and close around noon, but the general public is not admitted until 8:00 a.m. most days. **https://www.laflowerdistrict.com/**

LOCAL'S SECRET:
VISIT THE LAST BOOKSTORE

"This bookstore looks like it was built by fairies or was teleported straight from Narnia. Every little corner of The Last Bookstore is worth exploring and as soon as you enter, you'll get hit by that amazing, nostalgic old book smell. The main floor also has a vinyl area and some beautiful armchairs and sofas where you can sit down to gaze at the amazing world you have found yourself in. Upstairs there are amazing décor and art pieces to look at. Books, vinyl and art is not the only thing they have that makes this place so special, they also have a 'book labyrinth' where some hidden gems are waiting to be discovered. Don't forget to also visit the small art gallery on the second floor! Don't be alarmed if, by the end of your visit, you feel like you're coming out of a dream. This place is that magical, and somehow real." http://lastbookstorela.com/

— *Julian Sosa, spotter, Spotted By Locals,* https://www.spottedbylocals.com/blog/12-hidden-los-angeles-gems/

You've probably heard rumors that the newest way to get the greatest view of Los Angeles is **Skyslide,** an entirely glass slide that clings to the outside on one of the tallest buildings on the West Coast. The thrilling experience that opened recently is just part of the $100 million-dollar renovation of the iconic U.S. Bank Tower in Downtown Los Angeles, and has already proven a sure way to get people to the top for an experience of a lifetime. Skyslide is just one element of this all-new event space, **OUE Skyspace** LA that occupies the 69th and 70th floors, offering unobstructed, 360-degree vistas from the San Gabriel Mountains all the way to the Pacific Ocean. Your Skyslide adventure begins on the 70th floor of the U.S. Bank Tower, 1,000 feet above the city. The forty-five-feet long slide is made entirely of glass and takes intrepid sliders down to the 69th floor of the bank building, with unobstructed vistas along the way. You can take the one-story drop that lands at the 2,800-square-foot observation deck—the state's tallest outdoor observation deck—by purchasing a ticket. **https:// oue-skyspace.com/**

LOCAL'S SECRET: DINE ABOVE IT ALL

"71 Above is a perfect restaurant for a romantic date night, complete with 360-degree vistas over Los Angeles that reach out to Malibu and Catalina Island as well as the San Gabriel Mountains. Located in the US Bank Tower, your window seat towers 950 feet above downtown Los Angeles. Arrive in time to see the sunset for an unforgettable evening." https://www.71above.com/

–Brent & Daniela Strong, Santa Clarita

AUTHOR'S TIP: FREEWAY LANDSPEEDERS

Next time you watch Star Wars, listen carefully to the sound made by Luke Skywalker's landspeeder. It is actually the sound of rush-hour traffic on Harbor Freeway in Los Angeles.

Jeremy Bishop, unsplash.com

LOS ANGELES COAST, ORANGE COUNTY & CATALINA ISLAND

Miles and miles of pale yellow, finely textured sand are met by scenic, rocky cliffs and bright green to deep blue surf beginning along the Los Angeles area coastline on down through Orange County's South coastal villages. Summer or winter, hearty surfers congregate like groups of sea lions, bobbing up and down in the turbulent surf, waiting for that "big one." Quaint village communities attract tourists, artists and celebrities who come to share in the year-round activities of beach life: sunbathing, jogging, fishing, roller-skating, yachting and art gallery and boutique wandering. Numerous enchanting cafes and inns provide the perfect retreats for the romantic at heart; the atmospheric piers of the area provide local color and history.

This area is composed of some larger cities, as well: bustling ports-of-call and museum meccas with fascinating and diverse architecture, entertainment and restaurants. But in contrast, this coastal area is also a jumping-off base for one of Southern California's unique retreats, Catalina Island. California's own island paradise is surprisingly full of yesteryear and hidden treasures, despite its seasonal popularity with yachters and teenage sun worshipers.

The Los Angeles Coast

Malibu

Malibu, with its 23 miles of scenic coastline, has been immortalized in songs as a surfer's paradise; the media have kept the world informed of its celebrity residents, such as the late Johnny Carson, and Ali McGraw who shops in the local markets and eats in the local bistros of the "colony." But Malibu is foremost a stretch of Southern California coastline offering small-town charm and ambience. Homes, grand and modest, line the shore; the open beaches provide a refreshing lack of class distinction once you've slipped your bare toes into the soothing sand.

No matter how many times you have visited Malibu, you may be completely unaware of one of the most prestigious addresses in town. The **Adamson Home** and adjoining **Malibu Lagoon Museum** at 23200 Pacific Coast Highway are on an estate to match any in the exclusive area, and you are welcome to inspect almost every nook and cranny (even peruse the custom wardrobes in the closet) in docent-led tours. A part of the California State Park system but run entirely by volunteer docents, the house and museum provide a vivid history lesson of Malibu, from the presumed arrival of Cabrillo at this very spot, which is thought to have been a sizable Chumash Indian village, to the early development of the coast and Malibu. Visitors follow a dirt path past the lagoon, rose gardens and lawn to the courtyard of the thirteen-acre estate. The 1929 Moorish–Spanish Revival residence, with hand-carved teakwood doors and lavish use of exquisite ceramic tile produced on what was once estate grounds, is situated here with unparalleled views of the Pacific. http://www.adamsonhouse.org/

Almost directly across Pacific Coast Highway from the Adamson Home is the entrance road to what is now the **Serra**

Retreat, built from the remains of May Rindge's "castle on the hill." Mrs. Rindge's plans for a great house on Laudamus Hill overlooking Malibu Canyon included fifty rooms; in four years she had invested more than $500,000 in the castle-like structure, with elaborate tile work by her own Malibu Potteries for walls and floors. Because of financial problems, the house was never finished, nor was it occupied. In 1942 the mansion and twenty-six acres were sold to the Franciscan Order, to be used as a retreat, for $50,000. A fire in 1970 destroyed a great deal of the structure, but the Franciscans took over the laundry and nine-car garage and rebuilt. A winding road curves up to the quiet sanctuary, along the way granting dramatic hill and ocean vistas. The public is welcome to wander the tranquil grounds with panoramic viewing points as long as the retreat guests are not disturbed. If you are allowed to peek inside the Rindge Room conference area of the retreat, which was the former laundry of the mansion, you will see the remaining Dutch-patterned tile. **https://serraretreat.com/**

AUTHOR'S TIP: FINDING YOUR OWN BEACH

Although privacy is the watchword in Malibu, we all know the canyons and beachfronts are home to the famous, from Streisand to Goldie. But, surprisingly, the beaches that front the exclusive beach dwellings are all public below the mean high tide line. The dilemma is finding access to the more exclusive, non-public supported beaches between the sand-hugging dwellings without a hefty hike. Public staircases do exist along the beach highway, but the best and largest access beaches have names you know: Surfriders, Zuma and Leo Carillo beaches. Carbon or "Billionaire's" Beach is accessible near the newly renovated Malibu Fishing Pier. Just a few miles north of Malibu is a beach that locals love, but few visitors discover. El

Matador State Beach remains a secret, although it is a favorite destination for photographers and camera crews. Found down a steep descending trail with some stairs, the shallow beach is marked by giant rocks and natural caves and caverns that are nearly magical.

Malibu is filled with trendy bistros, but for an offbeat dining experience head to Paradise—Paradise Cove. It's definitely hidden and funky, but if you are in the mood for the best carrot cake waffle imaginable served with early Malibu history all around, then head to **Paradise Cove Cafe**. A dipping road off PCH takes you past wild canyon territory until the ocean finally emerges through the trees ahead. Set directly on the sand, the 1950s-built café is plastered in vintage black-and-white signed photos of celebrities, early surfers and fishing scenes going back to 1940's Malibu. The dining room, open to the beach and playing dolphins, serves all three meals. And, if you decide to make it a day, reserve a beach lounge and enjoy the idyllic stretch of hidden beach. **http://www.paradisecovemalibu.com/**

While Malibu is best known for its surfing and celebrities, one of its hidden charms lies in the **Malibu Hills** that embrace the community. Possessing a microclimate that mimics the Mediterranean coastal area, the rolling hills have become a fertile growing region for varietals. Boutique wineries and vineyards have gradually popped up in the area over the last 20 years, and wine-lovers are beginning to discover its allure. Tour on your own or take an organized tour the first time out. **Malibu Discovery Tours** offers a couple of fun wine tours that take you to a handful of the 50-plus vineyards and wine tasting rooms of the region. Tours are all booked in advance and are conducted aboard luxury vehicles; guides have passionate knowledge about all things Malibu—from history to celebrities. **http://malibudiscovery.com/**

A scenic side trip into **Malibu Canyon** is a worthwhile diversion from the coast. Turn off Pacific Coast Highway at Pepperdine University to Mulholland Drive. Wind through the canyon with its rocky cliffs and pass Tapia Park. Right before Cottontail Ranch, you will spot an elaborate, ivory-colored structure with ornate decorations and golden peaks. The unique cultural find is one of the first Hindu temples in the United States, the **Malibu Hindu Temple**. Visitors must remove shoes to tour the grounds but are free to linger by the roadside and take in the intricate architectural features of the temple: the embedded figures, columns, and scrolls, all cast individually in India and siliconed together. The **Hindu Temple Society of Southern California** is responsible for the construction of the temple, designed to be a legacy for their children so that their ancient cultural heritage may be passed on to future generations. No photography is allowed inside the building. **http://www.malibuhindutemple.org/home.aspx**

For a special dining experience, take a real off-the-beaten path trip through scenic Malibu Canyon to a secret gem, **Saddle Peak Lodge** restaurant. Twist through the winding canyon roads via the 101 Las Virgenes Road exit until you reach tucked away Cold Canyon Road. A short way up the rural passage is this former 1970's roadhouse turned exclusive bistro. It is a real case of rustic ambience meets sophisticated palate, making it a popular celebrity hideaway. An amazing and extensive wine list has a perfect match for any delicacy on the menu from New Zealand elk or Nebraska buffalo to mesquite-grilled antelope. Not into wild game? Then, settle for the frontier ambience granted by antlers on the walls and a cozy rock fireplace while you enjoy traditional gourmet fare, from striped bass to filet mignon. A lighter menu prevails as well, with vegetarian entrees and house specialties that include the bistro's own cured salmon and special carrot soup. **https://www.saddlepeaklodge.com/**

Santa Monica

On a coastline once dotted with piers, the 1909 **Santa Monica Pier** remains as one of the last of the great pleasure piers. A magnet for television, movies, whimsy and glamour, the pier has had more than nine lives, weathering storms, change, progress and economic struggles. Today, it stands as an action-packed centerpiece for this Southern California beach city. Almost like a small town within a city, everything a visitor craves lies within walking distance of this famous pier. A kaleidoscope of lights beckons you to explore the Santa Monica Pier, a pleasing blend of old and new. The original 1922-built carousel spins hypnotically at one end of the pier; looming nine stories above the pier is the Pacific Wheel, the only giant Ferris wheel over water in the state, and a five-story coaster swoops and clatters through the salt-laden air, granting night-time views of the twinkling Santa Monica Bay coast. More rides, shops and, of all things, a trapeze school that sends visitors "soaring" over the Pacific make this pier stand peerless.

AUTHOR'S TIP: LISTEN TO THE BEACH CHAIRS SING

Santa Monica is known for its public art, but there is just one that promises to give you a chance to harmonize. Located on Santa Monica Beach between Pico and the pier is "Singing Beach Chairs" by Doug Hollis. The unique steel and aluminum sculptures produce oboe-like tones when the wind blows through them, and each oversized chair is big enough for two to share.

For a glimpse at local history, the **California Heritage Square Museum** at 2612 Main Street offers a series of period rooms depicting the Santa Monica way of life from the 1890s through the 1930s. The restored Victorian, built in 1894 by the nationally known architect Sumner P. Hunt, was moved to its present location at Main Street and Ocean Park Boulevard in 1977. The house was the original home of Roy Jones, the son of the founder of Santa Monica. The California history museum is more than a tribute to the Jones family; it also serves to mirror life in the area throughout the decades. Each of the first-floor rooms has been reconstructed to show the lifestyle of a different period in the city's development, the second floor of the museum is dedicated to changing exhibits involving the history of California, and the museum also houses interesting photographic archives. **https://www.californiaheritagemuseum.org/**

Photo by Ann Kathrin Bopp, unsplash.com

AUTHOR'S TIP:
PERFECT ENDING OF AN
ICONIC ROUTE 66 JOURNEY

*The **Santa Monica Pier** importantly marks the western terminus of the iconic Route 66, where road and ocean meet. Walk along the pier to see the sign marked "End of Trail." After traveling nearly 2,500 miles from Chicago to the Pacific Ocean, it is a beautiful ending to a journey fueled on the promise of moving west. Those who are in the "know" profess that the real ending of Route 66 is located in the same spot occupied by the recently opened **Mel's Drive-In,** just prior to the pier.*

The city's greatest natural asset is, of course, its beaches—whether you care to plant yourself on the shoreline or admire it from Ocean Boulevard's scenic park that sits high atop the area's red sandstone cliffs. On any given summer day, the wide stretches of glimmering sand are brimming over in activity—from surfing to tanning. One beach, however, stands out from past decades: **Muscle Beach**. Attracting every gymnast, bodybuilder and weightlifter of the 1930s through 1950s, the beach was as big a part of the Santa Monica beach experience as the Pier. In its heyday, the stretch of sand attracted celebrities like Kirk Douglas, Jayne Mansfield and Steve Reeves. The equipment fell into disrepair through the years, but now, thanks to a beach improvement project, Muscle Beach is back—complete with fitness equipment and apparatuses.

Just above the coast, a park offers panoramic views of the Pacific as well as a delightful slice of recent history. The **Will Rogers State Historic Park** at 1501 Will Rogers State Park Road is the former 186-acre ranch of the "cowboy philosopher," who won the hearts of America with his humorous comments on the news of the day. Also known as the "cracker-barrel philosopher," the former rodeo trick roper made the ranch home in 1928, moving his family from their Beverly Hills residence. The ranch is open daily, and visitors may tour the buildings and grounds, maintained as when the family lived there. Indian artifacts, including many rugs; an extensive library of first editions; and paintings fill the thirty-one rooms of the spacious house. The mounted calf was given to Rogers for trick rope practicing. Will Rogers' typewriter sits awaiting his humorous anecdotes; the clock in the study is stopped at the time of his death. A short film showing Will Rogers's life story and his roping abilities (one room in the ranch house has a higher roof to accommodate his roping hobby) is shown at the visitor center. On weekends, weather permitting, stop by the old polo fields to watch a game in the same locale where movie greats such as Spencer Tracy played with Will in the twenties and thirties. Hiking trails and grassy picnic areas are scattered around the acreage. **http://www.parks. ca.gov/?page_id=626**

The oldest structure in Santa Monica, the 1910-constructed building called the **Channel Road Inn**, was moved to its present site at the mouth of Santa Monica Canyon. The three-story Colonial Revival, now a charming bed-and-breakfast inn, has been totally renovated and redecorated to reflect a fine Santa Monica home in the 1920s, with oak floors, birch woodwork and a stately fireplace. Guests here choose from fourteen suites, some with four-poster beds covered in lace or quilts. Bathrooms are stocked with bathrobes and bubble bath, and all accommodations offer armoire-tucked televisions and refrigerators, fresh fruit and flowers and romantic evening turndown service with berries and a tray of home-baked cookies. Breakfast is bountiful at Channel Road; wine and cheese are served each afternoon. The Channel Road Inn is located at 219 West Channel Road. **https://www.channel-roadinn.com/**

In this city where dining is an extreme sport, world-class chefs vie to outdo each other. Santa Monica hosts more than 400 restaurants in an approximate eight-square-mile area. Most of the local celebrity chefs, plus a many from as far away as San Diego, make a pilgrimage to the Downtown **Farmers' Market** each Wednesday for fresh produce, seafood and breads.

AUTHOR'S TIP: SENSORY DINING

For a foray into a one-of-a-kind dining adventure, make a visit to **Opaque** *where dining in the dark is an art. The first such eatery in Southern California, Opaque is located within the V Lounge in Santa Monica with limited days of operation. Guests enter a totally dark world that is designed to heighten the senses by eliminating sight. Each meal is $99 per person with a selection of choices that you just have to trust look as delicious as they taste!* **https://darkdining.com/santa-monica/**

Marina del Rey

Bordered by Los Angeles on three sides, minute 1.26-square-mile **Marina del Rey** is often swept up into the identity of its better-known neighbors, Venice and Santa Monica. However, the tiny city definitely stands alone on appeal. Within its intimate confines, Marina del Rey hosts the largest man-made yacht harbor in North America with over 5,300 vessels ranging from kayaks to mega-celebrity yachts. A laid-back South Seas ambiance permeates the golden sands of its main beach where swaying palms frame an azure lagoon. It is no wonder that the founding fathers gave it street names like Bora Bora and Tahiti Ways—it was a natural. Perched along this strand of harbor and waterfront are over 1,000 hotel rooms ranging from moderately priced to deluxe, nearly 30 bistros and idyllic parks and beaches.

You won't find any historic relics in Marina del Rey. Indeed, it stands as one of the younger communities in Southern California, but not any less interesting. It took over one hundred years for the vision of a harbor to be realized here. Visionaries of a commercial harbor on the spot lost out first to oil fields and then to nearby San Pedro, the final choice for L.A.'s prime commercial harbor. But, in 1960, the Army Corps of Engineers began dredging what would become Marina del Rey's yacht harbor—this time geared appropriately to recreation rather than commercial endeavors. The construction of the city's first restaurants and lodging establishments soon followed, and, in April 1965, Marina del Rey was formally dedicated, and the largest man-made recreational harbor in North America was open for business.

Uniquely owned by the city, the structures that line the harbor are undergoing an amazing resurgence at present with carefully planned renovation and updating underway. Always impressive, the area has much to boast about these days and is waiting for rediscovery.

The amazing **Los Angeles Coastal Bike Trail**, a paved waterfront bikeway which actually connects all the top beach communities for 22 spectacular miles, runs through the entire waterfront of Marina del Rey. A number of skate and bike concessions make it an easy-to-do outing; stay within the confines of the city or stop along the way to linger at a waterside cafe for a lengthier wheel-based journey.

AUTHOR'S TIP: SUNSET BEACH CONCERTS

Summer brings the small city to its feet along the waterfront. Marina del Rey's free summer concerts at charming Burton W. Chace Park features "Symphonic Thursdays" and "Pop Saturdays." Concerts begin at 7 p.m. so that concert-goers get the added bonus of watching the sun set over the water.
https://www.visitmarinadelrey.com/

You don't see many people walking in L.A., but In Marina del Rey cars are replaced by water buses during the summer months. For just $1, you can ride to seven popular stops, from Fisherman's Village to Marina Beach. The newest trend in waterfront dining is to paddle, swim or boat to dinner, with Marina del Rey one of the few Los Angeles coastal locations to offer "dock & dine." A local restaurant, **Killer Shrimp**, offers a public landing so that guests can arrive for dinner or sunset happy hour via kayak, jet ski, paddleboard or boat. Although you still need shirt and shoes to dine, the acceptable footwear is water shoes. The long-time favorite bistro is known for its irresistible shrimp prepared in a spicy sauce.

Playa del Rey

Playa del Rey, just south of LAX, has the feel of a small beach town, surrounded by towering bluffs on the east and precious Ballona Creek on its northern borders. Although airport hotels are plentiful, probably the only airport area lodging spot within walking distance to the beach is the praiseworthy **Inn at Playa del Rey**, a more recently built three-story Cape Cod–style inn that sits serenely overlooking the main channel of Marina del Rey as well as the 350-acre **Ballona Wetlands** and bird sanctuary, providing egrets, blue herons and hawks as welcome "backyard neighbors." The 22 guest rooms at the inn cater to both the business traveler and the romantic, combining both practical and aesthetic elements— from fresh flowers to data hookups. Try a romantic escape with an upstairs suite offering sunset views of the wetlands. The bathrooms contain some Jacuzzi tubs for two and some en-suite, see-through fireplaces. A complimentary breakfast is served in the inn's beach-themed dining room, with pleasing hues of sand, yellow and blue. The cozy living room, with appropriate waterfowl motif, is a comfortable retreat that boasts overstuffed sofas and view windows for bird-watching. **http://www.innatplayadelrey.com/**

At the west end of Los Angeles International Airport (LAX), is a surprising sand dune find, The **LAX El Segundo Dunes Preserve**. The largest dunes complex on Southern California's coast, it once extended from Palos Verdes to Santa Monica and is thought to have existed some 50,000 years ago. In fact, bones of an extinct member of the camel family have been discovered here. Today, the preserve consists of about 300 acres, providing protected wildlife habitat for more than 900 species of native animals and plants that once seemed destined for extinction – including the delicate, endangered El Segundo Blue Butterfly. Not only can you visit the dunes, you can get involved in its future with the LAX Adopt-a-Dune Program; volunteers are needed to help care for this natural environment by removing invasive plants. **https://www.lawa. org/-/media/lawa-web/volunteer-opurtunities/lax-dunes-home-page.ashx**

Hermosa Beach

It may be one of the smallest beach towns in SoCal, but **Hermosa Beach** packs the beach beat into every inch of sand. If you've visited the 1.4 square-mile beach village, you already know that. The city's pristine beach is what it is all about including its outdoor activities and nationally televised sporting events—especially volleyball. A visit to Hermosa Beach guarantees a sun-drenched beach experience that is highlighted by the casual coastal lifestyle we've all come to love. The mild weather patterns make it an ideal vacation spot all year round, but especially during the summer when the beach scene vibe is at its height.

For a truly authentic beach experience, choose a hotel that feels like your own beach cottage. The **Beach House Hermosa Beach** is a boutique hotel touching the sand between the busier towns of Manhattan Beach and Redondo Beach. Dining, nightlife and beachy boutiques are within strolling distance just two blocks from the hotel on Pier Avenue, making a surf board more of a necessity than a car during your entire stay. From the sand-touching terraces, guests look out onto the glistening expanse that provides non-stop people watching with a parade of bikers, skaters, surfers, volleyball players, dog walkers and sun worshipers. **https:// www.beach-house.com/**

Consider a bike ride along the Strand or simply take a leisurely stroll down the shoreline path. Hermosa Beach is the training ground for some of the world's best pro-circuit volleyball players, and the city's "laid-back" attitude allows the novice and pro to play together at the volleyball courts that lie directly in front of the hotel, which is also a front-row seat for the AVP professional tournament held each year. World famous surfing spots are just steps away, as well as yoga on the beach.

AUTHOR'S TIP: SEE JAY LENO ON SUNDAYS

Along with the "sandy" attractions, this lively beach village offers up ample nighttime entertainment, including The Hermosa Beach Playhouse and the Lighthouse with live music. However, the more than three-decade-old **Comedy and Magic Club** *is a must for anyone craving an evening of astounding magic and comedy from a variety of entertainers. In fact, many famous comedians choose this off-Hollywood club to hone their skills. Jerry Seinfeld and Bill Maher drop by regularly, and Jay Leno often performs here on Sunday nights. Make it a full evening with dinner and a show; the prices are surprisingly reasonable.* **http://comedyandmagicclub.com/**

There are dining options to delight every palate – from seaside bistros around the pier to a lingering dinner by moonlight. A surprising dinner discovery is **Chef Melba's Bistro**, a tiny eatery overseen by chef/owner Melba Rodriguez who churns out cutting edge, organic and fresh creations in her open demonstration kitchen to the delight of diners. Melba brings in fresh fish daily, uses only vine-ripened produce and puts it all together with a creative flair. **https://www.chefmelbasbistro.com/**

Almost as seductive as the waves and sand is the walk ability of Hermosa Beach. Within a few blocks in either direction of the Beach House, you'll discover not only quaint eateries but also surprising art and shopping. Although known for its beach vibe, the city is also gaining acclaim for its novel boutiques. High on your shopping list should be **Gum Tree Shop & Cafe**, just a block up from Pier Plaza. It's hard to miss the century-old Craftsman estate, now gift shop and cafe, filled with unique home decor and gift ideas, from pillows and rugs to picture frames and books. Grab a repast of avocado toast or meat pies in the adjacent cafe to fuel your browsing adventure. **https://www.gumtreela.com/**

Strolling around Hermosa Beach is also a visit to an outdoor art gallery, thanks to the **Hermosa Beach Mural Project**, with a goal to beautify the city with 10 murals in a decade. The eight murals now splashing city walls adorn unexpected artist contributions at every turn. The mural that captures the heart of Hermosa Beach best is composed of four giant photographs by photographer Bo Bridges. Bridges unveiled his ode to the beauty and athletic dynamics of volleyball in 2016 with images on the south and west side of Hermosa Beach's downtown Pier Plaza parking structure.

Redondo Beach

The historic 1892 coastal town of **Redondo Beach**, with its romantic seafront esplanade, famous Horseshoe Pier, early surfing legacy and charming shops and cafes, does a great job of capturing the nostalgic Southern California beach scene. Once a commercial port, Redondo Beach has been transformed to a safe, casual resort destination with watersports of all types and first-class resorts and restaurants.

In any coastal town, the pier is commonly the center of activity, from fishing to fun. The 1889-built **Redondo Pier**, once considered the pride and joy of the California coast, began a major renewal program a few years ago. The Redondo Landing, the gateway building to the pier, has a new façade that resembles the original Hippodrome—the landmark carousel building from the 1920s. Besides special events at the pier, take in the "Coney Island" atmosphere of the shops and restaurants, complete with funnel cakes and pearl-hunting oyster stands. Check out the International Boardwalk, a casual collection of ocean-view seafood storefronts and bars on the marina.

Plan to do some strolling or serious gift shopping at the Riviera Village in south Redondo, considered the most distinctive shopping area in the South Bay. Once dubbed the "Hollywood Riviera" as a popular entertainment hangout, the shopping village is comprised of six blocks filled with one-of-a-kind shops, boutiques and cafes that make a great lunch stop.

AUTHOR'S TIP: ALL ABOARD LOMITA'S RAILROAD MUSEUM

*Farther down the coast, about a mile past Redondo Beach, is the small community of Lomita. Nestled in a quiet residential area is one of the city's proudest attractions, known mainly to railroad buffs—the **Lomita Railroad Museum**. The only museum of its kind west of Denver, Colorado, Lomita's authentic salute to railroading is officially named the Martin S. Lewis Railroad Museum, in honor of the late Mr. Lewis. Mrs. Irene Lewis donated the museum to the city in 1966, and the Union Pacific and Southern Pacific Railroads, as well as the Southern California Live Steamer Club, have added to the railroading bounty. The Victorian-looking station house, surrounded by a wrought-iron gate, sits primly on a neighborhood corner at 250th and Woodward Streets. A quaint little park with tanker car, brick paths and a fountain lies across the street. The inside of the small building holds a conglomerate of railroading nostalgia, including some workable models. Stepping into the rear patio with its potted flowers, you're greeted by two authentic railroad cars that can be entered, a 1902 Mogul Engine and a 1910 Union Pacific caboose. A taped recording makes you feel a part of a "moving" experience as the conductor yells "all aboard" and the trains "get closer" to the station. **http://www.lomita-rr.org/***

Palos Verdes Peninsula

Steep, rocky cliffs that rise then fall to meet with the foamy surf give the 26-square-mile **Palos Verdes Peninsula** a wild NorCal coastal vibe. This unique enclave, once home to what many consider Southern California's first theme park, is nestled on a secluded and exclusive part of the state's enviable coastline. The fact that it is populated by more million-dollar estates and hidden beaches than visitors catching rays makes a visit just that much more alluring.

The serene, distinct beach community rewards those who escape here some of the most spectacular ocean vistas and sandy coves along the coastline—all just a short drive from the bustling LA scene—as well as an uncrowded outdoor paradise that happily possesses more hiking trails than tourist hang-outs. You might call it the best place in Southern California to watch the sun rise and set over the Pacific.

Approximately 1,400 acres with more than 30 miles of trails through rolling hills, steep canyons and rock outcrops make up the **Palos Verdes Nature Preserve** with spectacular ocean vistas and precious habitat. Here, you will discover a variety of preserves that range from sea level along the coastal edges of Vicente Bluffs to 1,300 feet above the surf at Vista del Norte. Plan a visit to the **Abalone Cove Ecological Reserve** here that features two beaches, Abalone Cove and Sacred Cove, tide pools to explore, bluff-top viewing points and bountiful trails. **http://pvplc.org/_lands/abalone_cove.asp**

Local Southern Californians going back a few decades remember the former occupant of 90 acres of this land that once reigned as the world's largest "oceanarium," **Marineland of the Pacific.** The theme park opened just one year before Disneyland with a $5 million investment aimed at making it the most unusual cultural, educational and entertainment center on the Pacific Coast. The location was chosen because of its overwhelming natural beauty, located adjacent to the

Pacific Ocean with undersea life displayed in huge tanks. The exhibits of ever-changing marine life—from dolphins to sea lions—meant a new show for park- goers with every visit. To the dismay of many, Marineland's doors closed abruptly in 1987 when the theme park was taken over by the owners of Sea World who moved the ocean animals to San Diego. The precious coastal property that brought busloads of students, families and even early-day explorers remained nearly aban-doned for the next two decades.

There is ample natural beauty and rich history to absorb in Palos Verdes, however, you can find bounteous portions of both in one destination resort. The Mediterranean-inspired **Terranea** resort now resides on the majestic 102-acre pri-vate peninsula once occupied by Marineland of the Pacific, yet the resort itself only occupies one quarter of the total area. Poised perfectly on the southern tip of the peninsula, the resort was ten years in the making to ensure that the beauty of the peninsula was absorbed respectfully and ecologically into the area's natural coastline setting. The untouched half-century-old trees, the use of local stone for construction, the creation of a two-mile hiking trail through the property and along the coast (which connects to the Palos Verdes Peninsula trails system) and the planting of 14 acres of natural Coastal Sage Scrub habitat are a testament to the area's graceful resurrection. Nelson's, a fun restaurant and bar, is a tribute to Mike Nelson, the character played by ocean preservationist/actor Lloyd Bridges in the 1950's tele-vision series, "Sea Hunt," filmed on the site and in the waters around Terranea.

The sandy **Cove at Terranea** is a magical spot nestled below the resort. Created by the resort's designers and overlooking the rocky tide pools, it is a great spot to watch dolphins at play, the winter migration of whales or just relax on the sand. For adventure, head to Pointe Discovery, the resort's activ-ity center, for a bounty of planned experiences—from tide pooling and nature walks to kayaking tours that depart from here regularly. **https://www.terranea.com/**

There is lots to explore in this area that once played host to Portuguese, Spanish and British adventurers who anchored in the sheltered coves of the Palos Verdes Peninsula. Plan some leisurely time in the **Point Vicente Interpretive Center**, located at 31501 Palos Verdes Drive West, where both nature and local history come together—with an emphasis on the Pacific gray whale. A top spot to see the winter whales and hike, you can also glimpse some nostalgic remnants of Marineland on display.

Designed by Lloyd Wright (son of Frank) and cradled in coastal redwoods is the **Wayfarers Chapel**, known as "the glass church." The historically designated chapel, built in 1951, is open to the public. You may recognize it as the filming locale for some scenes in the television show "The OC." Stop by to see the unique geometric architecture and take in the breathtaking ocean vistas; a visitor center and tower make the chapel very visitor friendly. **https://www.wayfarerschapel.org/**

Long Beach

The advent of redevelopment has changed the skyline around the **Long Beach** area dramatically. The old mansions along the Pacific are squeezed between high-rises; malls have usurped downtown shopping; and a vast convention center has helped bring in thousands of hotel rooms. But buried amid the old and the new are several treasures offered in this area, which includes nearby San Pedro, Wilmington, and Lakewood.

In 1851 Phineas Banning arrived in Los Angeles, a rural adobe pueblo with a mixed ethnic population of around 1,600. Banning went on to play an important part in linking the city to the port at San Pedro by rail, inducing the Southern Pacific Railroad to connect this area with the rest of the nation. Near the conclusion of the Civil War, Banning had a home built in Wilmington, and today the **Banning Museum** and surrounding twenty-acre park, with its mature trees and old-fashioned lampposts, are open to the public. The twenty-three-room mansion, a fine example of nineteenth-century Greek Revival architecture with brick steps and chimneys, has been carefully restored, and thirty-two pieces of furniture original to the house have been donated by Banning family members. Guests may tour the living museum's rooms and, on special occasions, even enjoy demonstrations of original Banning family recipes offered in the Victorian kitchen. **https://www. banningmuseum.org/**

AUTHOR'S TIP: THE GOOSE THAT FLEW AWAY

Howard Hughes's plywood seaplane, the Spruce Goose, was a top tourist attraction in the Long Beach area for most of the 1980s. The Goose held the distinction of being the largest aircraft ever built, yet it made only a single, one-minute flight in 1942. The remarkable aircraft had eight engines and a 320-foot wingspan. Alas, an economic situation forced the city to give up on the Goose. Two aircraft engineers, who had helped build the aircraft and had worked for Hughes for four decades, helped take the Goose apart for its final trip. In 1992 Evergreen International Aviation of Oregon purchased the Spruce Goose and placed it on permanent display in Oregon.

Other historical points of interest in the area include two adobes that link Long Beach to the past. The **Rancho Los Alamitos** adobe is the city's oldest domestic dwelling. Located today in the midst of a guard-gated residential community, the 1806 ranch house traces its origins from Indian settlement all the way to the state's rich ranching era in the early 1900s. Guided tours of the sprawling ranch house, surrounded by five acres of gardens studded with oleander and California native plants, are offered; highlights of the tour include furnishings collected by the Bixby family, who resided there for more than eighty years, as well as looks at the blacksmith shop and horse barns stocked with period equipment. **Rancho Los Cerritos**, a two-story Monterey Colonial adobe, is hidden from view by tall gates and dense foliage in its secluded location at 4600 Virginia Road. The adobe country house was once the headquarters of a 27,000-acre cattle ranch and now sits surrounded by close to five acres of peaceful gardens. Tours of the house, built in 1844, and its impressive Victorian furnishings are offered. **https://www.rancholosalamitos.com/ https://www.rancholoscerritos.org/**

AUTHOR'S TIP: FROM ODD TO AWESOME WORLD RECORDS

Long Beach holds interesting world records and distinctions. Think of the trivia you can pull out at your next cocktail party, such as:

The world's largest mural is located in Long Beach. Artist Wyland painted Planet Ocean, which covers the entire 116,000-square-foot surface of the Long Beach Arena. It took four weeks and three hundred gallons of paint to create.

Long Beach's breakwater stretches for 3 miles, making it the longest breakwater in the world.

Located at 703 Gladys Avenue is the world's skinniest house. The Skinny House was built in 1932 by Nelson Rummond on a bet that he could not build an inhabitable residence on a lot that measured 10 feet by 50 feet. He won the bet, creating a three-story-high structure with 860 square feet of living space.

Long Beach is home to the world's oldest tattoo parlor (established in 1927) still in business today.

Look out past the coast of Long Beach, and you'll think you're looking at tiny island resorts, complete with swaying palms, colorful lights and waterfalls. In fact, these are cleverly concealed offshore oil drilling stations, made soundproofed and pleasing to the eye by the THUMS Co. They are the only decorated oil islands in the United States.

Located on East Ocean Boulevard is the **Long Beach Museum of Art**. The used-brick and rust-shingled structure is one of several old mansions that line this picturesque stretch of the Pacific. The museum behind the ivy-covered brick fence was once the 1912 summer home of Elizabeth Milbank Anderson, a New York philanthropist, who purchased this prime piece of ocean bluff property in 1911. The house went on to become a private social and athletic club in the 1920s and later an officers' club in World War II. The city of Long Beach purchased the home and established the art museum in 1957. September 2001 saw the grand reopening of the museum. The multimillion-dollar expansion doubled the museum's size with a 12,800-square-foot exhibit building that merges beautifully with the existing 1912 mansion. The Arts and Crafts–style mansion went through an extensive renovation that revealed its original rich wood paneling and fireplaces. A first-rate museum store and garden cafe have been added, with awe-inspiring views of the ocean from their bluff-top setting. **http://www.lbma.org/**

Photo by Tyler Nix, unsplash.com

Exploring the diverse neighborhoods of Long Beach is a perfect way to find hidden treasures. Just three miles down Ocean Boulevard is the seaside neighborhood of **Belmont Shore** that features Second Street's quaint boutiques and outdoor cafes. Park the car and wander down one side and up the next, stopping for lunch at one of the trendy bistros. Tucked in this neighborhood is one of the most romantic destinations in Long Beach, **Naples Island**. The Italian-style gondoliers of Gondola Getaway take cruise-goers down the scenic canal waterways lined with million-dollar estates. It's also an ideal spot to ride a bike. Belmont's scenic three-mile **bike path** is a seventeen- foot- wide concrete trail on the beach, extending from Alamitos Avenue on the west to 54th Place on the east. The path starts at the lighthouse in Shoreline Aquatic Park, juts out and around the Aquarium and the Rainbow Park Lagoon, and then returns to the ocean. It also intersects the Long Beach Marina Bike Path in one direction, the Long Beach Bike Path and the Queensway Bay Bike Path. **https://www.belmontshore.org/**

AUTHOR'S TIP: NAPLES IN SOCAL

Cigarette manufacturer and visionary Abbot Kinney purchased this tidal flatland south of Santa Monica in 1904. He planned a subdivision based on Venice, Italy, that called for 16 miles of Venetian-style canals that would be traversed by an unusual form of public transportation—gondolas. Unfortunately, the canals interfered with oil drilling in the area and were abandoned. Today some of these canals have been revitalized and host romantic gondola rides. Kinney would have been pleased. **http://gondolagetawayinc.com/**

One of the more exciting neighborhoods to emerge in recent years is the **East Village Arts District**. The redevelopment area is populated with art studios, galleries, restaurants and art-related businesses. Plan a visit to the **Museum of Latin American Art (MoLAA)**, in this area a short drive from downtown. The only museum in the west to focus on the contemporary art of Mexico, Central and South America and the Spanish speaking Caribbean, it anchors a prominent corner of the village. **https://molaa.org/**

One emergent neighborhood pays homage to vintage clothing, mid-century furnishings, collectibles and antiques. **Retro Row**, located mostly along 4th Street between Cherry Avenue and Redondo Avenue near downtown, offers a handful of fun shops to explore. You'll find anything from rare albums and vintage roller skates to shabby chic. The 4th Street neighborhood is home to several eating spots and unique entertainment. **http://4thstreetlongbeach.com/**

San Pedro

Some people think of **San Pedro** as just a jumping off spot for a cruise—and it is. It is host to the largest commercial and cruise ship port on the West Coast, which has recently undergone a major rebirth—with more than $1 billion in further improvements planned in the **Port of Los Angeles** in the next few years. But a visitor will find more than that if they look beyond the ships to its Hollywood and maritime history. Think of it as a neighborhood embraced by both history and "sea breezes."

San Pedro may be the home of the nation's first Wienerschnitzel Restaurant, but its history goes much deeper than hot dogs and fries. Historic downtown San Pedro is a walkable stroll through the town where Richard Henry Dana set his novel, "Two Years Before the Mast." The area is in the midst of major transformation, adding lofts, businesses and shops. Without a doubt, the arrival of the **USS Iowa** battleship has infused warranted new interest in the city and provides another good reason to visit. Commissioned in 1943, the USS Iowa took part in every major military conflict from WWII and the Korean War through 1990 when it was decommissioned. The 887-foot long vessel was host to more U.S. presidents than any other battleship, earning the nickname "the battleship of presidents." It stands unique for having the only bathtub among battleships, installed for President Franklin D. Roosevelt in 1943. Now, a fascinating floating museum, the Iowa is open for touring its 70 years of history. Seven of the 19 decks are open with glimpses of the biggest guns the U.S. ever sent to sea. **https://www.pacificbattleship.com/**

Crafted, which opened a few years ago in a rambling former warehouse, is a good example of the area's rebirth. The craft marketplace is filled with stalls manned by artists, designers and artisanal food makers. Food trucks line the outside of the spacious shopping area; live entertainment makes it a fun weekend outing. **http://craftedportla.com/**

Two blocks downhill from historic old San Pedro, is the **Los Angeles Maritime Museum**, the largest maritime museum in California. Located in the art deco 1941-built Municipal Ferry Terminal, the museum's exhibits are focused on the maritime history of California's coast including ship models and navigational equipment. **http://www.lamaritimemuseum.org/**

The **San Pedro Trolley Red Car** will take you from the museum straight to the World Cruise Center. Stroll the one-mile promenade with art work and a history story "rope." Walk under the bridge from here to view the S.S. Lane Victory, a fully restored WWII cargo ship or continue on the trolley to the Cabrillo Marine Aquarium.

The **Cabrillo Marine Aquarium** is not the aquarium you might expect—it is so much better—especially if you are more interested in learning about the rich marine life that surrounds rather than killer whale extravaganzas. For the last 80 years, the modest aquarium has proven itself a first-rate educational facility for the public (at no charge) and for serious marine researchers and conservation programs. **https://www.cabrillomarineaquarium.org/**

AUTHOR'S TIP: WATCH THE GRUNION RUN

Yes, grunion do exist. Many people think they are just folklore or a novel excuse to take a date to the beach on a beautiful summer night. On the contrary, the silvery, elusive fish very much exist on the Pacific coast of Southern California, and they generally run several nights in July and August. The run consists of the fish's natural cycle to come on shore to spawn and lay eggs, usually following the full and new moons, when the tides are perfect. The Cabrillo Marine Aquarium in San Pedro hosts the most popular organized grunion run programs in Southern California. The grunion nights usually begin around 9:00 p.m., and participants are told to bring flashlights and warm clothing. Participants may take fish from the beach but only with their hands; everyone over sixteen must have a fishing permit to do so.

Long Beach's most recognized icon sailed into the city to stay, retiring after 1,001 crossings. **The Queen Mary**, on the National Register of Historic Places, stands as one of the last survivors of the great super liners and is, surprisingly, about twice the size of the infamous Titanic. The vessel has been preserved as a floating hotel with original "stateroom" accommodations and restaurants, but day-trippers turn out to take tours that guide them through parts of the ship that have been known for ghostly sightings. In 2018, the ship opened up its "most haunted" room to overnight guests: room B340. **https://www.queenmary.com/**

Catalina Island

https://www.visitcatalinaisland.com/

To a native Southern Californian, thoughts of San Pedro are often associated with the days of the great white steamer that linked the mainland of Southern California with the enchanted island of **Catalina** just 21 miles away. The huge steamer ship that deposited hundreds of visitors at a time to the state's one-time celebrity haunt had a lively dance floor and bands that greeted the voyagers at the Avalon dock, but the trip also took hours and usually under bumpy, crowded and chilly conditions.

It is far easier to reach Catalina these days, but not a lot has changed over the years—just small additions that make each visit more alluring. Strolls by the sea and charming bistros on the water still give you the romance you crave in this heavenly spot that USA Today calls one of the "best little-known islands." Add to that, no traffic to fight unless you count golf carts, little need for dinner reservations and only the sounds of the gentle crashing of waves on the rocky beach to lull you to sleep. Forget the plane ticket to the Caribbean. Just take a 45-minute **Catalina Express** ride from downtown Long Beach, and you have arrived on Catalina Island—your local island escape. **https://www.catalinaexpress.com/**

No matter how you get there, the beauty of Catalina Island will amaze you. The sparkling blue water that meets with the tiny Mediterranean village of Avalon is further enhanced by the green, towering hills that embrace the 1-square-mile city. But beyond Avalon lies the unspoiled beauty of the island, one of the few places in Southern California that is virtually the same as it was when the Spanish explorers landed in 1542. The beaches, sunshine and shops are enough to lure most visitors to Catalina, but it is the fortunate visitor who also takes time to explore the island's rich history, which is integrally linked to its off-the-beaten-path territory. A majority of the island is preserved nature, open only to permitted trips and island-run tours and great hiking forays.

AUTHOR'S TIP:
THE PLEASURE PIER

Under the ownership of the Banning brothers, who formed the Santa Catalina Island Co. in 1894, Avalon flourished as both a fisherman's and tourist's paradise. But by 1906 the beach was becoming overcrowded with boat stands, launches, glass-bottom boats, rowboats, racks of drying fish and sea lions waiting for handouts. A pier was built that was destroyed in a 1908 storm, so a new pier was planned and built in 1909, receiving the name "pleasure pier" a few years later. For many years it was the town's official weigh station for sports fishermen, including such notables as Zane Grey, Cecil B. DeMille and Charlie Chaplin. Seaplanes landed at the end of the pier in the 1950s and 1960s. Today, the pier in its distinctive shade of green is still a hub of activity as the departure point of tours and the home of the visitor center and boat rental and fish market business. Even if you don't partake of the pier's services, take the 407-foot stroll down its wooden planks and enjoy the clear water lapping at its nearly 100-year-old base.

Tours of Catalina Island provide one of the few ways you can glimpse the nearly 90-percent preserved portion of the island. A variety of fascinating tours take you through the inner-island paradise of deserted beaches met by emerald water, hillsides filled with Toyon and scrub oak and airplane-high vistas. The Catalina Island Conservancy maintains the trails through the ample wildlands of the island; hiking maps may be downloaded from the Conservancy's website. The popular **Garden to Sky Hike** trail begins at the Wrigley Memorial & Botanic Garden and leads to Divide Road at the top of Avalon Canyon. The roundtrip is 2 ½ miles of rugged, natural beauty. **https://www.visitcatalinaisland.com/**

LOCAL'S SECRET: CATALINA ISLAND AND THE WIZARD OF OZ

"According to The Telegraph, a United Kingdom-based newspaper, the sound director for The Wizard of Oz and his team spent a week on Catalina Island in 1939. During that time, they recoded the trills, chips and songs of each of the 8,000 birds in the Bird Park. The Bird Park off Avalon Canyon was created by William Wrigley Jr., and it became one of the Island's major attractions as well as the largest aviary in the world at the time. The sound crew recorded more than 15,000 feet of bird calls, the most complete collection of bird noises made up to that time. To create the eerie noises of the Haunted Forest for the film, the sound team distorted and overlapped the bird calls they had collected on Catalina Island."

–Alexa Johnson, Catalina Conservancy,
https://www.catalinaconservancy.org/

You might feel like one of the buffalo you are about to view when you board the coach for an **Inland Expedition Tour**, one of several unique tours offered on the island. But the ride in the shiny brown coaches, which look like cattle cars, pulled up the mountainsides by a semitrailer cab, is very comfortable, if not remarkable, as the full-length rig twists and climbs to the inner island. If you tend to be leery of heights, then sit on the left-hand side and relax—the drivers are experts who accomplish this feat daily. The unforgettable three-and-three-quarter-hour trip takes you along an early stagecoach route to a breathtaking summit at 1,450 feet. To reach the vista point with views of Mount Baldy and the Palos Verdes Peninsula on the mainland, the coach passes through a private gate (visitors are not allowed on their own beyond this point). The buffalo on the island today are descendants of fourteen buffalo (really North American bison) that were brought over in 1924 to "star" in a Zane Grey movie, The Vanishing American. The buffalo were so scattered about the island after the filming that the crew could not figure out how to gather them up; the island's owner, William Wrigley Jr. offered to buy the unusual animals and added more later— about 400 roam the island today. Wrigley bought the island in 1919, preserving the interior from commercial development. In 1972 Wrigley's son, who shared his father's ideals, turned over 86 percent of the island's 76 square miles to the Santa Catalina Island Conservancy, a nonprofit foundation dedicated to preserving and protecting the open space, wildlands, and nature preserves. **https://www.visitcatalinaisland. com/activities-adventures/land/inland-expedition**

Explore this terrain at night by **Hummer**. View the night lights of Avalon on this evening drive that is rife with breathtaking views and stops overlooking beautiful Avalon Bay. Your driver provides interesting Catalina Island highlights as the hummer winds its way through the heart of Avalon, down the coastline and into the hills under a canopy of stars. **https://www. visitcatalinaisland.com/hummer-tours**

If you prefer smaller groups and more freedom, book the incredible **Jeep Eco-Tour**, also offered by the conservancy, to explore the inner-island wonders. Granting the same awe-inspiring views as the Inland Tour, this open-air jeep tour is much more personal and intimate. The two-hour tour will depart with as few as two persons and is tailored to the group aboard. The state-of-the-art, four-wheel-drive vehicles climb and wind through the interior back roads of the island, stopping at archaeological and historical sites and irresistible viewpoints overlooking pristine beaches and coves. Tourgoers might glimpse bald eagles (recently reintroduced to the island), the shy Santa Catalina Island fox, bison, and rare plants. All proceeds from the Jeep Eco-Tours fund the conservation and education projects and programs of the

Santa Catalina Island Conservancy. **https://www.catalina-tours.com/tour/jeep-eco-tour/**

AUTHOR'S TIP:
NIGHTTIME ADVENTURE

So perhaps you've conquered the thrill of eco zip lining. Now, it is time to try it in the dark when speeds feel much faster and heights feel so much higher. Catalina Island has established the state's first night-time eco zip line tour for an adrenaline-pumping two hours of adventure. The **Night Zip** *begins with a step off of a platform high above the ocean, sailing into complete darkness, reaching speeds of up to 45 mph. Soar like a bird at heights up to 300 feet above the canyon floor and under the stars with only solar lighting illuminating each perch along the way. Listen for the sounds of the variety of creatures that come out at night including bats, foxes and owls. There's minimal lighting on the course for this thrilling adventure, so participants are outfitted with reflective strips and head lamps.* **https://www.visitcatalinaisland.com/event/night-zip-line**

The city of **Avalon**, where the population rises from 3,000 to 10,000 on summer weekends, is worth exploring, and this can be accomplished on foot for those with stamina. Taxis and golf-cart-type vehicles called auto-ettes are available but not necessary. To avoid the crowds and enjoy the island's off-season rates and warmer-than-mainland temperatures, visit Catalina Island in late fall and early winter. The lack of crowds will surely enhance your view of the charming mingling of small-town commerce, residences, fascinating historical points, recreation and nature spots.

The newly-constructed **Catalina Island Museum** is always interesting if you want to learn more about the fascinating history of the island. The new museum building with an Art Deco feel provides more than 18,000 square feet of exhibit space. The museum tour begins with a film about Catalina Island's history in the museum's Brown Family Digital Theater. The atrium boasts a mural composed of Catalina tile and the William Wrigley Jr. Gallery, the John and Hasmik Mgrdichian Gallery and the Artists' Plaza Gallery are all exhibition galleries dedicated to the island's history and to special exhibitions, many of which will travel to the island from collections throughout the world. More space is discovered on the building's rooftop and in the gardens immediately adjacent to the museum, used for dance and music concerts, as well as public and private events. **https://www.catalinamuseum.org/**

The white, rounded structure that juts out to sea in Avalon Bay is the island's best-known landmark, the **Casino.** The Mediterranean-style building with its Art Deco interior offers a fascinating legacy of pre–World War II memories, mostly associated with its upstairs dance floor, which held 3,000 dancers who moved to the 1930s big-band sounds broadcast on radios all over the country. The Casino, built by Wrigley, who never intended it for gambling, also holds a 1,200-seat theater, which was originally used by such motion picture greats as Cecil B. DeMille and Samuel Goldwyn to premiere their latest movies. Both the theater and the ballroom are focal points for island entertainment today. If you're lucky, you'll be able to attend a function in the Casino, but if not, take the visitor center's guided walking tour, which shows you everything from the large murals to the sounds of the rare pipe organ. The theater is still the island's only movie palace and offers weekend shows in the winter and nightly movies in the summer months. **https://www.visitcatalinaisland.com/activities-adventures/catalina-casino**

LOCAL'S SECRET:
LUIS AND HUELL ON BIRD ROCK

"In 2000, we went across the water near Catalina Island to visit a tiny privately owned island, Bird Rock, for an episode of "California Gold." Dive charter boats are frequent here since it is considered one of the best dive spots in the area. As Huell explored the island and marveled at the number of birds that call it home, I recall it was one of the messiest shoots I've done. The birds use the rock as their bathroom."

– Luis Fuerte, Producer/Cameraman,
"California Gold"; author "Louie, Take a Look at This,"
https://www.amazon.com/Louie-Take-Look-This-Howser-ebook/;
Prospect Park Books, https://www.prospectparkbooks.com/

Just beyond the famous Casino, the road and path lead to an idyllic cove and beach. **Descanso Beach** is one of the last private beaches in the state with public access. Pristine water for swimming and easy access to snorkeling, scuba and the zip line, make the beach a center of activity that goes from quiet, serene mornings to an energetic nightlife with an open-to-the-sea air restaurant and DJ tunes. Descanso Beach Club recently debuted a new look with private cabanas, chaise lounges and more pampering.

Standing in downtown Avalon, look to the hills southward for two mansions of significance. The **Holly Hill House**, an outstanding example of Queen Anne–style architecture, has been a local landmark since its completion in 1890. If you arrive by boat to Catalina, you will spot the hilltop structure immediately. Peter Gano, a retired civil engineer, bought this prime piece of real estate, and his talented, circus-trained horse, Mercury, made hundreds of treks down the steep mountainside hauling up construction supplies as they arrived by boat from the mainland.

Higher up in the hills, with panoramic views of the town and bay, is the **Inn on Mount Ada**. Named after Mrs. William Wrigley Jr., the imposing Georgian colonial mansion with shutters, moldings and trim in grays, whites and greens was the Wrigleys' Avalon home for thirty-seven years. The 350-foot mountain peak of almost solid rock was blasted to level the site for the house, and mules pulling scrapers graded the land in 1921. The mansion has seen guests such as the Prince of Wales and Presidents Coolidge and Hoover. After the death of Mrs. Wrigley in 1958, the mansion was acquired by the Santa Catalina Island Company. The Inn on Mount Ada offers six elegant guest rooms and suites on the second level of the house and a den, card lounge, sunroom, living room and dining room on the main floor. A hearty breakfast as well as lunch and evening appetizers are included in the very private stay here, which runs in the deluxe range. The inn allows a limited number of non-staying guests to join for lunch with prior reservation. **https://www.visitcatalinaisland. com/hotels-packages/avalon/mt-ada**

To experience the "other" island—its remote west end—in **Two Harbors**, take the Catalina Express from Long Beach's terminal directly to Two Harbors. No tourist facades greet you, just a few fishermen and some yacht owners anchoring there for the kicked-back ambience and minor services. This is Avalon as it once was, a boater's paradise surrounded by crystal-clear waters. The town is comprised of about six structures including visitor services for a couple of tours, water sports, a restaurant with a snack bar, bar and outside dining deck, general store and some public restrooms and showers. Travel up the dirt path from town and you will find the historic **Banning House Lodge**. Built in 1910 atop a hill overlooking both the Isthmus Cove and Catalina Harbor, it's a journey into the past. **https://www.visitcatalinaisland.com/ hotels-packages/two-harbors/banning-house-lodge**

Hiking and bicycle paths abound in Two Harbors, as well as land and sea guided tours. Sweeping views of the island's leeward coastline and pristine hillsides embrace every turn and twist, and it is not unusual to see hawks, foxes and mule deer. The Safari Bus Tour connects Avalon with Two Harbors for those wanting a day adventure.

The Orange County Coast
https://www.visittheoc.com/

The coastal cities and beaches that make up Orange County, tucked between the beach cities of Los Angeles and San Diego, are blessed with 42 miles of sparkling coast filled with surf history, art and amazing hidden gems.

Seal Beach

Pretty **Seal Beach**, the northern gateway to Orange County's coastline, provides a peaceful escape. Named after the seals that once populated its coastline, the charming city offers a special blend of quaint sites, history and ocean beauty. The city's old-fashioned downtown lies at the edge of the shoreline just off the pier at Main Street and Ocean Avenue. Wander Main Street's shops and restaurants and you'll discover why Forbes named it one of America's Friendliest Towns. At the end of Main Street is the **Seal Beach Pier**, framed by double Victorian lampposts. The 1,865-foot-long pier is the second longest wooden pier in California. It has also starred in several Hollywood films, including American Sniper and As Good as It Gets.

At the other end of Main Street lies an equally charming square that houses the **Red Car Museum**, located in an original red car trolley like those that brought city dwellers to the ocean beginning in 1904. Built in 1925, car number 1734 was actually a roving machine shop that was sent out to troubleshoot problems on the line when riders between Seal Beach and Los Angeles made the fifty-minute trip. The unique museum hosts different exhibits sporadically. **http://www.sbhs-red-carmuseum.com/**

Huntington Beach

What more do you need to say about a city that has a Woody as its official car? An abundance of wide, sandy beaches and California dreamin' surf culture draws millions of visitors to **Huntington Beach** annually to indulge in the consistently mild weather and amazing swells that make surfers and surf-lovers happy way past summer beach-going days. In fact, year-round temperatures rarely exceed 90 degrees and fall skies are bluer than blue. In addition to all of that, Huntington possesses one of the nation's largest recreational piers, a marina, a wildlife preserve, scenic trails for hiking, biking and jogging, as well as ocean-view shopping and dining that all add up to summer fun—well into fall.

The city that became legendary as "Surf City USA" opened its first surf shop along the white, sparkling strand of beach in 1953, a few years before the U.S. Surfing Championships were first held there and more than 25 years after Duke Kahanamoku brought the sport to Huntington Beach. Not surprisingly, most of the city's best action is centered around the beach and saltwater-kissed vistas. However, beach going in the city goes beyond surfers and surf watchers. It is known for its dog-loving surfers as well.

Head to a special section of Huntington Beach reserved for four-legged friends – even if you don't have a furry pal along. **Huntington Dog Beach** surf-watching is a popular pastime here as surf-riding dogs shoot the curl in tandem with their two-legged owners. The beach, free to the public, operates as a non-profit organization and furnishes complimentary biodegradable "doggie bags." The annual Surf City Surf Dog event at Huntington Dog Beach features a multi-heat dog surfing competition, guaranteed to entertain and impress each September. **http://www.dogbeach.org/**

But there is more to beach in Huntington Beach. It is home to around 70 parks, the largest in Orange County being **Huntington Beach Central Park**. Inside the park, **Shipley Nature Center** features 18 acres of California native habitat, a monarch butterfly waystation, educational center and charming gift shop. Flowing through the northern tip of town is the **Bolsa Chica Ecological Reserve**, the largest saltwater marsh along coastal California between the Monterey Bay and the Tijuana River Estuary. **https://www.huntingtonbeachca. gov/Residents/parks_facilities/parks/huntington_central_ park/index.cfm**

Balboa Island

Aside from Catalina Island, Southern California has another small island to offer with a slightly different experience. If you have ever bitten into the incredibly creamy, chocolate-covered block of vanilla ice cream called a Balboa Bar, then you have already sampled something native to this island, a stone's throw from shore. **Balboa Island**, a yachter's paradise and spring vacation hangout for teens, remains a Southern California symbol of island escape, even though a sleek bridge now connects it to land at one end.

Go along with tradition and ignore the bridge. Instead, head over to the car and pedestrian ferry that shuttles people, bikes, and cars over to the miniature isle continuously all day long. The nostalgic bargain costs just $1 per pedestrian. The open-air **Balboa Island Ferry** transports around three cars per

trip, so park the car and walk on if you're in a rush. **http://
www.balboaislandferry.com/fares.html**

The island itself is a wall-to-wall residential community, with a main street jammed with not only people but also swimsuit boutiques, restaurants and, of course, Balboa Bar stands. Wander for a while and take in the show before heading back to the mainland. The ferry docks at South Front; turn right and take a leisurely walk to the village past bay-fronting homes on the land side and the boat docks on the other. Abundant and colorful flower gardens along the way are reminders of affluent summer dwellers who have settled the island over the last century.

Most of the island's streets are named after precious stones. After passing by Topaz, Turquoise, Diamond and Sapphire, you reach the district's popular Marine Avenue, a shopping haven for one-of-a-kind gift items, art galleries and alluring bistros.

AUTHOR'S TIP: INDULGE IN THE NAMESAKE DESSERT

For under $5, you can savor two Balboa Island treats. Although the frozen, hand-dipped chocolate banana did not originate on the island, it gained real island fame on the television show "Arrested Development" that centered around a family who owned a Balboa Island frozen banana stand. However, the island is the birthplace of the ice cold, decadent Balboa Bar, a slab of rich vanilla ice cream slathered in rich chocolate and rolled in your choice of nuts and candy.

After your ferry returns to the bay, let the carnival atmosphere of the bay-front area, with its whirling Ferris wheel and crowds, sweep you along to the **Balboa Pavilion**, built in 1905 as the hub of the original Balboa Land Development. It stands as one of California's last surviving examples of early-twentieth-century, waterfront recreational pavilions. The building, restored in 1962, is now the headquarters of a summertime Catalina launch station, but the distinctive building with cupola was once the terminus for the Pacific Electric Railway from Los Angeles. The famed railway, with electric trollies known as "red cars," connected Los Angeles beachgoers with this desirable stretch of beach in one hour's time. But eventually the trollies ceased, bought up and scrapped by the new bus transit systems in the early forties. **http://www.balboapavilion.com/**

The Balboa Pavilion views the island and crisscrossing yachts on one side and the famed Balboa Pier in the opposite direction. The walk out to the end of the pier is a real taste of the Pacific, waves crashing on either side of the very spot that saw the first water-to-water aircraft flight in 1912, when a seaplane flew from here to Catalina. Enjoy another taste treat at the end of the pier at **Ruby's Cafe**. Ruby's greets you with a take-out window in front, but walk around to the back where the entrance to the cafe is located. Perched on the tail end of the boardwalk is the tiny diner right out of the 1940s. An intimate counter bar with swivel seats serves a few customers, while the remaining diners are seated at red vinyl chairs and chrome tables topped with vases of red carnations. The waiters and waitresses in red-and-white-striped uniforms offer friendly service in this fun eatery. **https://www.rubys.com/locations/balboa-pier/**

For a local's favorite haunt by the harbor, have breakfast or lunch at the tiny, unpretentious **Galley Cafe** that has been seeing generations since 1957. A frequent haunt of the late western star John Wayne, The Galley, sometimes called Eddie's, is a Balboa Peninsula institution with real milkshake machines, old-fashioned burgers, killer chili and bulging omelets. **http://www.thegalleycafenewportbeach.com/**

Newport Beach

Another pier worthy of exploration awaits nearby. A much different pier, **Newport Pier** is a conglomerate of businesses that line the shore as well as an active fishing area that boasts the only remaining dory fleet in California. Fishermen have been going to sea each day in these colorful wooden boats since the late 1800s, bringing back the fresh fish that becomes dinner in local restaurants and homes alike. The rainbow-colored boats dock at the pier at midmorning with their wares, setting up informal shops in the boats themselves. The fishermen-vendors weigh, scale and fillet the fish for you and also provide some handy advice on how to prepare their catch of the day.

Located near the dory fishing fleet is appropriately the **Doryman's Oceanfront Inn**, an interesting Italianate brick-and-marble building on a prominent corner. The bed-and-breakfast hotel at 2102 West Ocean Front was constructed in 1892 and has been beautifully renovated and decorated in carefully selected, Country French antiques. Each individually decorated guest room boasts ocean views, a fireplace and a marble sunken tub. An award-winning, gourmet seafood restaurant, 21 Ocean Front, in the bottom level of the hotel, offers dinner; a complimentary continental breakfast is offered to guests each morning in the parlor. **https://www.dorymansinn.com/**

AUTHOR'S TIP: BODYSURFING AT THE WEDGE

The Wedge Newport Beach is the perfect spot to watch body-surfers who know that a 30-foot wave is right around the corner, making it a better place to watch than participate unless you are a seasoned pro. Either way, this spot with the biggest swells in Southern California is a must see when you visit Newport Beach.

To capture the casual surfer feel of the Peninsula, consider staying at **Newport Beach Hotel**. Reminiscent of a seaside Cape Cod inn with wainscoting and pastel decor, it sits directly across from the sand and all the action. Part of the Four Sisters hotel collection, known for establishing the top bed and breakfast inns in the state, it combines luxury and personal service, along with carefree unfussiness. The guest rooms are finished with gleaming hardwood floors, flat screen televisions, some fireplaces and marble bathrooms with large Jacuzzi tubs (that soothe after a day at the beach). Extras mean an extended complimentary continental breakfast each morning, access to a beer and wine bar and the free use of beach towels, bikes and more. In an area tough to get parking, the hotel also offers private, remote-gate parking, which you will likely use just once. Park the car and stroll or bike to everything, from the beach to the lively boardwalk to some casual eateries. **https://www.thenewportbeachhotel.com/**

Cobblestone streets lead you to another waterfront area nearby, the **Lido Marina Village** on Newport Bay. The tree-lined streets are filled with boutiques and allow only pedestrian traffic to make for leisurely strolling. It's gone upscale with bistros such as Nobu and Malibu Farms, but if you slip around to the harborside boardwalk to see the yacht parade and take in some of the fishing and yachting atmosphere.

One of the best ways to achieve this is a stop for a meal or drink at **The Cannery** restaurant with more than 90 years of fishing history. This part of the harbor has been a major commercial fishing area in California for more than fifty years, and in 1921 a cannery was built on the site of the restaurant. The Western Canners Company took over operations in 1934 and increased production from over 400 cases of fish a day to more than 5,000 cases per day in later years. A recent employee of The Cannery restaurant also worked in the spot in its canning days. She remembered the women packers, all living walking distance away, being summoned to work by the sound of a steam whistle. Even though the cannery survived the Depression and World War II, pollution finally drove the mackerel out to sea, and the business closed in 1966. The fascinating interior of The Cannery is a living museum dedicated to the fish-canning industry. From the wooden plank floors to the open rafters hung with pulleys to the tables constructed of the original flooring to the original factory machinery in every nook and turn, the restaurant is comfortably realistic. **https://cannerynewport.com/**

Head south to discover two blooming garden spots, both tranquil retreats with beautiful displays, even if you are only a gardener at heart. Home of the nationally televised PBS show Victory Garden West is **Roger's Gardens** in Corona del Mar. The seven-and-a-half-acre botanical garden, boasting more than 50,000 plants, is also a nursery with indoor and outdoor plants; a florist; garden supply center; patio shop; how-to center; and gallery with one-of-a-kind antiques, artwork, and gifts of all sorts. Waterfalls, winding paths, slopes draped in a patchwork of blooms, and zoo-like topiary lead you through the immaculate grounds of the retail business that looks more like a botanical retreat. If you can time a visit to Roger's

Gardens between the second week of October and the holidays, you will be rewarded with the nursery's annual holiday extravaganza displays. Multiple trees are thematically decorated; unique Christmas accessories abound; and every night guests are enchanted by thousands of lights that illuminate the gardens. Plan to have lunch or dinner at the Farmhouse restaurant where locally sourced menus delight in a casual farmhouse setting with weathered wood and stone accents. https://www.rogersgardens.com/#

The **Sherman Library and Gardens** in Corona del Mar is city-block-long, Spanish-style research center and garden that provides an oasis of tranquility along this busy and congested stretch of the coast. Visitors entering the gardens first see the picturesque lily pond with fountain and surrounding poppies, a favorite artist's spot. The other garden areas, composed of more than 1,000 species, include a tropical indoor greenhouse with a koi pond, cascading waterfall, banana trees, and orchid blooms. The Discovery Garden was designed especially but not exclusively for the blind. The plants in this area emphasize the senses of touch and smell and are fashioned in an island-like shape for easy wheelchair access. The walkways of the gardens are lined with arbors, terra-cotta-potted plants, driftwood sculptures and statuary. Stop in outdoor Cafe Jardin for lunch Monday through Friday and Sunday brunch. **http://www.slgardens.org/**

Crystal Cove State Park, one of Southern California's most treasured gems, offers 3.2 miles of pristine beach. Take a docent-led tide pool walk on certain days of the week, relax on the beach, frolic in the surf or enjoy a great beach-themed meal on the sand at Beachcomber—top it off with a shake at Rudy's Shake Shack at the top of the hill on the PCH. Within the state park is a secret surf haven, Scotchman's Cove. Wooden steps lead to the beach near Reef Point that is a favorite of locals for catching a memorable wave when the tide is right. A more recent shopping complex sits across the highway with several new, trendy bistros—such as Javier's and Babette's. **http://www.crystalcovestatepark.org/**

AUTHOR'S TIP: STAY IN A HISTORIC BEACH COTTAGE

The **Crystal Cove Historic District** *is a 12-acre coastal portion of Crystal Cove State Park. The federally listed Historic District is an enclave of 46 vintage rustic coastal cottages originally built as a seaside colony in the 1930s and 1940s and nestled around the mouth of Los Trancos Creek. It remains one of the last remaining examples of early 20th century Southern California coastal development. The California State Parks and the Crystal Cove Conservancy has completed the initial phases of restoration in the Historic District, with 21 cottages of various sizes offered to the public for overnight stays with very reasonable rates. The hard part is getting a reservation which has recently been made easier with a six-month advance booking system.*
http://www.crystalcovestatepark.org/the-historic-district/
https://crystalcove.org/beach-cottages/reserve-now/

Not as well known by visitors is **Little Corona Beach**, however, it may offer the best tide pool bounties in the OC. The secluded beach off Ocean Boulevard is another great place to observe small fish of all varieties, crabs, starfish and sea urchins. Relatively small, the beach is flanked on both sides with rocky reefs that offer the spectacular diving well known to local divers. The beach is very well protected from swells and surf, making it one of the easier beach diving sites and a great beach for families. **https://www.parks.ca.gov/?page_id=652**

Laguna Beach

In **Laguna Beach**, gentle ocean breezes combine with some of the cleanest beaches, water and air on the coast to make the area a magnet for water-play, hidden coves, tide-pool exploring in "nature's aquarium," rugged canyon hikes, bird watching and simply enjoying the refreshing coastal temperatures. However, it is the art that keeps people coming back each summer with a one-of-a-kind art and theater presentation: the **Pageant of the Masters** and an entire summer of art in many other forms, the **Festival of Arts**. https://www.foapom. com/

More than eighty years ago, the country was still reeling over the Great Depression. Offering a bounty of uplifting natural beauty, Laguna Beach became a popular refuge for artists who were inspired by the glistening coastline, the rambling hills and the soothing sounds of the waves. By 1932, a group of those artists banded together to find a way to raise spirits and money by selling their art.

In the summer of 1933, the Laguna Beach Festival of Arts was born when around two dozen artists hung their paintings on fences, trees and buildings along Laguna's main street, hoping to lure visitors to the first Festival of Arts, while some artists opened their home-studios to the public. Music, colorful signs and banners, parades and entertainment added to the celebratory ambiance of the event, which turned Laguna Beach into one enormous art gallery. In 1935, "living pictures" were transformed into a full production with music, narration and painted backdrops, giving birth to The Pageant of the Masters which rapidly evolved into a popular summer tradition. Not surprisingly, the pageant now draws an audience of more than 200,000 and the Festival of Arts Fine Art Show prevails as one of the longest-running art exhibitions in the state.

AUTHOR'S TIP:
LET YOUR MUSE EMERGE

What do Bette Davis, a music-loving skunk and a pigeon with make-up on its claws have in common? They have all played parts in the lore and legend of the Pageant of the Masters, established more than eight decades ago to bring paying customers to Laguna's art colony. Evolving into the acclaimed fantastical theatrical event it is today, the pageant leaves most patrons wondering how art masterpieces magically become living pictures, complete with narration and costuming.

If you're an art lover, don't wait for summer's Pageant of the Masters. The city has more than 30 art galleries as well as the well-known Laguna Art Museum for perusing. There are more than 85 works of public art that you can tour on your own. **https://www.visitlagunabeach.com/blog/10-must-see-public-art-pieces-in-laguna-beach/**

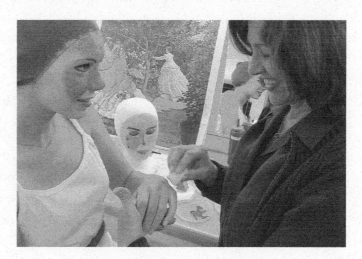

Courtesy Visit Laguna Beach

LOCAL'S SECRET:
EXPLORE A SUNKEN SHIP

"At Cleo Street, just a few hundred feet offshore, rests the Foss 125. Built in 1942, The Foss was a barge that the Coast Guard used to ferry supplies ashore. In typical Laguna Beach fashion – remember this is a town once full of brigands and rumrunners – the details of the ship-wreck are murky. Some say it hit the rock reef during a storm, while others argue that it was part of an insurance scam. Over the years, divers have scoured for treasures among the Foss's sunken remains – with a fair degree of success. The real allure of the wreck is the artificial reef that the bones of the ship have created. Halibut, sand bass, and rockfish explore the wreckage, while spiny lobsters make their homes in the wreck's nooks and crannies. If you're diving and plan to enter the wreck, make sure you have experience or are being led by an experienced wreck diver. Otherwise, swimming around the outside of the hull should offer plenty of visual entertainment."

– Ashley Johnson, President & CEO, Visit Laguna Beach,
https://www.visitlagunabeach.com/

Founded in 1887, Laguna Beach was first named Lagonas (lakes) by the early California Indians, who were inspired by the beauty of Laguna's two freshwater lagoons. Nature's beauty, from the crashing surf to the mountains to intimate coves in between, is evident today from several viewing points. Called the "Top of the World," **Alta Laguna**, a park at 900 feet above sea level, grants views of the sunset over Catalina Island and sunrise over pretty Saddleback Valley in the distant east. Pack a picnic lunch and head north on Alta Laguna Boulevard. Another viewing spot, Emerald Vista Point, offers more than 200 miles of coast to savor.

AUTHOR'S TIP: GOATS AT WORK

Low scrub brush that grows in Laguna is particularly suscep-
tible to burning out of control. To keep people and property
safe, preventative measures have to be taken. With the ground
too rocky for machines, the city has turned to goats. Each year,
Peruvian goats visit Laguna Beach to eat, mowing the canyon
hills bare one section at a time. To see the goats in action, walk
along the fire access roads between Moulton Meadows and Top
of the World parks.

Set amid 20,000 acres of wilderness, Laguna Beach is a perfect choice for all ages. Sink your toes in the sand, embark on a whale watching adventure or learn to surf or paddleboard. If you bring your favorite pooch along, beaches and many hotels and restaurants are dog friendly. There's even a dog park in Laguna Canyon, where pups can run off leash on a two-acre grassy lawn. Plan on exploring Laguna's tide pools or visit the **Pacific Marine Mammal Center** to view rehabilitating seals and sea lions.

Thousand Steps Beach Cave might be the most impressive cave in the county. You'll find it at the south end of **Thousand Steps Beach**, a beautiful sandy beach that requires going down a very long set of stairs. A bonus with this beach is the rock arch at the north end of the beach that leads to a hidden beach on the other side. Be sure to visit at low tide so you can see both natural features.

The residential area of Laguna Beach is worthy of inspection. Take a self-guided trip, courtesy of the **Laguna Beach Historical Society**, through Laguna North past many interesting 1920s bungalows that housed some of the first year-round residents of the ocean community. At 390 Magnolia is the first cottage built in the Laguna Cliffs subdivision. Building it in one weekend, the Spots family won a $100 prize for being the first to construct. The prize probably covered most of their expenses. The Spanish Revival Mediterranean estate at 482 High Street, built in 1938, remains one of the most impressive in the city.

At Laguna South, known as Arch Beach, residences are marked by an abundance of 1920s summer cottages and artists' studios, but several notable one-of-a-kind homes are sprinkled throughout this area. The only remaining Victorian home in Laguna is located at 411 Arroyo Chico. The 1884 house has been moved from its original location on a bluff above Main Beach and restored as a part of Laguna's pioneer days. The 1920-built home at 530 Mountain was originally the home of Hollywood film star Polly Moran, who stayed after shooting a film on location in Laguna Beach. A fascinating pamphlet guide to individual homes in both these districts is available at **http://www.lagunabeachhistory.org/self-guided-tours**.

Dana Point

A multimillion-dollar marina jammed with luxury yachts, just south of Laguna Beach at picturesque **Dana Point**, is also a spot filled with early California history. Take a turn off the Coast Highway to the far western end of the Dana Point Harbor to view an exact replica of author Richard Henry Dana's vessel, the **Pilgrim**. The Pilgrim sailed around Cape Horn to this point in 1835, trading New England goods to nearby Mission San Juan Capistrano and area ranchos for cowhides tossed from the cliffs above. The full-scale model was made famous in Dana's American seafaring classic of the 1800s, Two Years Before the Mast, and is docked in this location except for its annual entry into the Tall Ships Festival in September. The 100-foot schooner is also utilized as a unique floating theater in July and August, when it serves as the stage for nautically themed live productions.

Right next door to where the Pilgrim is docked is the Cape Cod–style **Ocean Institute**, a nonprofit educational facility. The small museum, free to the public, offers books, maritime gifts, and a lab room with whale jawbones, fossils, sea turtle shells, fish tanks, and tapes of the various Orange County Marine Institute programs, such as living history programs held on the Pilgrim and a floating marine laboratory open only to schoolchildren weekdays throughout the year. **https://www.ocean-institute.org/general-information/about-pilgrim**

LOCAL'S SECRET: HIDDEN WATERFALL

*"One of my favorite hidden gems of Orange County is the secret **Dana Point waterfall**. Ever since I was a teenager, I would always jump into the car on a rainy day to admire the splendor of this natural beauty. Now that I have kids, our favorite thing to do on a rainy day is going to see the Dana Point waterfall. After we are done watching the waterfall in the rain, we warm-up with a cup of hot cocoa and breakfast at **The Harbor House Cafe**. Runoff from the city of Dana Point is the cause of the waterfall – so do not go near the water. While it is not the kind of waterfall that you can swim in on the islands of Hawaii ~ it is just as beautiful to admire." 24413-24469 Dana Point Harbor Dr, Dana Point*

– Shelby Barone, OC Mom Blog, **https://ocmomblog.com**

Inland Orange County

Irvine

A carefully sculpted, master- planned community, **Irvine** in Southern California's OC has it all. As home to more than 100 company headquarters, a University of California campus, some of the nation's leading family-friendly destinations nearby—from Disneyland to Knott's Berry Farm—recreation and lifestyle amenities are plentiful. However, Irvine has a "wild" side too. The Irvine Company nicely created a balance between the calculated lifestyle necessities and the natural space and beauty that also defines the city and its surroundings. For the visitor that translates to a bounty of hiking, biking and nearly endless nature trails in what has been coined "America's safest big city."

You may not remember Lion Country Safari since its lifespan was relatively short. The 140-acre attraction opened in 1970 in the rolling hills not far from the giant Ferris wheel marking the Irvine Spectrum entertainment complex. With the desire to bring the exotic side of an African safari to visitors to Orange County, the drive-through zoo allowed cars (or rented safari Jeeps) to traverse the four-mile preserve trail populated by free-roaming lions, hippos, elephants and more for truly up-close wildlife experiences. Even though the park was a success, drawing more than one million visitors during its first year of operation, the challenging economy of the mid-1970s, along with some bad publicity from escape attempts by some of the animals, brought an end to the park in 1984.

You may not see any African animals roaming the hills of Irvine these days, but you are sure to find plenty of wildland country to explore. Having ranched and farmed here for generations, the Irvine family was close to the land, and the city's original planners understood the importance of preserving wildlands, parks and places to connect with nature as a respite from urban life. Irvine offers more than 40 miles of off-road bike trails and 280 miles of on-road cycling lanes.

One of Orange County's most beautiful nature escapes, **Irvine Regional Park**, was once the private picnic grounds of James Irvine, Jr. and offers 160 picturesque acres a flush with trees and trails for biking and hiking. City planners also understand the ecological importance of open land, creating preserves like the **San Joaquin Wildlife Sanctuary** that serves as a refuge for local and migrating wildlife. **http://www.cityofirvine.org/open-space-trails**

Few places in the developed areas of the southland remain the same as they were 100 years ago. In the unincorporated foothills of the Santa Ana Mountains in the southeastern part of Orange County is a 4,000-acre preserve dedicated to the early ranching days that defined the OC and Irvine. Bordered by the Cleveland National Forest on the north and east and a regional park to the south, the **Starr Ranch Sanctuary** makes a perfect wildland escape. Owned by the National Audubon Society, the ranch is a throwback to the OC's ranching days with ancient orchards, farm buildings and a scenic creek that reaches down to woodlands. Over the years, hard work from volunteers and managers has made rustic Starr Ranch a well-kept and accommodating research station. The sanctuary has gradually rolled out more public programs and opens to the general public with its Family Nature Workshops. In this area that is populated by lions of the mountain lion genre, educational talks on local wildlife, nature walks and rides into Bell Canyon are highlights. The workshops are free, but registration is required, and there's no way to get to the ranch otherwise. **http://www.starrranch.org/index.html**

Secluded in the canyons of the Santa Ana Mountains in eastern unincorporated Orange County is a private resort and zoological garden, **Rancho Las Lomas**, surrounded by exotic animals such as tigers and zebras and historic Old California structures that are often used for weddings, filming and photo shoots. Wildlife tours are offered by reservation only; tours offer families and friends the opportunity to get up close with the animals as well as admire the elegant architecture and the beautiful botanical gardens throughout the property. The rancho's knowledgeable tour guides are dedicated to educating and inspiring visitors while promoting wildlife protection and education. **https://www.rancholaslomas.com/**

Old Towne Orange

Not far from Disneyland is an oasis of yesteryear: a one-hundred-year-old village that could have been the model for Walt's Main Street a few miles away. Unlike Main Street Disneyland, **Old Towne Orange** is not a fanciful fabrication, but a real old-fashioned downtown with surrounding Victorian neighborhood, preserved like an antique jewel that is surrounded by generations of progress and change. In fact, you can't help but wonder if Disney got his inspiration here—in his own backyard.

The one-mile-square village off the Chapman exit on the 55 freeway is instantly recognizable. The focal point of the historic district is a central park plaza, Plaza Park, with antique fountain and surrounding towering pines. Known as "Plaza City," the 1869 former fruit packaging and shipping town is California's largest historic district.

Today, a stroll around reveals both quaint and cutting-edge restaurants, interesting gift boutiques, myriad antique and collectible shops and intimate Victorian homes, all within walking distance of each other. Not surprising, the area is a favorite locale for movie and television filming, with many of the local businesses touting their part in productions, from "That Thing That You Do," filmed largely in the village, to "Cannonball Run." Old Towne Orange may be the antiques capital of Southern California. Dozens of antiques stores fill the historic streets here, offering every kind of antique and collector item imaginable. Many of these shops are cooperative, with several antiques dealers under one roof, adding even more selection to a fun day of scouting the past.

One of the best ways to tour this slice of early California is take an **Old Towne Orange Walking Food Tour** offered by sisters Deanna and Renee who unite their love of food (Italian) and history in three deliciously designed tours that include a large dose of Old Towne history. The siblings, who also produce a radio talk show about Orange, are longtime residents with years of knowledge to impart between steps and tastes. Appealing to foodies and visitors alike, the tours introduce goers to Orange's food culture on a neighborhood level, according to the sisters. From one-of-a-kind ethnic eateries to contemporary fine dining spots and retro Americana, there is something for everyone. **http://www.oldtownorangewalkingfoodtours.com/**

It would be an oversight not to mention a casual spot for breakfast or lunch. **Watson's Drugs and Diner** at 116 East Chapman is the oldest soda fountain in Orange County and the oldest ongoing business in the city of Orange. Established in 1899, Watson's serves breakfast all day, along with shakes, onion rings, and burgers for lunch. Diners sit on swivel chairs at the counter or at the red-and-white booths. A 1950s-tunes-filled jukebox serenades diners and drugstore shoppers, who can still pick up their prescriptions here along with an order of S.O.S. (biscuits with gravy). **https://www.watsonscafe.com/**

AUTHOR'S TIP: HIDDEN PARK

Pitcher Park *is a tucked away park is nestled in a quiet residential neighborhood, and it is one of the city's best kept secrets. The park was built on land donated by the Pitcher Family on the site of their former home and farm. The park's barn is a replica of the family's homestead and is home to a Fire Museum and memorabilia of Orange's agricultural roots. The Pitcher Park Community Foundation assists in maintaining the park by hosting a series of neighborhood fundraisers throughout the year.*
https://www.pitcherparkorange.org/

Old Towne Orange is more than just great food and antiques—it is also known for the arts. **The Exchange** at 195 South Glassell Street is a fine example of what the area offers. Located in the 1922-constructed Sunkist Orange County Fruit Exchange building, the fine arts gallery exhibits work by Orange County and other California artists. The carefully renovated the historic structure is marked by Italian Renaissance flourishes. The central atrium of the gallery features four large Honduras mahogany columns, and a masonry and iron fence was added at the entrance to the gallery using the original 1921 plans. A ceiling painting in the atrium measures 7 by 16 feet, the work of local artist Gary Armstrong, and was inspired by works of an Italian master.

San Juan Capistrano

It is no wonder the swallows return to **San Juan Capistrano** each March 19 (St. Joseph's Day), as the popular song of the 1940s recounts. The small, history-packed California village is almost idyllic and a wonderful getaway off the beaten path—unless you arrive at the same time the graceful birds flutter through town and perch on the church ruins.

Around the Mission San Juan Capistrano are several charming boutiques and cafes. A short walk away is the carefully preserved **Capistrano Depot**, built in 1894 by the Atchinson, Topeka and Santa Fe Railroad. The depot, with distinctive red-tile roof and hand-fashioned bricks, is the oldest Spanish Colonial Revival station in Southern California.

San Juan Capistrano is alive with history; its glorious **1776 Mission San Juan Capistrano**, with serene gardens and impressive adobe structures, has remained an outstanding archaeological, native Californian, and early Californian historical influence on the entire Orange County area from its historic founding. But within walking distance of the sacred grounds are a multitude of historical sites that you may view on your own or as a part of a walking tour. Each Sunday at 1:00 p.m. (or on arrangement), volunteer members of the San Juan Capistrano Historical Society lead visitors on a fascinating, one-hour-plus walking tour of the early adobe structures nearby. Nearly all the adobes you will view were built by the Indian neophytes of the mission as a part of the mission's establishment in the late 1700s; the Rios Adobe was the state's smallest land grant and was continuously occupied through the years by the Rios family. The tour includes a visit to an underground jail and buried treasure hiding places, as well as some exciting bandit tales. **https://sjchistoricalsociety.com/programs/historic-walking-tours/**

AUTHOR'S TIP:
TUNNEL UNEARTHED

According to Len Hall in a Los Angeles Times special article, local gallery owner Sue DiMaio was renovating the 19th-century home of Judge Richard Egan when workers uncovered the remnants of a long-sealed tunnel that appeared to lead under Camino Capistrano. Historians say there was a maze of tunnels in old San Juan, most of them used for irrigation and connected with Mission San Juan Capistrano. Hall reported that experts are not sure where the latest find leads or what it might have been used for--only that it adds to the "rich history and mystique of this mission city."

Travel down historic **Los Rios Street** in your car or on foot to learn about the various adobes and significant surrounding structures. Look carefully as you follow the county's oldest residential street; local lore has it that the street has a number of ghostly inhabitants. The Albert Pryor Residence, built in the 1870s at 31831 Los Rios Street, was restored in 1979 by the historical society and serves as the society's office and the O'Neill Museum; it has been rumored that Albert Pryor could be seen rocking on the porch of the pretty gray Victorian with white gingerbread trim long after his death.

THE DESERTS

https://www.visitgreaterpalmsprings.com/

The High Desert

Southern California's high desert has historically lured travelers in search of vast fortunes in gold and silver and a fresh start out west, but today's travelers are lured by the awesome beauty and vastness of space that the deserts of the Mojave and Death Valley promise. Winter and fall explorers experience a desert of cool starry nights and wind-swept plains and canyons, while summer and spring visitors feel the scorching midday sun and balmy evenings. No matter when you choose to visit Southern California's high desert, you will delight in the history that abounds: ghost towns that tell stories of exciting, earlier times; trails that follow in the footsteps of our pioneer ancestors; and fossils of early humankind. Nature's bounty in the high desert is plentiful as well: view fascinating sand dunes, unique rock formations, soda lakes, desert hues of purples, reds, and browns and so much more.

Barstow

Barstow is a perfect starting point for exploring points in the Mojave Desert, as well as the famous Route 66. The once thriving mining town is at the junction of three major highways, Interstate 15, Interstate 40 and Route 58, and now survives on the constant flow of visitors on the way to Las Vegas and other destinations. A must before entering the Mojave Desert is a stop at Barstow's **Desert Discovery Center** at 831

Barstow Road. The center, in an attractive Southwestern-style adobe, has fascinating exhibits on the natural history of the desert and abundant visitor information. A large relief map is helpful, as are the advice and resource material. The Bureau of Land Management offers books you may buy from a fine selection of publications available in the racks. **http://desertdc.com/**

Barstow is named after its founder, William Barstow Strong, who was the president of the Atchison, Topeka and Santa Fe Railroad. The Southern Pacific built a line from Mojave through Barstow to Needles in 1883, and, even today, much of its economy depends on transportation. Before the advent of the interstate highway system, Barstow was an important stop on both Route 66 and Interstate 91.

Probably the most recognizable symbol of Barstow's train heritage is the **Harvey House**, built in 1910. Listed on the National Register of Historic Places, the once elegant rail depot, restaurant and hotel complex was designed by the renowned Fred Harvey Company with a blend of Spanish Renaissance and Classical Revival architecture styles. Today, the structure functions as an Amtrak stop, visitor center and locale of the **Barstow Route 66 Mother Road Museum**. The museum displays an ever-growing collection of historic photographs and artifacts related to Route 66 Main Street in Barstow, and exhibits give a fascinating historical view of the development of the roadway, from early pioneer trails to the railroads and the automobile.

Barstow is also known for its historic **murals** that line the old town area along Route 66's Main Street. Take a self-guided tour of 15 murals that grace the sides of downtown structures for a drive-by history lesson of the area. **http://www.barstowharveyhouse.com/**

Courtesy photo

A slight detour west out of town will lead to a unique outside art "gallery." As a child, Elmer Long would travel through the open desert near Barstow with his dad who would collect discarded objects they found. When his father passed away, he left behind a sizable collection of colorful bottles and Long struggled to decide what to do with the unusual collection. One day, the artist decided to build his first bottle tree on his desert ranch. Today, **Long's Bottle Tree Ranch** on Route 66 west of Barstow contains hundreds of imaginative scrap metal bottle trees made from recyclable discoveries, from typewriters to saxophones. There is no charge to wander the outdoor glass and iron "gallery," and Long is often there to greet the thousands of guests who stop by each year and to chat about his treasured creations. **https://www.facebook. com/ElmerLongsBottleTreeRanch/**

Route 66

A sign bearing the words "Start of Historic Route 66" can be found at the junction of Adams Street and Michigan Avenue in Chicago. From that point on, the highway passes through landscapes of often missed Americana from flowing agricultural fields to nearly abandoned towns now bypassed by modern highways, as well as amazing natural landmarks from the Grand Canyon to ancient lava flows. Although you could take the 2,400-mile journey from this Chicago intersection all the way to Santa Monica —and some "66" aficionados make the eight-state pilgrimage annually—you can still get your "kicks on Route 66" with a road trip that spans a fascinating part of California's road history.

The less traveled Southern California portion of the route in the high desert, also called America's Highway, offers a wondrous look at an important portion of the highway (with just a few detours) beginning in Barstow and ending in Needles. Not unlike travelers 60 years ago, the easy road trip is filled with new discoveries each day, from geological wonders to funky roadside cafes and landmarks with a bounty of California history—all dedicated to the traveling freedom that was revolutionized by car travel.

A short side trip from Barstow on I–40 will take you to the historic town of **Daggett**. Take the Daggett interchange to the 1860s town that was a way station on the San Bernardino–Daggett–Post Office Springs Freight Line. Look for the landmark Stone Hotel, as well as Fouts Garage on Santa Fe Street that has a particularly interesting history, with past uses that include a roundhouse for narrow-gauge railroad equipment, a livery stable, a garage for "gas buggies," a grocery store (with a dirt floor!) and a garage from 1946 to the present. The 1894-built blacksmith's shop on First Street constructed the wagons that hauled silver and borax from desert mines; such a wagon sits in the yard.

In **Newberry Springs**, at the foot of the mountains on the south side of Route 66, you will find another landmark of the roadway—the **Bagdad Café**. Mention the name to French tourists who come by the busload, and they will tell you about its cinematic cult allure. Formally known as the Sidewinder Café, the tiny café gained international fame when the movie "The Bagdad Café" was filmed there. Its flamboyant owner, Andrea Pruett, holds court and is a celebrity in her own right.

Ludlow is not quite a ghost town. The once welcoming stop for passing motorists with a motor court, café and gas station no longer exists, however a newer Ludlow just north of the off-ramp of Interstate 40 reemerged in the 1970s to serve the traveler once again with gas stations, a small motel and a newer Ludlow Café and a Dairy Queen.

Designated a National Natural Landmark in 1973 and located just off historic Route 66, **Amboy Crater** is an almost perfectly symmetrical volcanic cinder cone. This 250-foot-high geologic wonder in the Mojave National Preserve landscape provides panoramic views of some astounding features, including a 26-mile lava flow, Bristol Dry Lake, and the Marble Mountains.

LOCAL'S SECRET:
AMBOY IN THE SUMMER

"In 1993, Huell Howser and I traveled to the Mojave Desert in the heat of summer to explore the old Highway 66 town of Amboy for his television show "California Gold"; he also explored the huge Kelso Dunes and climbed the extinct Amboy Crater. Following him with all the camera gear, I almost passed out in the heat climbing up Amboy Crater. It was 115 degrees with no shade. The things I did for Huell."

– Luis Fuerte, Producer/Cameraman, "California Gold"; author "Louie, Take a Look at This," https://www.amazon.com/Louie-Take-Look-This-Howser-ebook/; *Prospect Park Books,* https://www.prospectparkbooks.com/

Originally a town that supported the nearby mines and railroading, **Amboy** still boasts the 1938-established **Roy's Café** and Hotel and gas station with famous sign. Now owned by Albert Okura of Juan Pollo restaurant fame, plans are underway to restore the businesses.

AUTHOR'S TIP: ANCIENT VOLCANO REMINDERS

Traversing the backroads of the Mojave Desert along Interstate 15 or Kelbaker Road rewards desert wanderers with countless geological wonders. Among these treasures are the dramatic remnants of an earth that spewed hot molten lava millions of years ago, resulting in expansive lava flows that enveloped huge masses of land, as well as volcanic cones that rise abruptly from the desert floor today. Since volcanoes don't happen just anywhere, these prime specimens surrounded by a sea of hardened lava are amazing sights in California's high desert.

Watch the horizon dotted with thirty-two unique cone-shaped mounds of red and black volcanic rocks. These petite volcanoes, called cinder cones, began erupting nearly 8 million years ago, emitting their last lava flows about 10,000 years ago. These well preserved and precious reminders of a time long ago were designated as **Cinder Cone National Natural Landmark** *in 1973.*

Scientists believe that a dynamic period of volcano activity happened in this area due to the region's dynamic fault activity that cracked the earth's crust into blocks that slid and rotated to create a tremendous amount of heat—enough to melt rocks forming magma that pushed to the surface. You may not realize that not all lava is equal. Some lava is thick and gooey, flowing shorter distances. However, these ancient lava flows in the **Mojave National Preserve** *were smooth and thin like syrup, streaming out across the desert (and, at times, on either side of* *the road you traverse). Interestingly, these molten flows cooled on the surface, but underneath, the still flowing lava formed tunnels and tubes.*

*For those seeking an extra dose of adventure, you can get really up close to lava's creations in the Mojave. You have the rare opportunity to make a descent into an ancient **lava tube** off Kelbaker Road, about 15 miles north of Kelso. Reaching the tube is a little tricky, however. Travel about five miles on Aiken Mine Road (off Kelbaker), passing an old water tank and corral. About 4 ½ miles down the mining road, bear left at a fork and continue to a parking area. From there, you need to walk uphill about 300 yards to a fence. Then, turn right and follow a path to a metal ladder that descends into the lava tube. The climb into the collapsed hole in the tube's roof reveals a perspective of volcanic activity rarely seen. But note, since the National Park Service does not regularly maintain the tube, adventurers enter at their own risk—and, yes, there can be snakes!*

Northwest of Essex is the **Providence Mountains State Park,** home to the recently reopened Mitchell Caverns, is well worth a detour on Route 66. The Providence Mountains nestled within the state-run recreation area, in a region otherwise surrounded by National Preserve land, is its own unique desert destination, distinguished by a range of mountains that bring cooler air and a botanic garden of cacti and pinyon. The bright red rhyolite in the higher elevations is home to Bighorn sheep and pinyon pines. Edgar Peak soars 7,000 feet above the desert floor and is populated by oak trees. Numerous paleontological and archaeological finds, from prehistoric animals (namely the sloth) to Chemehuevi Indian tools and fire pits, have been made through the years both in the caves and in the surrounding area. Considered a sacred place for the tribe, the Chemehuevi referred to the caves as "the eyes of the mountain" due to the two prominent entrances atop the mountain. But most visitors say it resembles a very large nose with nostrils.

However, the caverns did not acquire their name from the tribe but from the caves' first owner, Jack Mitchell, who operated the caves from 1934 to 1954 as a rest stop and attraction magnet for travelers on Route 66. Mitchell took visitors on cave tours and also held mining rights to the property, digging holes and tunnels that can still be seen. The enterprising Mitchell leaned about the caves while prospecting for silver and moved his family from Los Angeles to live on the property. Although Mitchell later built a series of paths through the main cave for his tours, his first brave tour-goers were lowered on ropes to reach some of the most scenic chambers. During WW II, the rationing of gasoline meant few visitors for Mitchell's Crystal Caverns, and, after the war, Mitchell approached the State to take over 82-acre site as a state park.

Mitchell Caverns, California's equivalent to the Carlsbad Caverns, has been closed to the public for nearly a decade to allow for extensive upgrades and safety precautions. As the only limestone caves in the California State Park system (and only one of two you can enter), the natural attraction offers fascinating stalactite and stalagmite formations going back to the Pleistocene epoch when ground water ate into the surrounding marble and sedimentary limestone. There are three caves in all, but only two are available to the public. Winding Stair Cavern has long been regarded as unsafe for most explorers, but El Pakiva (Devil's House) and Tecopa (named for a Shoshone Indian chief) caves that are connected by a man-made tunnel reward present-day explorers with a rare desert experience. The ranger-led tour of Mitchell Caverns involves a 1.5-mile moderate roundtrip hike to and from the caverns and an hour guided tour of the cave. Reservations are required and accepted only by phone: (760) 928-2586 (speak with a staff member; messages not accepted). **http://www.parks.ca.gov/?page_id=615**

Back on Route 66, turn left at Goffs Road and continue to the **Goffs Cultural Center & Mojave Desert Archives.** Goffs was a stop along famous U.S. Route 66 prior to 1931, when a more direct route between Needles and Amboy was built. Goffs was also home to workers of the nearby Santa Fe Railroad. The town was known as Blake between 1893 and 1902, named for Isaac Blake, the builder of the Nevada Southern Railway that began here. Visit the historic schoolhouse, built in 1914, that has been renovated to its original plans by the Mojave Desert Heritage and Cultural Association (MDHCA). The schoolhouse and grounds now house a fascinating museum primarily specializing in the area's mining history. Remnants of Goffs' mining days still dot the town. **https://www.mdhca. org/cultural-center/schoolhouse**

Not far from the Arizona border into California take the Moabi exit that leads to Route 66 to the right. A left at the white bridge will take you to the **Topock Maze**, a 15-acre geo-glyph consisting of patterns of parallel lines thought scraped into the desert by the Mohave Indian Tribe more than 600 years ago. The modern Mohave people believe the maze was a portal to the next life. **https://newsmaven.io/indiancoun-trytoday/archive/sacred-sites-topock-maze-needles-califor-nia-k9tJ7OTeG0igSibA-rur7A/**

Mojave Desert

As you leave the Barstow area, the Mojave Desert unfolds. This desert area is credited with more prehistoric art than any other area in the world; rock drawings that date from 200 to 5,000 years old, arrowheads, pots, and other imple-ments reveal ancient patterns of humanity. The **Calico Early Man Site**, 15 miles east of Barstow at the Minneola exit, is the earliest known site for man-made artifacts in North America.

Noted anthropologist Dr. Louis Leakey served as the project director of the fascinating quarry and stone toolmaking site for many years, discovering scrapers, chopping tools, axes, blades and other stone tools that were used by early nomadic hunters and gatherers and are dated from 20,000 to 200,000 years old. **http://calicoarchaeology.com/**

Early human beings may have wandered the hills that make up **Calico Ghost Town** off Calico Road in Yermo, given its proximity to the Early Man Site nearby. But we do know for a fact that Wyatt Earp once walked the streets of the 1880's silver-mining boomtown. As you wander through town, you are bound to wonder why Calico became a ghost town. It wasn't due to fire like many others, although part of the town had experienced fires and been rebuilt. And, it wasn't due to an illness that spread through so many other towns during the era. The reason Calico closed down was simply economics. The price of silver declined to the point that mining was no longer practical.

Calico was resurrected in 1950 by Walter Knott of Knott's Berry Farm fame. The ghost town could have become the Knott's Berry Farm of the desert, but he later donated the town to San Bernardino County as a regional park. The "quasi-tourist attraction" does see a fair share of tourists on the weekend, unlike other ghost towns that populate the Mojave, but the town is far from a commercial attraction.

One-third of the original structures of the hillside town exist; others have been recreated. The main street of Calico, lined in wooden sidewalks, is populated by shops, a few informal eateries and people decked out in period costumes. It is not unusual to catch a gunfight here at any time. On top of one hill overlooking Main Street is the one-room schoolhouse; hills on the other side are the site of former miners' shacks and numerous abandoned shafts. Take a "Ghost Tour" to absorb all of the local history; Maggie's Mine is an interesting walk through one of Calico's rich silver mines. A narrow-gauge railroad carries passengers out to the heavily mined mountains. **http://cms.sbcounty.gov/parks/Parks/ CalicoGhostTown.aspx**

AUTHOR'S TIP:
GIGANTIC THERMOMETER

The Mojave Desert seems a natural spot to find the world's largest thermometer. Although, sometimes, when it's that hot, we really don't want to know. Located in Baker, at the junction of I-15 and Highway 127, the 134-foot-tall thermometer stands—a beacon to motorists venturing through the arid climate. Erected in the early 1990s, the thermometer cost around $700,000 but went dark for several years when the property changed hands. The original owner's daughter, Barbara Herron, used her savings to reclaim the thermometer in 2014 and reopen the thermometer's gift shop for the first time with t-shirts, keychains and even the original lightbulbs from the thermometer for sale.

In eastern San Bernardino County lies the **Mojave National Preserve**. At 1,600,000 acres, it is the third largest preserve in the National Park System in the contiguous United States. As you travel the I-15 in this area, a sign for Zzyzx Road pops up, drawing curious road trippers. Follow the 4.5-mile road and you will reach an area that was once known as Soda Springs and is the home to Lake Tuendae. What you'll discover at Zzyzx today is the **Desert Studies Center**, a research facility operated by the California State University system. Though the biological studies of the Saratoga pupfish happening now are interesting and important, they are not nearly as fascinating as the crazy history of the locale known as **Zzyzx**.

AUTHOR'S TIP:
ZZYZX MINERAL SPRINGS

*Curtis Howe Springer, a radio evangelist and self-proclaimed medical doctor and minister, founded and named the **Zzyzx Mineral Springs Resort** in the locale now occupied by the Desert Studies Center. In fact, he named the settlement Zzyzx as a gimmick to ensure that it would be "the last word" in health. He may have been one of the last old-West medicine men because he was neither a doctor or a minister which led to his eventual eviction from the land and his brief imprisonment.*

In 1944, Springer filed a mining claim on the federal land that contained the remains of an 1860 Army post and a railroad station on the defunct Tonopah and Tidewater Railroad. Springer created a bogus hot spring by using a boiler to heat several pools. In time, Springer erected a sixty-room hotel, a church, a health spa with mineral baths, a radio broadcast studio, a private airstrip and several other buildings—even a castle. From Zzyzx, Springer continued his syndicated radio program, at one point carried by 221 stations in the United States and 102 more abroad, mixing religious music and his own radio evangelism. Along with his broadcasts came his requests that listeners send him "donations" to get his special cures for everything from hair loss to cancer. The potions were actually little more than a blend of celery, carrot and parsley juices

The town of **Nipton** is near here, reached by the Nipton Road turnoff from I-15; head straight for the hills, and the tiny railroad whistle-stop of a town is situated right over the tracks. The town possesses a colorful history of visiting outlaws who hid out in the nearby mountain backcountry, and it was a wagon road before the railroads arrived. In 1985 two Santa Monica, California, transplants, Gerald Freeman and Roxanne Lang, bought the 1885-founded town lock, stock and barrel, or, rather, hotel, saloon, store and assorted small buildings—all in need of restoration. Gerald Freeman, a Los Angeles geologist who liked to look for gold in his spare time, rediscovered it in the 1950s. He and his wife spent the next 30 years restoring its hotel, trading post and its handful of houses. The couple put the town up for sale after Freeman's health began to fail; Lang sold it after her husband passed away. The entire town was purchased by a new owner in 2018 with current plans to resurrect tourism with various events and businesses. **https://www.nipton.com/**

A loop trip from Nipton along the Kelso-Cima Road will give you a good overview of the scenic area and some ideas for other side trips, if you have a four-wheel-drive vehicle. Take I–15 from Nipton to the Cima Road exit. Follow the brown East Mojave signs off the interstate as you go. The town of Cima, which consists of a post office and railroad crossing, is known for its nearby **Cima Dome** and adjacent cinder cones. The 75-square-mile dome, which resembles an upside-down pan, is covered by an impressive Joshua tree forest and is made up of symmetrically weathered and smoothed granite.

Photo by Derek Thomson, unsplash.com

Continuing the loop toward Kelso, you will eye the **Kelso Dunes** straight ahead. You might expect to see camels and nomadic tents traversing the steep slopes of Kelso, one of the tallest dune fields in America and one of only two dune systems in the continental United States that boom a deep, resonating sound when a sand slide occurs. Winds that carry sand from Soda Dry Lake, the Mojave River Sink and the Devil's Playground to the base of the Granite Mountains have created Kelso Dunes. Rising up to 700 feet and covering 45 miles of glistening rose quartz and feldspar, the dunes are the largest in the Mojave National Preserve. These shifting dunes, like Eureka, are known for their "singing" as hikers climb to the top and slide slowly down. Over the past few thousand years, plants such as the evening primrose and rice grass have covered and stabilized areas once only covered by drifting sand. As you explore the dunes look for tracks left behind by the many creatures that call these dunes home, such as the sidewinder, kit foxes and Mojave fringe-toed lizard.

The historic town of Kelso holds the 1924 **Kelso Depot**, a gracefully arched, Spanish-style depot that served the Union Pacific Railroad. The tile-roofed, cream-colored structure hints of its one-time elegance; ghosts of 1920s passengers haunt the handsome brick platform, lined with Victorian lampposts and mature trees. With the passage of the California Desert Protection Act of 1994, the East Mojave National Scenic Area became the Mojave National Preserve, and the Depot passed into the hands of the National Park Service. Needed renovation of the Kelso Depot began in 2002 with the building reopening to the public as the new visitor center for Mojave National Preserve in 2005. Tour the former depot with exhibits describing the cultural and natural history of the surrounding desert. The baggage room, ticket office and two dormitory rooms have been furnished to illustrate life as it was in the depot during the first half of the twentieth century. A short film is shown in the theater. **https://www.nps.gov/moja/learn/historyculture/kelso-depot.htm**

The eastern Mojave has much to offer, but the rest of the Mojave and neighboring Death Valley have tales to tell and scenery to be seen. Take Highway 58 to Highway 395 just beyond Johannesburg. **Randsburg**, with one main street, is a perfect example of a living ghost town. In 1895 three prospectors discovered gold at the base of Rand Mountain here, and the mine, named the Yellow Aster, turned the town into a boom area with more than 4,000 inhabitants. Butte Avenue in town is lined with stores of the gold-rush days still in use, even a prospecting supply store and the original post office, established in 1856; the tiny Randsburg Desert Museum (open on weekends) is nestled in the heart of town, offering interesting mining artifacts and history. Miners' shacks, many surprisingly inhabited, can be found in the hills around town. The surrounding hilly terrain resembles Swiss cheese, reflecting the intense mining activity that occurred in Randsburg; many of the mines bear signs warning of dangerous shafts.

Death Valley National Park

The history of Death Valley dates back to Indian cultures that existed there up to 9,000 years ago. The first white people to enter the valley were a group of around one hundred emigrants in search of a shortcut on their way to the Mother Lode Country in 1849. The hardships they endured before leaving earned the valley its gruesome name. By chance one of these first "tourists" discovered silver, and soon the valley became a boom area for gold, silver, copper and lead. But it was borax that proved to be the most profitable find in the area. Today visitors congregate in the 300,000-square-mile area, a popular winter destination, to view the historical remains and the interesting topography of the region, created by millions of years of slow but massive change. In fact, rocks are still changing in Death Valley as sudden, torrential rains beat out paths altering the dramatic scenery.

There are several ways of reaching Death Valley, but one back route with interesting scenery is through **Emigrant's Pass**. Take Highway 395 to State Highway 178 to view the **Trona Pinnacles**, about 500 tufa pillars that shoot up from the desert floor to heights of more than 130 feet. These calcium-carbonate formations, not as well-known as those at Mono Lake, are located straight ahead when you see the Leslie (Salt) Road. Created by dried lakes, the tall salt rocks form shapes that will give your imagination a workout. You'll see castles for sure and perhaps a royal drawbridge, as well.

After viewing the Pinnacles, head into the town of Trona for a refueling stop, if necessary, and then continue on, taking the Trona Wild Rosa Highway to Emigrant Canyon in Death

Valley. Watch for the wild burros that roam the scrubby flats. Soon the mid-valley floor emerges, with some changes that you will want to experience.

Photo by Rachel Baskerville, unsplash.com

Goodbye Furnace Creek Resort and welcome **Oasis at Death Valley**. Just a short while ago, the venerable lodging icon of Death Valley had a $50 million rebirth and, with it, a new name. The newly coined Oasis at Death Valley includes a 66-room inn that is now the Inn at Death Valley and the 224-room ranch, now the Ranch at Death Valley. Owned and operated by Xanterra Parks & Resorts, those who crave nostalgia would still have the golf course (214 feet below sea level) carrying the Furnace Creek name. Also seeped in history and lore, the new name is very fitting. Set in the middle of Death Valley, the resort with date palms, ancient waters that bubble to the surface, birds and wildlife is anyone's idyllic concept of a desert oasis. The more intimate Inn at Death Valley, built into the mountainside where the precious waters originate, offers an additional 11 two-room casitas surrounding the spring-fed pool with sweeping vistas. Speaking of inspiring views, the dining room of the historic retreat has undergone a complete restoration including a turquoise ceiling that matches the Death Valley sky and banquettes that capture every sunset from high above the desert floor. **https://www. oasisatdeathvalley.com/**

An early waking hour at **Stovepipe Wells** will let you in on a special view of the 14-mile-square expanse of sand dunes across the way. The footprints of the desert's many nocturnal animals can be spotted, and the sunrise casts dramatic shadows on the contours and ripples of the eroded quartz dunes. Sunset and moonlight provide their own special effects on the flowing slopes as well.

AUTHOR'S TIP: 23 SKIDOO

In 1905 gold was discovered in Death Valley. A man named Bob Montgomery purchased the discovery from miners and began the town of Skidoo. Skidoo was a full company town, with Montgomery at the helm. The town acquired its name after a popular saying at the time, "twenty-three skidoo," a reference to the mileage (23) that water needed to be piped in from a spring in the Panamint Mountains. At its peak the town's population was about 700, and profits filtered in until about 1917. It stands as one of the rare Death Valley mining operations that made a profit, more than $3 million. A few people stayed to get the last of the ore, but by 1950 Skidoo was officially a ghost town. To reach the ghost town, take Skidoo Road down a curvy dirt path that feels very much like a ride on an old-fashioned washboard. Those with imagination can feel somewhat as the pioneers in covered wagons must have felt on this route, which curves through the mountains and grants impressive views of the canyon and beyond. The bumpy ride appears to end at a sign that gives the history of the mining town. Although the *signs do not indicate the remains, you'll see a stamping mill and mine. Note: For safety's sake do not attempt to enter any of the abandoned mine sites.*

A paved road cuts through the middle of the valley to **Scotty's Castle**, another Death Valley icon. In October 2015, the desert legend closed after a massive flash flood changed the surrounding landscape, destroying roads and utilities. Scotty's Castle has ranked as a "must-see" in Death Valley, not just for the amazing Spanish Colonial architecture, but more for the rich and colorful historical stories and lore. Walter Scott (Scotty) came out west to join the Buffalo Bill Wild West Show and later became a clever con man, extracting grubstake money from wealthy businessmen he had convinced of the existence of a secret gold mine in the valley. One such businessman was Albert Mussey Johnson, a wealthy but sickly life insurance company owner in Chicago, who in healthier days had been a mining engineer. Johnson became the main backer of Scotty's "mine" but never saw the results. The story of their unlikely friendship and the estate that was built in the valley is endearing. Closed to the public since the devastating flood, the Death Valley Natural History Association has made it possible to tour once again. But this isn't the same tour that hundreds of thousands took in years past. This one gets a handful of guests up close to what the power of water can do to shape the desert scape in just a few hours. Although Scotty's Castle is still not projected to open until 2020, join in a Flood Recovery walking tour to get a first-had look at the ongoing recovery efforts; the small fee will be used to help with the ongoing preservation work. Tickets must be purchased in advance; only 13 "lucky" people allowed on each tour, only offered on selected weekends during the year. **https://www.nps.gov/deva/learn/news/flood-recovery-tours.htm**

Heading south again, you will reach the **Harmony Borax Works Ruins**. Follow a short footpath past the ruins of the refinery that was used to process borax from 1882 to 1889, as well as original twenty-mule-team wagons on display. The Borax Museum itself is located in Furnace Creek and displays the mining machinery and historical exhibits from the borax-mining days, emphasizing the underground mining period. The twenty-mule team tandem transportation that carried the borax across the desert is well-known, but the many uses of borax, in the glass industry, soap, fertilizers, ceramics, cosmetics and even nuclear reactors, is amazing. The exhibit and living monument remains show the history of an industry that has grown from a 2,000-ton output in 1882 to well over a 1.5-million-ton production today. **https://www. nps.gov/deva/planyourvisit/indooractivities.htm**

Situated at historic Death Valley Junction is a unique cultural offering for this part of the desert, the **Amargosa Opera House**. Painter, dancer and performer Marta Becket transformed this one-time movie theater into her own opera house. In 1968 Becket began the overwhelming task of painting the murals on surrounding walls, which depict a permanent audience of sixteenth-century Spanish royalty, gypsies, clergy and revelers, as well as a domed ceiling mural that illustrates sixteen ladies playing antique musical instruments. Surrounding the dome are bands of dancing cherubs, representing the four winds, and seven doves of peace. For 40 years Becket presented varied performances of ballet and pantomime to the public. Although Becket passed away at age 92 in 2017, the show goes on. **http://www.amargosa-opera-house.com/**

Death Valley's borders expanded sizably in 1994 with the passage of the California Desert Protection Act. Among the additions to Death Valley National Park are the nearly 10,000-year-old **Eureka Dunes** and **Darwin Falls**, an incredible oasis in this desert. Eureka Dunes are the second tallest dunes in the country, towering more than 700 feet. The dunes are huge, created by sand carried by winds from the northern end of the valley. The early-morning and late-afternoon shadows make an impressive mark on the soft flowing edges. The dunes are located about 10 miles off Eureka Valley Road and provide easy wandering or strenuous climbing if you are going to the top, but the views of the reddened Last Chance Mountains make the sandy trudging worthwhile. The Darwin Falls, an easy drive off State Highway 190 just west of Panamint Springs, offers a parking area at the trailhead. The trail follows a creek lined with lush greenery that leads to the striking, 30-foot-high falls. The 2-mile trip is a refreshing departure from the scrub and sand, and the falls offer a rare wetlands experience in the midst of the untamed desert scape.

AUTHOR'S TIP: MAJESTIC VISTAS IN THE VALLEY

We all possess that intrinsic desire to see the world displayed below us, in front of us and under our feet--all at the same time. And, there is not a more magical, mystical place to satisfy that need than in California's scenic deserts where city lights are replaced by some of nature's most majestic and sculptured beauty. See the world from one of these Death Valley vista points:

Zabriskie Point: This popular scenic vista point in Death Valley National Park offers such striking vistas that a 1970 movie of the same name was filmed here. The vista was built by the Pacific Coast Borax Company in the 1920s and was named after the company's vice president and general manager, Christian Zabriskie. The site was originally intended as a way stop for visitors in automobiles to see Manly Beacon, the prominent landmark in Death Valley's "Badlands," but the amazing vistas overlooking the badlands, gulches and canyons have made it a reason in itself to visit. A favorite spot for photographers, the lookout provides some of the most remarkable colors and landforms in the entire southwest desert—not to mention one of the most impressive sunrise spots in the world.

Dante's View*: This vista point is one of the most popular sites in the park, and every year over half a million people make the drive up to Dante's to see Badwater Basin a mile below them. Located over 5,600 feet above Badwater Basin, Dante's View provides sweeping panoramic views of Death Valley. A recent remodeling has made the experience more pleasurable with new barriers, a newly added flat viewing area, benches and railings.*

Father Crowley Vista*: This vista is not nearly as well known. In fact, you may just find you have it all to yourself. Located near the top of switchback between Owens Valley and Death Valley, you'll first note a historical marker commemorating the vista's namesake, the local Catholic pioneer priest, John Crowley, as a memorial. The views from Crowley Vista stretch out over Rainbow Canyon with its 1,000-foot walls striped in red and yellow volcanic rock, as well as over the vast horizons of northern Panamint Valley.*

For a self-guided automobile tour of the Death Valley and Mojave Desert region, you can start at the **Shoshone Museum**, where a free tour map is available. The 550-mile loop through Death Valley and adjacent areas is an ambitious journey, so pick out some side trips and enjoy. The first thing you will discover at the museum is that no Shoshone Indians ever lived in this former mining-town area, but visitors to the region can still walk through the hillside caves where the first residents made their homes. A few years back scientists from Sonoma State University uncovered the skeleton of an entire prehistoric mammoth here. After completing their studies of the mammoth, the university recently returned it to a new wing at the museum that was built specifically to accommodate this exciting discovery. **http://www.shoshonemuseum.com/**

About 9 miles from Shoshone, the tiny town of **Tecopa** sits on a hot springs-rich stretch of desert. This small berg offers multiple campgrounds and RV resorts boasting private hot pools and opportunities for bathing. For those seeking a budget-friendly option for soaking, consider the free **Tecopa Mud Baths**; the Tecopa Hot Tub is currently closed. The mud baths are a collection of springs that bubble up into a shallow pool with temperatures well over 100 degrees. Near Tecopa is a hidden gem of an oasis, **China Ranch Date Farm.** The China Ranch formation is one of the oldest conglomerate formations on the planet; geologic students and professors come from all over the world to study it. The canyon hosts old gypsum mines and opens up to a beautiful and totally unexpected oasis. The family-owned and -operated small farm is not a resort or much of a tourist destination but does deserve exploration. The unusual setting provides a lush getaway in the harshest part of the desert. Towering cottonwoods and willows follow a meandering stream, and date palms and wildlife abound. The Old Spanish Trail is within walking distance, as is the historic Tonopah and Tidewater railroad bed. You can hike to the abandoned mines nearby or just browse around the store at the farm. The store features homegrown dates, great date bread and shakes and creative crafts made from materials grown at the ranch. **https://www.chinaranch. com/**

Located 35 miles from the Furnace Creek Visitors Center, but not actually within the boundaries of Death Valley National Park is an abandoned mining town worth a visit. In 1904, two prospectors found an abundance of quartz filled with gold in this remote nearly uninhabited area. Soon, a townsite was established nearby and given the name **Rhyolite** after the silica-rich volcanic rock found there. More than 2,000 claims in the region followed, and Rhyolite became a bustling town with three-story buildings, hotels, a school, foundries and even a hospital. In 1906, a miner built a Bottle House out of 50,000 beer and liquor bottles; 1907 saw the construction of a mill that handled the vast ore coming from the nearby Shoshone Mine. It was the financial panic of 1907 that signaled the beginning of the end of the bustling town. Mines and banks closed with production following. In 1916, the light and power were officially turned off. Today, you can see remnants of the town's glory days, including some of the walls of the three-story bank building and the jail. The Bottle House was restored by Paramount Pictures in 1925 for a movie and stands today as one of the most interesting structures of its kind. **https://www.nps.gov/deva/learn/historyculture/rhyolite-ghost-town.htm**

Deserts of Los Angeles County

Deserts can be remote, as in Death Valley or the Mojave, but they can become meccas for subdivisions and shopping centers as well. A few high-desert communities closer to the Los Angeles commuting fringe are examples of combined urban sprawl and high desert beauty.

Lancaster

https://www.destinationlancasterca.org/

It seems there's lots more sprouting in the high-desert city of Lancaster than its signature orange poppies. Nestled in the Antelope Valley known for its aviation history, Lancaster is making its own history these days as a progressive California city that also offers a weekend getaway full of surprises. Poised on the edge of the Mojave Desert, the region possesses forests of Joshua trees, steep canyons lined with red rocks and funky roadside stops. However, Lancaster also stands as the first U.S. city to require solar in every new house that is built. And, it is Lancaster's newly reinvigorated downtown, rivaling more cosmopolitan destinations, that has inspired new reasons to visit the destination's desert bounty.

Photo courtesy of Destination Lancaster

All too often, we are witness to resurrected downtown areas that never quite make it. Suburban sprawl and box businesses often overwhelm small businesses that struggle to lure diners and shoppers to what was once the pulse of a city. In 2010, Lancaster sought to beat the revitalization odds with the **BLVD**, a one-mile stretch of Lancaster Boulevard that had been virtually closed down. Inspired by the high-desert setting, city planners rolled out a vision for the nine-block area prime for strolling. Palm trees, art, pavers and plenty of seating areas line the avenue that encourages walking and gathering. In fact, it is all "orchestrated" by musical stations, including a piano you can stop to play, and anchored by new shops, impressive dining choices, community-engaging annual events and the coupe de gras: a state-of-the-art performing arts center and a mega art museum, both attracting Los Angeles' best talent.

In 1991, the city opened the **Lancaster Performing Arts Center (LPAC)** in the heart of the BLVD. With a seating capacity of more than 750, the attractive, sleek live- entertainment venue was interestingly built on the site of the valley's first movie house that was owned by Frank Gumm, also known as Judy Garland's father.

Certainly, the other big attraction on the BLVD is **MOAH, Lancaster's Museum of Art & History**. The multi-story contemporary building arrived in 2012 just a block from LPAC and has been opening eyes and imaginative minds ever since. MOAH draws from artists both locally and around the country with more than 10,000 objects on display at any given time, consisting of both permanent and special exhibitions that change often. You will discover an eclectic art scene here that blends some local history with collections of contemporary art makers of Southern California. **https://www.lancastermoah.org/**

The BLVD's newest artistic roll-out is **POW!WOW!,** bringing art by notable artists to the streets in the form of murals splashed on building walls. The on-going public art program already boasts nearly two dozen murals to surprise and catch the imagination sprinkled about, from pop spiral designs to aerospace-inspired large works. Take an easy self-guided tour while shopping and dining on the BLVD. **http://www.lancastermoah.org/powwow**

MOAH's sister art gallery, **Cedar**, is just down the avenue and was long ago the city's jail. Cedar is the community's forum for art with many local artists and students displaying their works. The gallery encourages progressive ideas and new and experimental genres of artwork which highlight education, including a room filled with free art supplies for creating your own masterpiece.

Just across the street from Cedar is the **Western Hotel Museum**, dating back to 1888. As Lancaster's oldest surviving building, the museum is filled with artifacts from the city's Native American days to miners, ranchers and farmers.

Boeing Plaza, straddling the far edge of the BLVD and signaled by an F-4 Phantom, marks the **Aerospace Walk of Honor**. The plaza and surrounding monuments feature plaques commemorating the accomplishments of 100 notables, including Chuck Yeager, Neil Armstrong and Jacqueline Cochran. Five honorees are inducted each year in a special ceremony held in September.

The **Antelope Valley** has long been recognized for its abundant and unique "natural" side, from **Saddleback Butte State Park** and **Red Rock Canyon State Park** to the San Andreas Fault-created Devil's Punchbowl. Climbers, hikers and bikers have trails aplenty—all set within Joshua trees and twisted sediment. But, now, you can explore very close to town with the recently acquired **Prime Desert Woodland Preserve.** Located in the midst of urban development is this highly walkable 100 acres of desert wildlands that is like no other city park you are apt to visit. Three miles of trails and a kid-friendly visitor center with ranger make it a great family destination. Trails run north and south and are lined with forests of Joshua trees that mingle with low-lying desert scrub and an assortment of scampering wildlife from jackrabbits to lizards, as well as hawks and owls. Once a month, the local astronomy club hosts a "Moon Walk" at the preserve for stargazing. **https://www.cityoflancasterca.org/about-us/departments-services/parks-recreation-arts/parks/prime-desert-woodland-preserve**

LOCAL'S SECRET:
FOLLOW 'THE MUSICAL ROAD'

"By far, the best secret in Lancaster is **The Musical Road** is located on Avenue G between 30th and 40th Street West. Originally designed and constructed by Honda as part of an advertising campaign, The Musical Road became the first road of its kind in the United States. The popularity of the musical road began shortly after the original stretch along Avenue K was launched and word quickly spread of its new groove. The roads feature intermittent grooves similar to rumble strips found on highways. The grooves are spaced so that a series of pitches play when a car drives over them at around 55 mph. It was designed to replicate the finale of William Tell Overture. Due to the noise complaints filed by local residents who lived alongside the original road, the city was forced to repave the old road and cut the music short. Eager to keep the Lone Ranger spirit alive, the city relocated the road to a more secluded area and brought the attraction back! To see this one-of-a-kind attraction for yourself, head out to Avenue G and experience the music in motion!"

– Angela Clayborne, Executive Director Destination Lancaster,
https://www.destinationlancasterca.org/

The **Antelope Valley Indian Museum**, set against a dramatic backdrop of towering rocks and Joshua trees, has been a public museum since 1932. However, it has also been a homestead, a theater, a dude ranch, a Hollywood set and an attraction. Situated on 147 acres of state desert parkland, the museum's unique architecture and creative engineering earned it a spot on the National Register of Historic Places, and the Native American Heritage Commission designated Piute Butte as a sacred landscape. Wander the museum which exhibits over 3,000 objects, including many rare and outstanding objects from the Antelope Valley, California coast, Great Basin and the Southwest that reflect the important four-way trade route developed in the Antelope Valley at least 4,000 years ago. The park also features a picnic area, historic grounds, historic cottages and an outdoor ceremonial arena. Around the museum is a ½- mile self-guided nature trail. If you time your visit for the holidays, you are in for a treat with a celebration of the museum's homestead origins that includes a chili cook-off and music during "Holidays on the Homestead." The historic grounds are draped in vintage holiday decor, with cowboy poetry sung around a campfire, tours of the grounds, a country craft boutique and real cowboy coffee brewed over the fire. The museum is located at 15701 East Avenue M in Lancaster. **https://www.parks.ca.gov/?page_id=632**

Your eyes in in for a "feast" in the spring around Lancaster as the desert bursts forth with wildflower displays. In fact, to handle the thousands of visitors who arrive in April and May to see the brilliant hues of deep purple lupine, bright yellow seahorse-like coreopsis and striking orange poppies, the state operates the **Jane S. Pinheiro Interpretive Center**. The center is equipped with volunteers who staff a special hotline with the latest poppy-viewing information; call the hotline at (661) 724–1180. Surrounding the center is the **Antelope Valley California Poppy Reserve**, a part of the state park system. The reserve, with 1,700 acres dedicated to the poppy, offers 8 miles of walking trails and is open year-round for hiking and picnicking. **http://www.parks.ca.gov/?page_id=627**

Between Victorville and Lancaster is a stretch of road known for its roller-coaster bumps and some great fruit and vegetable stands. One small area along this Pearblossom Highway route is the town of **Little Rock**. Once a stagecoach stop, the town boasts several antiques shops (the Old Stage Coach Stop House on Seventy-Seventh Street north of Pearblossom Highway is the historical landmark stop), a small museum with Indian history memorabilia and **Charlie Brown Farms**. You won't see the "Peanuts" cast or even a cartoon reflecting the store's name, but the fresh fruit and vegetable store is well-known by those journeying this highway linking desert spots. In fact, you'll swear you've found the "Brown Derby of the desert" when you eye the walls behind the cash register here, lined with the autographs of performers who stop on their way to headline in Las Vegas. What you won't find in this rambling maze of buildings is simply fruit and vegetables. The 1929-begun fruit stand has diversified in recent years to offer pottery, syrups, olives, teas, bulk grains, homemade candies, an all-year Christmas store, boutique items, toys, ice cream, a cactus garden and more. **https://charliebrownfarms.com/index.php**

AUTHOR'S TIP: HOUSES SPUN OUT OF POETRY

In **Hesperia** you'll discover a sort of "micro-town" of what could be called "earth architecture." **CalEarth**'s complex of eco-friendly structures was founded by the late Nader Khalili who created this seven-acre compound in the modest high-desert community of Hesperia as an alternative school of architecture. However, his approach went past "alternative"-- it was steeped in the philosophy and poetry of the thirteenth-century Persian poet Rumi. "Rumi's poetry," Khalili told us on a tour years ago, "teaches the architect that earth, water, air and fire are the basic elements of life." This led Khalili to create the "domes of earth" rising up in Hesperia today. His domes may have spiritual roots, but they are surprisingly practical as well. They are easily built with a minimum of technological expertise, are inexpensive, may be built quickly and stand up to earthquakes, wind, fire, floods and hot temperatures. Visitors may schedule a tour of the domes at **https://www.calearth.org/**.

If the skies overhead along the route nearing **Palmdale** resemble an ongoing air show, the reason is your proximity to **Edwards Air Force Base**. Chuck Yeager marked his historic faster-than-sound flight at Edwards in the same location where gold-mining wagons used to "sail" across dry lakes. The **NASA Armstrong Flight Research Facility** on the base develops and tests flight operation techniques and new aircraft and hosts a visitor center with model aircraft and a gift shop. Since NASA Armstrong Flight Research Center is located on Edwards Air Force Base, only military, those who can access the base as credentialed civil service and government contractors, or those who have visitor permits are admitted. There is a NASA gift shop and Visitors' Center that you can visit if you are on the base, and public tours of Edwards Air Force Base are still being offered by the Air Force Test Center's public affairs office. The Edwards tours include a visit to the Air Force Test Center museum as well as a bus tour of the main base area. **https://www.edwards.af.mil/**

About II miles from Lancaster, in the **Rosamond** area, take in a show of speed and daring at the **Willow Springs International Raceway** off Rosamond Boulevard. Declared a California Point of Historical Interest in 1996, the raceway claims to be the "fastest 2 ½- mile nine turn road course in the West," and you won't disagree, as blurry race cars zip around the sloped course in front of you. Although the raceway does charge an entrance fee for weekend special events, the public can catch the exciting practice runs almost any other day here free of charge from their cars in the spectators' parking lot. If you care to sign a release, you may watch from the pit area closer up. The track with challenging dips, curves, and climbs gave birth to road racing west of the Mississippi when it opened in 1953; the facility also offers a driving school that goes from basic vehicle control to professional race strategy, in case you want to join in. International Raceway is open every day, with action every Saturday and Sunday. **http://www.willow-springsraceway.com/**

A bit down the road from the raceway at the end of Manley Road, look for a monument on the left side of the road. The engraved plaque explains that Willow Springs was a stage station on the Los Angeles–Havilah Stage Lines from 1864 to 1872. Past the historical monument is the main street of **Willow Springs Ghost Town**. Old adobes, fascinating stone structures and remnants of old stone walls sit unattended; abandoned silver mines top the hills.

In this same area near Rosamond off of the Mojave Tropico Road is a chance to go eye-to-eye with a tiger at the **Exotic Feline Breeding Compound**. Nicknamed "The Cat House," this nonprofit institution is the only private facility involved in artificial insemination research on exotic cats and boasts an impressive inventory of rare felines that includes, among others, northern Chinese leopards, the almost extinct Temminck's golden cats and a snow leopard. It is only one of a few small such preservation compounds in the nation and accepts nocturnal felines, unlike many of the larger zoos. The natural habitats here are part of an ongoing construction project on about three rustic acres. Visit during the week to see the cats up close and have them pretty much to yourself. The compound with gift shop is open to the public for tours. **http://www.wildcatzoo.org/**

Just south of Rosamond, find another creature delight at the **Quail Run Ostrich Ranch** near Lake Hughes. This unique ranch venue for the entire family brings together education and fun that goes along inevitably with these wacky birds. Three generations of family ranchers, here since 1988, impart interesting information on their "herd" of more than 20 bird giants. You'll learn facts such as the ostrich is the largest bird on the planet (some of the ranch's ostriches are 10 feet tall!) and are also the third fastest land animal, just behind the cheetah and antelope. Get up close for ostrich feedings and take home some unique ostrich oil, so good for your skin. Tours are a modest fee, and only groups need to reserve. http://www.quailrunostrichranch.com/

The Low Desert

Southern California's low desert is an area of fascinating contrasts. Visitors here experience views of boulder-covered hills with purple mountain backdrops, crisp blue skies and dramatic red-hued sunsets, open desert plains splashed with purple and yellow wildflowers and championship golf courses. Add to that, tall palm groves by roadside date stands and gourmet bistros and designer boutiques and rural camping and hiking retreats, as well as celebrity hideaways and spas. The low desert, boasting a year-round summer climate, is also the gateway to mountain playgrounds—a snowball's throw away. Agriculturally and naturally rich, this portion of Southern California's desert offers a diversity of pleasures to fit almost anyone's idea of a perfect desert getaway with some surprises waiting around every corner.

Greater Palm Springs

https://www.visitgreaterpalmsprings.com/

The nine cities that make up **Greater Palm Springs** in the Coachella Valley are perhaps best known as a winter retreat for the snowbound, but things have changed in recent years to claim the region as a year-round playground for all ages. Blame the area's popularity on many things: its year-round summer weather; hundreds of acres of green, flowing golf courses; and an abundance of manicured flower gardens, palm-lined streets, hot water spas, luxury resorts, farm-to-fork restaurants, Modernism architecture, world-class concerts and events and designer shops. The city is known for its celebrity residents, who discovered the beauty of this sparkling jewel in the desert just two hours from Los Angeles decades ago.

There was a time when the sight of giant dinosaurs would surprise visitors headed to Greater Palm Springs on I-10, but surrounding development has made spotting the quirky road-side dinos a little more difficult. In fact, the iconic statues that were featured in "Pee Wee Herman's Big Adventure" are still there but now a part of a larger park. **Mr. Rex's Dinosaur Adventure** has expanded to 50 dinosaurs and activities such as fossil digging. The Dinosaur Adventure is open seven days a week; there is an entrance fee. **https://www.cabazondino-saurs.com/**

Palm Springs

Not long after the dinosaurs welcome you to the val-ley, another landmark signals your arrival in Greater Palm Springs—the more than 2,000 towering "ambassadors" that make up the wind-powered energy farms of the region. Even if you've never been to the area, you've probably seen them in movies, recently in the newest "A Star is Born." Much bet-ter than marveling at the fascinating windmills as you pass at 70 mph is taking a **Palm Springs Windmill Tour**, the only tour with exclusive behind-the-gates access to the mysteri-ous turbines. In fact, the two-hour tour includes extensive knowledge about the wind energy industry that dates back more than 130 years. Tour-goers are oriented with interesting movies that show the daring technicians who maintain the windmills, scaling to heights more than 350 feet and dangling on the edge of propellers. The in-room information continues outside with walks through the giants for up close views and then an expertly guided bus trip that includes visits to solar and natural gas facilities, high-up vistas of the wind farms and a stop at the famous Windmill Market for date shakes and samplings. **http://www.windmilltours.com/**

LOCAL'S SECRET: BEST DATE SHAKE AT WINDMILL MARKET

"As a tour guide on the Windmill Tours, a stop at the Windmill Market nearby is always a pleasant surprise for my tour guests. The old-fashioned country market makes the best date shake in the valley—even better than many of the better-known date gardens in the east valley. They use Thrifty ice cream and the freshest dates to make a rich, sweet shake for enjoying on the little outdoor courtyard. Many of my guests end up taking dates home with them to keep the sweet taste going."

– Randy Buckmaster, Palm Springs Windmill Tour Guide,
http://www.windmilltours.com/

An exit on the I-10 marked Whitewater Canyon, delivers you on a rugged canyon road aligning a fast-moving river to a surprising wilderness not far from the desert floor. The **Whitewater Canyon Preserve** still hosts some trout reminiscent of its more than six decades as a pay-to-fish hatchery, but, now, the rainbow specimens are dedicated to a catch-and-release educational fishing program. The area is still surrounded by an abundance of natural beauty, but the weathered trout farm days have wonderfully given way to the farm's careful preservation as the Whitewater Canyon Preserve, a recreational destination idyllic for families, hikers and nature lovers. The 291-acre preserve is now a part of the Wildlands Conservancy's 2,851-acre Whitewater Preserve, dedicated to preserving this important ecological corridor for all generations now and in the future to enjoy. Through a partnership with the Friends of the Desert Mountains and the Coachella Valley Mountains Conservancy, these scenic acres north of Palm Springs off the I-10 have been maintained as an important portal into the San Gorgonio Wilderness.

The preserve is a testament to nature's incredible beauty. The year-round Whitewater River runs through the preserve, and surrounding vegetation serves as habitat for many endangered species, as well as bear, deer, bighorn sheep and mountain lions. A prosperous blooming area for native plants and flowers, the preserve is filled with native sycamores, cottonwoods and narrow leaved willows. Even though the end of April is past the high- bloom season of the area, an abundance of colorful wildflowers, such as bush poppies and coreopsis, can be spotted throughout the canyons well into May. The preserve is open seven days a week from 8 a.m. to 5 p.m. for camping, picnicking, hiking and a variety of special programs. And, there is never a charge for use of the facilities or any of its programs. A trailhead for the Pacific Crest Trail in the San Gorgonio Wilderness can be found here as well for hikers wanting a major challenge. **https://www.wildlandsconservancy.org/**

Another wilderness experience awaits, this one with a desert floor-to-mountaintop climb on the revolving cars of the **Palm Springs Aerial Tramway**, the world's largest rotating tramcar. This spectacular journey that climbs steeply up the rugged San Jacinto State Park on dramatic pulleys is breathtaking and represents state-of-the-art technology. The tramway is not news to anyone who visits this area, but what lies at the top of the mountain is a surprise well worth investigating. A fine dining restaurant, Peaks, is worth the journey alone, but daytime visitors will also rejoice in the hiking and wildflower viewing opportunities of the state park in the summer and snow play in the winter. Fifty-four miles of hiking trails grace the pristine wilderness, all accessed by exiting the tram's Mountain Station. Scenic overlooks and climbs from easy to strenuous await the visitor. Make it an entire day's outing and finish with an inspiring dinner at the bistro overlooking the lights of the valley. **https://www.pstramway.com/**

LOCAL'S SECRET: WHERE TO SPOT CELEBS IN GREATER PALM SPRINGS

*"When I head out for a night on the town, I usually drop by **Melvyn's**, the piano music is great, the cocktails generous, and the clientele hasn't changed much from the Hollywood Heyday… Peter Farrelly (Director, Best Picture Winner Green Book) spotted me singing a few Sinatra tunes there once (which was pretty cool, but he still didn't cast me). Other good spots for celebrity spotting are **Le Vallauris** (but don't interrupt dinner). I often see valley legend Suzanne Sommers and her hubby Alan Hamel there, but the amazing food and top-notch service attract A-Listers. You also might stroll the ground at the **Parker**, where celebrities stay behind the hedges and lounge at the pool (and enjoy Chef Herve Glin's incredible cuisine). Or pop in the **Purple Room** and enjoy the Rat Pack vibe. I go for the incredible selection of bourbons, and Michael Holmes' great music!"*

– Patrick Evans, KESQ News Channel 3, President, Fulvio's Foods

Greater Palm Springs did not begin as a movie star mecca. To discover its distant past, a step away from the glitter of Palm Springs' downtown shops, escape to the area's Indian roots and observe some of the desert's finest untouched beauty. A detour off the city's posh Palm Canyon Drive right in the heart of things leads you to the Agua Caliente **Indian Canyons**. An informal toll booth attendant collects a modest fee per person for entry into the Palm, Murray and Andreas Canyons, which may be explored on foot or by horse. **Smoke**

Tree Stables nearby the canyons can provide you with horses and trail rides. **http://www.smoketreestables.com/**

The Agua Caliente Cahuilla (kah-wee-ah) Indians settled in Palm Springs and developed complex communities in these canyons with the aid of abundant water, plants and animals. Listed on the National Register of Historic Places, the three southern canyons hold many traces of these early Indian communities: rock art, house pits and foundations, dams, trails and food processing areas. The lush canyons hold the distinction of possessing the most, second most, and fourth most palm trees in the world, respectively. The road into Palm Canyon leads to an Indian trading post and the last remotely commercial sight on the reservation. The authentic shop hosts Indian workers beading and a nice selection of hand-made pottery, jewelry, baskets and weavings. The trail, which dips dramatically into the 15-mile-long canyon here, leads to some of the most beautiful scenery in Southern California. Hike through easy paths past a scenic stream and stately groves of palms that contrast with stark, rocky gorges. Plan to enjoy a picnic at one of the picnic sites along the way and take off your shoes to wade in the inviting stream.

Andreas Canyon, just a half-mile from the entrance to the reservation, is a lush oasis boasting more than 150 species of plants and magnificent fan palms. A scenic foot trail leads past groves to unusual rock formations containing some Cahuilla rock art and to the Andreas Creek, where one can still see the bedrock mortars and metates used centuries ago for preparing food. **Murray Canyon** is an easy walk south from here; good foot and equestrian paths lead to the canyon's secluded beauty, containing an endangered species of bird, the least Bell's vireo, and views of wild animals that roam above the canyon. **https://www.indian-canyons.com/**

A detour into the heart of Palm Springs is not all shopping and bistros. Right in the midst of designer boutiques at 221

South Palm Canyon Drive is the small **Village Green Heritage Center**, home to a handful of historic buildings preserved from or dedicated to Palm Springs's past. Here Miss Cornelia White's House, built in 1894 from railroad ties, sits next to the McCallum Adobe. Displays include the first telephone in Palm Springs. The McCallum Adobe, built in 1885 from native soil, contains a portion of the Palm Springs Historical Society collection, as well as personal memorabilia belonging to Pearl McCallum McManus. Ruddy's General Store Museum on the green is an authentic, re-created 1930's general store stocked with owner Jim Ruddy's collection of showcases, fixtures, signs, and products that were purchased from a real general store. After exhibiting the store contents in his basement for more than forty years, Ruddy moved his museum to the Village Green. The museum boasts one of the largest and most complete displays of filled and unused general store merchandise in the country—notice one medicine vial labeled 1897. **https://www.palmsprings.com/attractions/village-green-heritage-center/**

Known world-wide for an abundance of exemplary midcentury modern architecture, Greater Palm Springs is the perfect home for the country's first free-standing architecture and design museum. The **Palm Springs Art Museum Architecture and Design Center, Edwards Harris Pavilion** is a must-see for architecture aficionados. Housed in the historic 1961 Santa Fe Federal Savings & Loan building designed by E. Stewart Williams, the museum showcases classic midcentury design exhibits.

The **Modernism Week** annual celebration each February of all things midcentury modern includes 11 days of design, architecture, art, fashion and culture with hundreds of events, including films, double-decker architectural bus tours, a Modernism Show, vintage fashion, a vintage travel trailer exhibition and much more. The unique celebration and its fall preview counterpart have earned Greater Palm Springs the distinction of being the "Modernism Capital of the World," luring period aficionados from all over the world. **https://www.modernism-week.com/**

LOCAL'S SECRET: VISIT FRANK'S HOUSE

*"During Modernism Week in Palm Springs I like to visit the **Frank Sinatra Twin Palms Estate**, my favorite midcentury modern house in the desert. The house was built in 1947 and designed by desert modernist architect, E. Stewart Williams. The home has been lovingly preserved and is on the National Register of Historic Places. It is beautifully sited with its "twin palms" (hence the name of the estate) placed next to the piano-shaped swimming pool. San Jacinto Mountain creates the perfect backdrop in the distance. I love to stand in Frank Sinatra's bathroom (which has not been renovated) and gaze into the mirror, hoping my eyes meet the same spot on the mirror as Frank's or Ava Gardner's. At that moment, I feel a swell of excitement as if I am in Frank's presence, or standing in his footsteps. You should try it sometime when in Palm Springs."*

– Lisa Vossler Smith, Executive Director of Modernism Week,
https://www.modernismweek.com/

A historic inn beckons traveler off the well-worn path of Palm Springs's quaint village streets to a hilltop perch that's within walking distance of those very sidewalks. **The Willows Historic Palm Springs Inn**, at 412 West Tahquitz Canyon Way, is a charming, 1927-built Mediterranean villa that has hosted the notable likes of Albert Einstein, honeymooners Carole Lombard and Clark Gable and Hearst mistress Marion Davies. Lovingly embraced by Mount San Jacinto, the inn was originally the winter estate of Samuel Untermyer, former U.S. secretary of the treasury. Exquisitely restored to the nearly identical ambience of its 1930's elegance, this private, posh inn is a romantic delight. Mahogany beams grace the great hall, frescoed ceilings fill the veranda and the estate's 50-foot waterfall spills hypnotically into a pool outside the dining area. The decor of the inn is a pleasing blend of antiques and Neoclassical elements, complemented by muted walls, coffered and vaulted ceilings, natural hardwood and slate floors and an ample supply of stone fireplaces. Einstein's Garden Room was the original guest room of the house (where Einstein stayed as a guest); the Marion Davies Room is an ultraromantic pick, with its elegant antique furnishings, fireplace and "fantasy" bathroom containing a two-person claw-foot tub, silver chandelier and marble-floored shower. A gourmet, multicourse breakfast is included in the stay. **https://thewillowspalmsprings.com/**

Climb into the cockpits of the legendary fighters and bombers of World War II, as well as Korea/Vietnam era aircraft, and see some of the world's greatest fighting planes in Palm Springs. Named in 2014 as one of the top 14 aviation museums in the world by CNN Travel, the **Palm Springs Air Museum** is a fascinating tribute to these craft and is dedicated to the restoration and preservation of this collection. It contains one of the world's largest such collections of flying World War II airplanes, including the Robert J. Pond collection of planes and automobiles, and aircraft on loan from the National Air and Space Museum, the U.S. Navy and private owners. Every week brings a new experience at this unique museum: flyovers, aviation celebrities and special happenings on military occasions. A visit to the attractive museum, with giant hangars and glistening floors, includes information by volunteer docents, many of whom flew in the very planes you will visit. Original combat photography is used to take viewers back in time, along with a variety of memorabilia to make the experience complete. The Buddy Rogers Theatre, a gift from Hollywood star Buddy Rogers, who served as a navy pilot during World War II, regularly presents epic flying features. The ten-acre museum site is located near the Palm Springs Airport. **https://palmspringsairmuseum.org/**

You've seen the planes that fought valiantly during one of the world's greatest wars, so now imagine that today's desert playgrounds were once the site of the largest military training installation in the world. It was right here that General George S. Patton trained American forces to fight the German army in North Africa during World War II. The **General Patton Memorial Museum**, a small museum at Chiriaco Summit, commemorates the real man and his mission. Head east on I-10—about a forty-five-minute drive out into the desert scape that was once this training ground—to the Chiriaco Summit exit and cross the highway to the museum fronted by a bronze statue of the man with terrier Willie obediently at his side. The interior of the museum reveals an interesting collection of World War II memorabilia, all donated by museum supporters. The newly added Matzner Tank Pavilion allows visitors to actually sit inside a tank. A half-hour video about Patton traces his life from his beginnings to his military achievements, highlighting his career in the desert. It reveals how he chose the desert regions of California, Arizona and Nevada, with headquarters near here at Camp Young, to train nearly a million troops in the hot sun with little water, tanks and machinery that clogged with sand, and a challenging terrain of sand dunes. Outside the museum, tanks are on display and a stone altar replica reminds museum-goers that the golf courses and resorts nearby were once home to courageous soldiers learning to fight in North Africa. **http://generalpattonmuseum.com/**

Desert Hot Springs

A drive out Gene Autry Trail in Palm Springs cuts through the city's light industrial area at its fringes and connects with the neighboring desert community of **Desert Hot Springs** to the north. This small, tucked-away desert town is known for its healing mineral hot springs that sprout from Miracle Hill, as well as sweeping vistas of the Coachella Valley. About 22 hot water resorts fill the area, the ancient underwater springs, enriched with valuable minerals, providing pure, healing waters that flow like silk over your summer- scorched skin. The most renowned of the resorts boasting crystal-clear, hot, healing mineral water is **Two Bunch Palms**, the 1930s hideaway of mobster Al Capone. The resort, with Grotto and outside mud baths, is a popular celebrity hideaway and a quiet refuge for all its guests. It is also the first carbon-neutral resort in America. **https://twobunchpalms.com/**

AUTHOR'S TIP: TAKE THE ROAD TO MOROCCO

*Transport yourself to an exotic, hot water oasis for romantic nights and indulgent days, Casablanca style. This luxury boutique hotel, **El Morocco Inn & Spa**, is filled with authentic Moroccan treasures, rich flowing fabrics, Casablanca romance and, of course, the incredible award-winning mineral waters. The tranquil oasis grants twelve distinct guest rooms decorated in hand-crafted brocades, flowing canopies, sitting alcoves, copper sinks—and even some round beds. The stay includes free movies and snacks, a bountiful breakfast with desert treats in the Kasbah and an evening happy hour with intoxicatingly refreshing Morocco-tinis by the pool.* **https://www.elmoroccoinn.com/**

One hot springs experience is really an adventure that combines a wildlife preserve and nursery with acres of privacy. In the midst, is a private hot mineral water escape sunken in the earth for just a few privileged adventurers at a time. **Monarch Hot Springs** is a sanctuary dedicated to the Monarch butterfly and its preservation, and it is also an Airbnb campsite. Take a journey through the open desert and through the Monarch habitat to reach a small natural spring that is all yours for a night of star watching while soaking in this tranquil preserve. **https://www.monarchhotsprings.com/**

While in Desert Hot Springs, pay a visit to **Cabot's Pueblo Museum**, a thirty-five-room adobe built entirely by one somewhat eccentric man. The four-story pueblo with 65 doors and 150 windows was built by Cabot Yerxa over nearly three decades, using abandoned materials—in other words, trash! A visit to the museum is a little like going on an archeological dig—layer upon layer of amazing and diverse finds. It is a museum dedicated to much more than one person (although Cabot's legacy could fill a small Smithsonian), one period of history or one genre of artifacts. It is all of that combined, plus a nifty gift shop with handmade jewelry and art. The fascinating Hopi Indian- style conclave carved into the hillside was built by Cabot Yerxa, who is considered the "Guiding Light of Desert Hot Springs."

He was an adventurer, artist, naturalist, utopian and conservationist. Though bred from Boston culture and society, he was born on a Sioux reservation in 1883 and eventually traveled to Mexico, Cuba and Alaska. After losing a fortune in the 1913 California citrus frost, Cabot headed to Desert Hot Springs to homestead. He discovered what he considered healing and spiritual hot mineral waters on his homesteaded property in 1914, when the city's population was only 20, and encouraged his developer friend, L.W. Coffee, to open the first spa. Cabot, deeply entrenched in his early roots, built the museum to honor all Native Americans and created an art colony on the premises. **https://cabotsmuseum.org/**

LOCAL'S SECRET:
'SECRET' HIKE TO VISTAS

"Of course, we love Cabot's and the water tours there, but right next to it (to the right as you face the pueblo) is a grouping of very large boulders. These mark the parking area, although it's not official, for a wonderful hillside hiking area that leads folks up and beyond several ridges (not mountains so it's an easy hiking adventure) and affords breathtaking views of the valley along the way. Remember, this is the valley from a unique and different viewpoint, one which can also be seen if you were to travel on over to Joshua Tree National Park...and go out to the overlook called Key's View- but without the drive! It's the perfect quiet spot for an early morning or late afternoon hike as you'll rarely see another hiker, yet it's a real treasure because it's already located in one of the higher neighborhoods called Miracle Hill in Desert Hot Springs."

– Bruce Abney, Owner/Innkeeper El Morocco Inn & Spa,
https://www.elmoroccoinn.com/

Highway 62 from Desert Hot Springs winds farther into the desert through the Morongo and Yucca valleys on the way to Joshua Tree National Park with its headquarters in Twentynine Palms, nestled between the Mojave and Colorado Rivers. The nicely paved highway cuts through scenic hills.

In the outskirts of tiny **Morongo Valley**, take East Drive to the **Big Morongo Canyon Preserve** adjacent to Covington Park. Nestled among the Little San Bernardino Mountains in the **Sand to Snow National Monument**, the desert oasis at Big Morongo Canyon is one of the 10 largest cottonwood and willow riparian habitats in the state. At 31,000 acres with elevations ranging from 600 feet on the canyon floor to 3,000 feet at the top of the ridge, this diverse landscape has been an important part of the Morongo Basin's natural and cultural history for almost two billion years. The natural oasis supports more than 300 species of plants and many animals in their natural habitat but is a favorite of bird-watchers. The former Morongo Indian village and cattle ranch is a bird-watching site, with more than 250 species of birds (the names of those spotted in the preceding week are posted in the exhibit area) and hosts a series of rural hiking trails. Bird walks are conducted weekly so check the calendar. **https:// www.bigmorongo.org/**

LOCAL'S SECRET: VISTAS, DEER & WHEELCHAIR HIKING

"My husband Kuba and I live in the area, and one of our favorite spots is Big Morongo Canyon Preserve. We are amazed by the abundance of deer there, and the bird watching and hiking are wonderful. But just as inspiring are the incredible views!"

– Krystal Kusmieruk, Social Media Manager, Greater Palm Springs CVB

"We've never had a guest who wasn't pleasantly impressed and say it really added to their overall experience to visit Big Morongo Canyon Preserve. Our secret is that it's simple to spot even though it's off the main road and down a lane. Why? Because the little lane is directly across from a large restaurant and bar called Willie Boys on that highway. There are numerous trails to walk and hike, even a wheelchair-accessible boardwalk through the marsh and riparian habitats. We love this aspect because it is so unusual and not widely advertised but is perfect for our senior guests or those who may use a walker, cane or wheelchair."

– Bruce Abney, owner/innkeeper, El Morocco Inn & Spa,
https://www.elmoroccoinn.com/

Yucca Valley

As Highway 62 reaches **Yucca Valley**, turn left on Pioneer Road for an adventure straight out of the Old West. The roadway winds through hills stacked high with balancing boulders and studded with Joshua trees, sagebrush and jutting cacti. You might expect to see Gene Autry or Roy Rogers galloping along the desert scape; and, in fact, you probably have. **Pioneertown**, an occupied "ghost town" of former Western movie sets, was built by the two cowboy stars in the 1940s for location filming of their movies and television shows. Today some location work still goes on, but the railroad tie and adobe structures are inhabited by a few residents who buy real food at the little general store, mail real letters at the post office and live in the little houses on "Mane Street." Occasional reenactments of Old West gunfights also take place some weekends; the free shows give the town a real feeling of the Wild West. **http://www.gunfightersforhire.com/**

However, the town's main claim to fame is the popular saloon and casual restaurant **Pappy & Harriet's Pioneertown Palace**, which fits right in with the vintage western motif of the town but adds its own popular draw to this remote getaway. Pappy & Harriet's has become a favorite place for musicians to jam, from country to rock. In fact, its list of illustrious drop-ins includes Paul McCartney and Eric Burdon of Animals fame. Forget the diet here—the restaurant specializes in mouth-watering western barbecue chow. **http://www.pappyandharriets.com/**

LOCAL'S SECRET:
STAY IN PIONEERTOWN

"Old Heard Ranch, now an AirBnb, is located on a quiet 20-acre home-stead steps away from the internationally famous Pappy and Harriet's bar and saloon in Pioneertown. Joshua Tree is now is popular destina-tion for Angelinos looking to get away from the hustle and bustle of city life. The ranch-style house has modern twists of western design with a secluded backyard and hot tub...perfect for soaking away daily stress under the vast desert sky. You'll leave with a different and slower perspective." https://abnb.me/tU5bdqvquS

– Annette Said, A | S Marketing Services,
https://asmarketingservices.com/

The 25,500-acre **Pioneertown Mountains Preserve** descends from the high piney 7,800-foot ridges into the Pioneertown Valley, with Pioneertown surrounded by conservancy-owned volcanic mesas, the Sawtooth Mountains and preserve lands leading to the San Bernardino National Forest. The preserve has year-round riparian corridors in Pipes Canyon and Little Morongo Canyons. The preserve is open daily from dawn to dusk for hiking the region's diverse geology; free interpre-tative programs are offered. **https://www.wildlandsconser-vancy.org/preserve_pioneertown.html**

AUTHOR'S TIP: DISNEYLAND OF BEAUTY PARLORS

Jeff Hafler began collecting hair and beauty artifacts and mem-orabilia nearly two decades ago while he was in beauty school. His impressive collection now totals more than 3,000 "hair-ti-facts," from a circa 1940 permanent wave machine that styled

*Veronica Lake's famous waves to antique hair dryers, that are part of his Yucca Valley **Beauty Bubble Salon and Museum**. And, yes, you can also make an appointment for hairstyling in the salon!* https://beautybubble.net/about-beauty-bubble/

The **Hi-Desert Nature Museum** is a small gem of a museum in the heart of **Yucca Valley**. A changing exhibit room offers myriad traveling exhibits and some annual exhibits for holidays and seasons. A glow room shows off local gems, and a miniature desert critter "zoo" housed within is fun for all members of the family. Children of all ages get a close-up peek at lizards, snakes, kangaroo rats and orphan desert tortoises and rabbits. The children will delight in the hands-on exhibits devoted to different aspects of science and nature. There is no admission fee, but donations are happily accepted. **http://hidesertnaturemuseum.org/**

LOCAL'S SECRET: CLASSIC MOVIES AT THE BIJOU

*"My talented son, Chris Perry, has always had a fascination for classic films—even as a child. Now, he shares his love of the medium at his own theater in Yucca Valley, the **Bijou Cinema**. The theater is filled with vintage décor and an intimate 35 old-fashioned wooden seats. It is a great place for people who want to learn about classic film from Chris and watch them on the big screen-- the way they were meant to be viewed!"* https://www.meetup.com/desert-classic-film-society/

- Joyce Bulifant, actress/author, https://joycebulifant.com/

Twentynine Palms

Many of the desert's cities support aggressive community art programs, some of which include the creation of murals. However, it all began in the high desert community of **Twentynine Palms** when local residents heard about the overwhelmingly successful mural program in the city of Chemainus in British Columbia. Twenty-five murals later, the city of Twentynine Palms has earned its reputation as **"An Oasis of Murals."** Take a self-guided drive through town to see the colorful, historic murals. **http://action29palmsmurals.com/murals.html**

About 20 miles north of Joshua Tree National Park is **Landers**, known for a roadside attraction called the **Giant Rock**. At about seven stories high, it could qualify as the largest free-standing boulder in the world, but more impressive is its movie-style history that includes purported spies and UFO sightings. It has been a Native American spiritual site for thousands of years. In the 1930s, a German immigrant and miner, Frank Critzer, built a small home underneath the rock with a radio antenna on top. The antenna led to the hermit's suspicion of spying, which was never substantiated. After his death, his friend George Van Tassel, a pilot, reopened an old airfield at the Giant Rock in the 1950s, naming it Giant Rock Airport. Van Tassel was an avid believer in aliens and began holding extraterrestrial sessions in the underground home to receive alien messages.

Eventually, Van Tassel constructed a one-of-a-kind all wood dome structure here, supposedly based on the design of Moses' Tabernacle, the writings of Nikola Tesla and telepathic directions from extraterrestrials. The **Integratron** was designed to be an electrostatic generator for the purpose of rejuvenation and time travel. Built on an intersection of powerful geomagnetic forces that, when focused by the unique geometry of the building, concentrate and amplify the earth's magnetic field. Magnetometers read a significant spike in the earth's magnetic field in the center of the Integratron. Today, the Integratron is owned by three sisters who have been part of the restoration and maintenance of the structure and property for more than 30 years. Their focus is to restore and preserve the structure while sharing it with the public for the first time.

AUTHOR'S TIP: RELAX IN A SOUND BATH

To experience the Integratron is to immerse yourself in an hour-long "bath" of soothing sounds that produce deep relaxation and introspection that leads to rejuvenation. All Sound Baths consist of a history of the structure, the playing of quartz crystal bowls and ambient music. The singing bowls are each keyed to the energy centers of the body, based on the belief that sound is "nutrition" for the nervous system. All sound baths must be reserved. **https://www.integratron.com/**

Not far from the Integratron is another unexpected experience in Landers. Aisles and aisles of beautiful orchids of all colors fill the harmonious environs of **Gubler Orchids**. Three generations of the Gubler family have loved and grown orchids, originally beginning in Switzerland where Heir Gubler opened his orchid nursery in 1918. It was his second son, Hans, who moved to California to chase the American dream and in 1954 started Gubler Orchids selling the orchids from his station wagon. Now it is Hans' son Chris who continues the legacy, along with his sister, Heidi. Now Gubler is one of the top orchid growers in the world, and you can visit to admire the flowers or buy your own piece of flower heaven. **https:// www.gublers.com/**

The small resort community of Twentynine Palms is the gateway to **Joshua Tree National Park**, comprising more than 800,000 acres of wilderness that hosts wildlife, flora, vistas, camping, hiking and history. Open daily, the Oasis Visitors Center for the park offers unique three-dimensional exhibits of animals and plants found in the desert here, a push-button desert climate movie and a wide selection of brochures and pamphlets. Two deserts come together at Joshua Tree. The lower Colorado Desert, occupying the eastern half of the monument, is dominated by bush and jumping cholla cactus; the slightly higher, cooler and wetter Mojave Desert is the habitat of the Joshua tree, sprouting profusely throughout the western half of the monument. Geographically, the monument encompasses rugged mountains of twisted rock, granite monoliths, arroyos, playas and alluvial fans.

Pinto Man, one of the Southwest's earliest inhabitants, lived here, gathering along a river that ran through the now dry Pinto Basin; rock paintings and pottery found in the monument are reminders of Indian civilizations that followed. A day at Cottonwood Spring in the southernmost section of the monument gives you a chance to explore these remnants, as well as the spring itself, which served as a popular stopover for freight haulers, prospectors and desert travelers at the turn of the nineteenth century. Several interesting trails wind through the canyons and washes of Cottonwood past abandoned mines and mills. The **Lost Palms Oasis Trail**, one of the most memorable hikes in the park, is a strenuous 4-mile hike through canyons and washes to an inspiring and remote native fan-palm oasis. More than one hundred fan palms are found in the deep canyon, which is surrounded by walls of quartz monzonite. This area is also occupied by desert bighorn sheep and many other forms of wildlife; sheep are seen around the oasis in summer months. **https://www.nps.gov/jotr/index.htm**

Photo by Sandra Selle-Rodriguez

AUTHOR'S TIP: TOUR DESERT QUEEN RANCH IN JOSHUA TREE

In the late 1800s, explorers, cattlemen and miners began venturing into the desert. The Desert Queen Mine, rich in gold and ore, was discovered near a working cow camp, but the mine's riches diminished, and its owner died. Ownership of the mine passed on to mine worker Bill Keys in exchange for back wages. Keys, who had collaborated on several "deals" with dubious miner "Death Valley Scotty," also filed a homestead on 160 acres of land that included the old Queen Mill, an ore processing site. Keys and his new wife, Frances, built a home, the Desert Queen Ranch, on the isolated homestead on the southern edge of the Mojave (just north of the Hidden Valley campground) and raised a large family. By the 1930s when the Depression hit the nation, a few more families homesteaded near the Desert

Queen Ranch, ending the Keys family's isolated life, and the Keyses constructed several guest houses for their new company. Bill Keys, who served a short jail sentence for shooting a neighbor in a gunfight, died in 1969, preceded in death by his wife six years earlier, and is buried in the family cemetery on the ranch. Visitors to the monument can wander the ranch today by National Park Service tour only; you will notice that grass and shrubbery have taken root in the old corrals and rust is covering the machinery, but the National Park Service is working to preserve the Desert Queen Ranch as long as possible as a tribute to humankind's adaptation to the desert. The views from this perch atop the Little San Bernardino Mountains, encompassing the entire Coachella Valley from the San Gorgonio Pass to the Salton Sea, are unsurpassed.

If camping isn't part of your trip here, try an overnight stay at **Joshua Tree Inn**, an Old West-style bed-and-breakfast inn just a few miles from the gateway to the park. The gracious brick hacienda on the highway offers both suites and cottages, all outfitted with antiques and western memorabilia. The main structure hosts a comfortable living room, a dining room, a study, a patio and an oversized lap pool. Those into eerie ambience might meet a ghost, that of country rock pioneer Gram Parsons, who died in the house after a bout with alcohol and drugs in 1973. The inn is located at 61259 Twentynine Palms Highway. **https://www.joshuatreeinn.com/**

Another alternative to camping in the park, is staying at the **29 Palms Inn**, a super-laid-back, rustic enclave on seventy acres that since 1928 has been taking in those in need of relaxation. The family-run hostelry and dining spot is friendly and casual, and its guests bask in the solitude, which is enhanced by no telephones and minimal television. Charming adobe casitas with private patios and fireplaces and vintage framed cabins dot the property, as do an inviting pool, a privately housed hot tub, and a popular restaurant. A stroll around the grounds leads you to the inn's own natural oasis, the **Oasis of Mara**. This serene pond inhabited by fowl of many species and surrounded by ancient palms is the only privately-owned natural oasis in the high desert, and it is shared with Joshua Tree National Park. An impressive vegetable garden on the premises provides the ultra-fresh produce for the rustic restaurant's impressive menu. A light breakfast is included in the stay here; the inn is open to the public for meals. **http://www.29palmsinn.com/**

AUTHOR'S TIP: NOAH PURIFOY'S OUTDOOR ART

Los Angeles artist Noah Purifoy craved the wide-open spaces of the desert where he could realize his dream of creating bigger-than-life art. The desert surrounding Joshua Tree, just a few miles from Joshua Tree National Park, was ideal. The late Purifoy spent the last 15 years of his life producing ten acres of sculpture on the desert floor, all constructed from discarded objects he found there, from toilets to tires. The result? Astonishing. **http://www.noahpurifoy.com/joshua-tree-outdoor-museum/**

Rancho Mirage

Returning to the lower communities of Greater Palm Springs, take a short ride from Palm Springs to **Rancho Mirage** for a new and unique experience. Known as the "Playground of Presidents," the city has recently debuted the valley's first observatory for state-of-the-art stargazing. Travelling along Highway 111, you can't miss the **Rancho Mirage Observatory**.

Its dome roof automatically spins and opens to the night sky with a touch of a button and can spin 360 degrees in either direction without stopping. The observatory that was constructed adjacent to the city library's western entrance offers onsite tours, telescope viewing and group stargazing with individually owned telescopes. The observatory also has its own resident astronomer. **https://www.ranchomiragelibrary.org/observatory.html**

LOCAL'S SECRET: GO BEHIND THE PINK WALLS

*"For years I had wondered what was hidden behind the pink walls of this massive, historic property located some ten miles from my home. With camera in tow, I drove to the public entrance to **Sunnylands Center & Gardens** in Rancho Mirage. At the end of the driveway, I found a parking place near the start of one of several perfectly-landscaped walking paths. I spent the next hour hiking the mile-and-a-half labyrinth of trails, taking pictures all along the way. The beauty and serenity made the setting a photographer's paradise. I could have immersed myself in this natural habitat all day but talked myself into learning what else Sunnylands had to offer. What I found was overwhelming, to say the least. The rather unassuming visitors' center building housed art galleries, a theatre, an al fresco café and a rather eclectic gift shop. A docent told me there were Friday yoga classes and Sunday concerts on the lawn behind the center. She also mentioned a variety of tours of the Annenbergs' private property, including a ride around the grounds as well as a guided tour of the interior of their historic 25,000-square-foot home. I decided to save that for a future visit, which actually came sooner than I thought. After my enthusiastic review of Sunnylands, a couple of neighbors were anxious to accompany me on the 90-minute private home tour. Reservations are a bit tricky, but I remembered*

the advice given to me by the docent on my first visit. Tickets are only available online on the 15th of the month beginning at 9:00 a.m. Since there are a limited number of tours offered during certain hours Thursday through Sunday, they tend to sell out very quickly. Fortunately, I was persistent (and flexible on dates) and managed to acquire a few for a tour at the end of March. It was well worth the wait. We drove to the estate an hour early and had a cafe lunch on the patio overlooking the expansive lawn. Our tour guide, a Rancho Mirage native who also taught tennis lessons on the Annenberg property, picked us up in an eight-passenger shuttle cart and whisked us around the pool, guest houses and private golf course. The rest was literally history...as we walked from room to room, learning all about the daily life of Walter and Leonore Annenberg and the hospitality they offered to so many U.S. presidents, foreign dignitaries and celebrities over the four decades they used the home as a winter retreat. The Annenberg residence, the grounds, the art and furnishings were nothing short of amazing, not to mention our tour guide's anecdotes about the elegant soirees that took place there. Without a doubt, Sunnylands has become my happy place for sharing good vibes."

– Audley Upton, columnist, http://howaud.blogspot.com/

Palm Desert

Palm Desert, home to the upscale "Rodeo Drive of the desert"—**El Paseo**, is also home to one of the low desert's unique tributes to nature. Visitors to **The Living Desert** may view hundreds of fascinating desert animals, walk through eight different deserts, hike along miles of scenic trails and enjoy a variety of special exhibits. The private, nonprofit wild animal park and botanical garden is dedicated to conservation, education and research. Self-guiding hiking trail guides and a plant trail guide navigate you along the sandy and paved, meandering paths of the 1,200-acre facility with gift shop and handsome Meerkat Cafe. The paths take you past an expansive walk-through aviary, a coyote grotto, kit fox sanctuaries, plains of Arabian oryx—the "unicorn of the desert" (only 400 exist in captivity)—and bighorn sheep, whose colors blend with the sand-colored rocky hills. You will also see slender-horned gazelles, an endangered species (fewer than one hundred remain in existence), which have been brought to this ideal desert refuge for preservation. Occasionally the open, pristine desert path is traversed by a roadrunner carrying its prey; flowering aloe and graceful smoke trees fill the void between exhibits. A lake with local water inhabitants, a refreshing oasis with a desert pupfish pond and sand dunes (raked frequently to display small animal tracks) are also a part of this haven for nature's activity. Visit Eagle Canyon, a state-of-the-art wildlife exhibit and conservation center containing more than thirty animal species in lushly landscaped "open desert" settings, and the cheetah exhibit. Village Watutu, an enchanting African village is complete with African animals, a petting zoo, the Thorn Tree Grill restaurant and the Kumbu Kumbu Market African gift shop. Its Gecko Gulch is an interactive play area for children with a "cactus" slide, "tortoise" shells to crawl on, and a coiled "king snake" to straddle. Kids also delight at the park's Starry Safaris, which allow the unique adventure of experiencing the sights and sounds of the desert at night. Special programs are plentiful, including giraffe feedings and camel rides. **http://www.livingdesert.org/**

LOCAL'S SECRET:
GOLF FANS MUST-VISIT

*"The desert has no shortage of respectable on-course dining to go with great golf. For me, there's no question that the patio perch at **Desert Willow Golf Resort** in Palm Desert is a must-visit for guests. Offering an impeccable view of the manicured golf grounds, it's engaging to watch how players take on the tough, water-laden Nos. 9 and 18 on the Firecliff Course in the backdrop."*

– Judd Spicer, golf journalist and radio host, **https://www.juddspicer. com/ https://www.1039espn.com/shows/the-press-box/**

If you'd like to see the desert much the way the early pioneers viewed it, then head to the 20,000-acre **Coachella Valley Preserve**. In 1984 the Nature Conservancy purchased this pristine acreage just outside Palm Desert to protect its threatened inhabitant, the fringed-toed lizard. The preserve also contains several palm oases, formed because San Andreas Fault lines allow water flowing underground to rise to the surface. The spectacular **Thousand Palms Oasis** here includes a mile-long trail that winds past pools containing endangered desert pupfish and submerged in native vegetation such as creosote, burro bush, smoke tree and desert lavender. **https://www.blm.gov/visit/coachella-valley-preserve**

LOCAL'S SECRET: EAT LOCALLY

"**Luscious Lorraine's Organic Juice & Eatery** in Palm Desert is one of my favorite places to eat "clean" in the Greater Palm Springs area. Chef Lorraine Ornelas has been serving up delicious fresh fare in Palm Desert since 1999, and has recently expanded her Palm Desert eatery. The menu features a comprehensive selection of fresh juices, smoothies, coffees and elixirs, breakfast items, sandwiches, salads, wraps and cold and hot bowls. I'm partial to The Monkey smoothie and Blanca Tuna sandwich, but pretty much everything on the menu is amazing. When it comes to promoting sustainability and sourcing fresh local ingredients, Chef Lorraine most definitely walks the walk. I've often seen her at local farmer's markets." https://www.lusciouslorraines.com/

– Jan Maguire, writer/editor/public relations,
https://jan-maguire.com/

A spectacular 130-mile-long highway that connects the desert floor with snow-topped mountains and then continues on into the San Gorgonio Pass and Banning claims its desert terminus in the heart of Palm Desert. The **Palms to Pines Scenic Highway** (Highway 74) leading to the charming mountain retreat of **Idyllwild** is a scenic side trip that may be a full day's outing or a romantic overnight respite from the desert heat. Highway 74 from Palm Desert ascends the dramatic rocky hills behind the city briskly. Look behind you and see the panoramic desert views, and look all around you and see vast hill scapes of cacti, scrub, balancing boulders and rocks in shades of pale burgundy and peach. Don't be surprised to catch glimpses of brightly colored "birds" circling in the thermals around these hills as you approach one of the first vista points over the valley frequented by hang gliders who jump from the parking area cliffs. Another vista point near Palm Desert is a spotting place for the bighorn sheep.

Just as you begin your ascent up Highway 74, make a short stop at the **Santa Rosa and San Jacinto Mountains National Monument** at 51500 Highway 74 (on the left). The 1,800-square-foot, stone-constructed center is tucked into the natural desert terrain and features exhibits highlighting the geology and natural culture and history of the desert. A garden displaying plants that Native Americans used for medicine and food is also here, as well as several popular trails for exploring. **https://www.blm. gov/programs/national-conservation-lands/california/ santa-rosa-and-san-jacinto-mountains-national-monument**

AUTHOR'S TIP: MOUNTAIN SIDE TRIP

Continue your climb up Highway 74 from the national monument and the road begins to climb and curve on its way to the mountain town of **Idyllwild**, just 45 minutes from the desert floor. Tall pines with mountain cabins dominate the entrance to this tiny town surrounded by the San Bernardino National Forest. The charming mountain retreat's crisp alpine air mixed with burning timber smoke puts you in the mood to snuggle by a fireplace or take a walk wrapped in heavy cotton sweaters—an abrupt contrast to the bathing suit you left drying by the pool in the melty midday sun. Drive into the quaint village for a stroll around the alpine cabin–like assemblage of shops, restaurants and art galleries. Idyllwild's open play areas beg you to throw a snowball or take a nature hike, while at the same time learning a little about the area's Indian, mining and early resort days. Directly off the main highway is the **Idyllwild Nature Center**, which has exhibits and photographs of early area history, including Cahuilla Indian displays. A self-guided nature trail at the center leads through the pine forest. **https://www.rivcoparks.org/idyllwild-nature-center/**

La Quinta

The city of **La Quinta** has delicately balanced the new with the old for many years, from a legacy of golf greats such as Arnold Palmer to the historic elegance of the famed La Quinta Resort & Club, known for attracting Hollywood royalty. Major golf tournaments fill the area's flowing green fairways today, and art has taken a major role in capturing the beauty of the Santa Rosa Mountains that embrace the city.

Visitors still escape to the historic **La Quinta Resort & Club**, a refuge on 45 acres of citrus-laden grounds filled with casitas, fountains and pools. The resort stands as one of only two hotels in the country to have a city named after it – the other being Beverly Hills. La Quinta Resort's rich history is filled with colorful stories, beginning in the early 1920s when Walter H. Morgan, son of a wealthy San Francisco businessman, purchased 1,400 acres to create what he envisioned as a private getaway in this remote area of the Palm Springs desert. In 1925, he retained Pasadena architect Gordon Kaufman to design six adobe casitas, an office, lobby and dining room utilizing more than 100,000 handcrafted adobe bricks, 60,000 roof tiles and 5,000 floor tiles. It was not long before Hollywood discovered its charisma. Garbo came for the isolation; Gable came to socialize with friends; and Frank Capra found creative inspiration. That magic still pervades in the resort that includes a world-class spa; 41 pools and 53 hot spas; five on-site restaurants; and five championship golf courses. **https://www.laquintaresort.com/**

LOCAL'S SECRET: CAPRA'S MOVIE MAGIC IN LA QUINTA

"Frank Capra (1897-1991) Academy Award winner, film director, producer and writer and his wife Lucille were frequent visitors to La Quinta Hotel (today known as La Quinta Resort & Club) beginning in the Golden Era of Hollywood. Through the years, many of Hollywood's elite followed the Capras to La Quinta. In 1980 after retirement from Hollywood, Frank and Lucille moved into La Quinta Hotel's three-bedroom casita #136 and lived there for a decade. On the colorful grounds of La Quinta Hotel, near the Capra ballroom and at the front of casita #136 sits a garden bench today dedicated to Frank and Lucille Capra, a lovely place to sit and enjoy the beauty of the historic hotel."

– Judy Vossler, Manager of La Quinta Hotel from 1980-1993

If you are yearning for a more intimate, secret getaway, consider the next best thing to a French chateau on a tranquil lake. Don't worry if you forgot your passport, this French chateau is your private entry into another world. The **Chateau at Lake La Quinta**, hides behind closed gates, and offers just two dozen charming guest rooms, each one with a serene lakeside view and private patio. The romantic restaurant at the Chateau, MÉLANGE, offers delectable items that will have you returning for breakfast, lunch and dinner. Dine on the patio and enjoy breathtaking views. **https://www.thechateaulakelaquinta.com/resort.html**

Not far from the Chateau is **Old Town La Quinta**, its cobbled street lined with bistros and boutiques. Interestingly, it is not really "old" at all, just inspired by the art and architecture of Santa Barbara and other central coast towns to be molded into La Quinta's "Main Street" and a gathering space for concerts and events, such as a regular farmer's market in season. **https://oldtownlaquinta.com/**

Indio

Neighboring **Indio** is newly famous for its music festivals these days, Coachella Valley Music and Arts Festival and Stagecoach, that fill weekends each April and overfill hotel rooms throughout the valley. Indio has also gained notoriety for its polo grounds that, when not being filled with music fans, is home to championship polo matches at **Empire Polo Club** and neighboring **El Dorado Polo Grounds**. Spectators during polo season are treated to a unique sport known for its fast-paced action, champagne divot stomps and tailgate picnics on lush grounds. **https://empirepoloevents.com/ http://eldoradopoloclub.com/**

LOCAL'S SECRET: POLO UNDER THE STARS

"The Empire Polo Club is one of two polo facilities in the world that has a fully lit grass polo field for night polo. The "Polo Under the Lights" games are a unique experience that offers spectators field-side tailgating at one of the most beautiful polo clubs in the country. You can pack a picnic basket loaded with your favorite snacks and a nice bottle of wine to enjoy while you watch the horses gallop down the field. It is a thrilling experience to watch the teams compete in a fast-paced match. There is nothing else like it. The Friday night "Polo Under the Lights" games take place on select dates in February and March; they are free and dress is casual." **https://empirepolo.com/**

– Lynn Bremner, Digital West Media, Inc., **https://www.dwmi.com/**

Heading south along Highway III you'll discover a section of the Coachella Valley that boasts soil and climate closely compared with that of northern Egypt. So, it was that in the early 1900s, farmers planted the popular Egyptian crop of dates in this desert land, and majestic date groves domi-nated the once barren landscape. Date farms and vendors dot this area heading southward, as does an abundance of undeveloped desert scenery marked by yellow and lavender wildflowers in the spring and dramatic, rocky hill backdrops.

An Indio landmark along the highway, for those who love the sweet, energy-packed fruit, is **Shields Date Gardens.** Begun in 1924 by Floyd and Bess Shields, this spacious indoor date shop is a step back in time. Sit down at the long counter and have a refreshing date shake; buy a bag of sweet grapefruit; peruse the candy counter full of date confections; or watch a unique show on the history of dates, "The Romance and Sex Life of the Date." The Café at Shields sits surrounded by groves and offers breakfast and lunch; don't be surprised to discover some date recipes you won't find anywhere else, from date pancakes to salads topped in Deglet Noors. **https://www.shieldsdategarden.com/**

AUTHOR'S TIP: DATE SHAKES

The arrival of the first date palm from the Middle East in the 1890s brought about large-scale date farming in California. No place does it better than the Coachella Valley, where date farms line the agricultural byways. Don't pass them by with-out trying the area's own "date shake." This combination of ice cream or frozen yogurt mixed with milk and chopped dates is whipped into a rich delight that promises to cool you off on those "Arabian" summer days.

*If you happen to visit in February, a day of date feasting will have you in the mood for the **National Date Festival**, Indio's annual Arabian romp. Without a doubt, what most distin-guishes the decades-old county festival from the fast-food* *booths and carnival rides and games are the daily races. No, not horse races, but—what else in the desert?—camel and ostrich races!* **https://www.datefest.org/**

The "real" desert can seem like one of life's harshest places to tour, but on closer inspection this world is anything but dry and colorless. A tour on **Desert Adventures Red Jeep Tours & Events** will reveal the lush, biologically diverse and "lively" world that lies a jeep ride away. The cherry-red jeeps of the tour company are your desert "limos" into Indian canyons with palm groves, waterfalls and sparkling pools, and high mountain hiking and touring; seasonal tours might include wildflower extravaganzas and the desert by night. Go into an "earthquake zone" on its signature tour of the San Andreas Fault Zone. Extraordinary scenery abounds as your Big Red Jeep winds its way through the labyrinth of geological cuts and canyons of the San Andreas Fault Zone while your naturalist guide entertains you with stories about the plants, animals, geology and history of the California desert. You'll even walk between steep walls of deep canyons that have been created by the powerful forces of the plate tectonic, water, wind and time. **https://red-jeep.com/**

Coachella

The small agricultural town of **Coachella**, known as the valley's Heritage City, is undergoing a cultural renaissance of sorts highlighting its art and food. Take a self-guided walking tour of its historic structures and art with a map found on the website. Called the **"Pueblo Viejo"** tour, visitors tour the historic downtown blocks. **https://www.coachella.org/home/**

Salton Sea

South of Coachella on Highway 86, stands of date palms and lush citrus groves fill the open desert—a sampling of how the entire Coachella Valley must have looked in the early 1900s. **Thermal** is home to the valley's largest Medjool date crop; informal fruit and produce stands selling wares fresh from the fields appear along the stretch of highway between Thermal and the Salton Sea. Views of green, bushy citrus trees with limbs dripping in oranges and palms silhouetted against the hills dominate the pastoral drive. Some U-pick groves are located near the junction of Highways 86 and 195.

Going further south, you may think you are seeing a mirage. A vast sparkling "ocean" emerging from the dry desert. You haven't reached the Pacific, but you have reached the **Salton Sea**. The Salton Sea, lying 228 feet below sea level, was once a part of the Gulf of California and stands as one of human-kind's biggest "accidents." In 1905 a dam diverting water from the Colorado River accidentally broke, flooding the desolate salt basin, the old Salton Sink. The 38-mile-long by 9- to 15-mile-wide inland sea earns its name by becoming "saltier" each year because of the salt left behind when water naturally evaporates. From the highway, you will spot the sea past fields of citrus; it looks much more like a huge mirage. A glance to the hills alongside the highway will reveal the former waterline of the "sea" before it began its retreat.

The **Salton Sea Recreation Area** occupies nearly 18,000 acres along the lake's northeast shore, which is unfortunately diminishing with time due to a diversion of fresh water. While a solution to save the sea is ongoing, the area is worthy of a day trip to look at its stark beauty and quirky offerings, from unusual birds to mud pots and one man's vision of outdoor art. For a special day outing, take a trip around the sea to take in its many wonders.

Veering east at Westmoreland, nestled within the fertile Imperial Valley, you'll reach the **Sonny Bono Salton Sea National Wildlife Refuge** on the southern tip of the lake. The 2,200-acre wildlife refuge, just 40 miles north of the Mexican border, was named to honor the late celebrity politician after his untimely death. Located along the important course of the Pacific Flyway, the refuge's feathered visitors have learned to adapt to the changing face of the Salton Sea—from the water's salinity to shrinking marshland. Today, thousands of waterfowl and other birds spend the winter at the refuge, including some endangered species such as the Yuma clapper rail. You may spot white pelicans basking in the setting sun, yellow-footed gulls or black-bellied plovers; more than 70 percent of the California Burrowing Owl population is found within the Salton Sea's ecosystem. Bring your binoculars and climb the observation tower here or enjoy an easy hike on trails leading from the visitor center. **https://www. fws.gov/refuge/sonny_bono_salton_sea/**

Your next stop is harder to find, but worth the trouble. The amazing **Mud Volcanoes** and **Mud Ponds** have been formed by geothermal seismic activity, complete with gurgling mud pots and mini volcanic motion that radiates serious heat. To experience this phenomenon, drive straight on Sinclair from the refuge center a few miles before linking to Highway III, going north. Located about nine miles through the town of Niland is Davis Road. The road leading to the seismic area is paved for a half mile, but just past the paved portion is a sign for the Imperial Wildlife Area, Fish Ponds and Mud Pots. The Mud Volcanoes, on private property, are reached by going back to Davis Road, and turning right to the intersection of Davis and Scrimpf roads.

Photo by Randy Laybourne, unsplash.com

Your next stop was actually declared a national treasure by the Congressional Record of the United States after Senator Barbara Boxer described it as "a unique and vision-ary sculpture." **Salvation Mountain** is unlike any other out-door art installation you are apt to see. The colorful creation by the late Leonard Knight is part mural, part Bible verses and totally folk art, made from adobe, straw and paint. Since

Knight's death in 2014, volunteers have maintained the site, and a charity has been established to support its future care. Adjacent to the Mountain is a community known as **Slab City,** often referred to as one of the last free cities in America. The abandoned Marine facility that hosts remnant slabs from the original base is home to winter inhabitants who are mostly retirees as well as some fulltime residents that relish life "off the grid." Makeshift campsites, library and even a nightclub and golf course in pure desert fill the large expanse that was once Camp Dunlap.

The Salton Sea that many remember experienced its resort heyday in **Bombay Beach**. Guests swam, golfed and water-skied all day and partied at night at the Yacht Club. The beach, once populated by celebrities, now reveals sad remnants of days gone by—from fish carcasses to abandoned piers. Further up the northern coast, the restored North Shore Yacht Club is now a community center that represents a bright spot in the faded scenery.

Nine miles before Mecca, is a world-famous phenomenon— the **International Banana Museum**. The museum that was born out of owner/curator Fred Garbutt's need to "collect" is one of a kind. With more than 20,000 banana-related items— from toys to books—the museum is a bright yellow salute to the fruit in every conceivable way. You can even celebrate with a banana split—if you haven't indulged on too many date shakes along the way. **http://www.internationalbananamuseum.com/**

Borrego Springs https://www.sandiego.org/

From the Salton Sea going south, make a turn on Route S22 leading to **Borrego Springs** on the edge of the **Anza-Borrego Desert State Park**. This scenic 21-mile route to the state park is referred to as Erosion Road. The first scenery along this roadway is riddled by fractures and faults, abundant evidence of earthquake motion. The twisted sedimentary layers resemble a miniature Grand Canyon of washed-out, rainbow-colored hills. The town of Borrego Springs at the end of the trail has been called an oasis in the desert. Christmas Circle in town leads to a mall, a theater, shops, small hotels and cafes. The quiet resort community is the logical home base for exploring the state park, unless you are camping. Campers have free access to the 600,000-acre state park (except for the vicinity of the visitor center and developed campgrounds), as the only state park in the system that maintains such liberal camping regulations.

LOCAL'S SECRET: A MAGICAL ESCAPE

"Borrego Springs is more than the unbelievable 600,000-acre Anza Borrego State Park; it's a magical place in the desert where time stands still. As one of my favorite getaways and a destination where I can truly relax while there, Borrego Springs is only 90 minutes from the Coachella Valley where I live, and yet it feels worlds away. Exploring downtown you'll find one main street, no traffic signals and a community park called Christmas Circle. Venture out a little farther and animals sculpted from metal freely roam the desert landscape. Expect to meet visitors from around the world who come to experience these desert creatures. As one of the few Designated Dark Sky Communities in the world, don't forget to look to the skies each night for a star-studded event." http://www.visitborrego.com/

– Françoise Rhodes, Host of Traveling With Françoise television and radio shows/ Travel blogger, https://travelingwithfrancoise.com/

It was through Borrego Valley that Juan Bautista de Anza discovered the first land route to California. This happened five years after Father Junípero Serra had founded the first mission in San Diego. In 1774 Anza led a party of explorers from Arizona down into Mexico and up along to the Colorado River, then finally north across a dead sea into California and the Borrego Valley. The north end of the valley was called Coyote Canyon, and it provided a natural staircase over the mountains. These early explorers were pleased to find a softening climate, water and trees. More than 200 years later, Borrego Springs is a coveted resort hideaway, although, to the traveler's delight, the secret is not completely out.

LOCAL'S SECRET: GAZPACHO AND LEMON DROPS

*"For foodies, **Carlee's** is THE place to go for the absolute best gazpacho you've ever had! Their lemon drop martinis are pretty tasty as well."*

– Robert Arends, Public Relations Manager,
San Diego Tourism Authority, https://www.sandiego.org/

As you wind through the rural roads of tiny Borrego Springs, you'll think you're seeing a mirage—actually, a multitude of mirages. The town that is home to Anza-Borrego State Park is also home to **Galleta Meadows**, an outdoor sculpture extravaganza that surprises at every turn. The one-of-a-kind, giant metal sculptures by Ricardo Breceda range from a 350-foot-long fantasy-like serpent that winds across a roadway to recognizable prehistoric creatures. Breceda's sculptures fulfilled the vision of the late Avery label heir, Dennis Avery, who wanted to establish an outdoor art gallery for all to enjoy. Visitors will encounter more than a dozen large free-standing metal sculptures of prehistoric animals such as mammoths, giant birds and saber-toothed cats at Galleta Meadows. **https://www.visitcalifornia.com/attraction/ricardo-breceda-sculptures**

Photo by Stan Ford, www.fotosbyford

AUTHOR'S TIP:
HIDDEN EXPLORATIONS

· Take a free self-guided hike along the **Ghost Mountain Pictographs Trail**, encountering historical "forgotten artist" rock paintings created by Native Americans and the ruins of a Depression-era mountaintop homestead, Yaquitepec.

· **The Wind Caves** and the **Anza Borrego Mud Caves** are phenomenal natural wonders for visitors to view and explore. The Anza -Borrego Desert State Park has one of the most extensive mud cave systems in the world, containing

*approximately 22 known caves and 9 slot canyons. Some
extend over 1,000 feet, varying in width, with ceilings as high
as 80 feet.*

· **Coyote Canyon** *and* **Shell Reef** *are top destinations for viewing wildlife. Coyote Canyon is one of the few places in the
desert that contains a year-round running stream, making it
a prime location for watching wildlife. Visitors can view the
fossilized remains of prehistoric oysters at Shell Reef, which
was formed nearly four million years ago.*

A historic, off-the-beaten-path spot to overnight is **The Palms
at Indian Head**, located at the dead end of Hoberg Road. It
has been referred to as "one of the oldest and newest" resorts
in Borrego Springs. Old-time visitors to this desert recall the
twenty-acre property as the Old Hoberg Resort. In its heyday,
the Hoberg was a hideaway for movie stars and was served
by its own landing strip. Much of the resort, which included
fifty-six bungalows, burned down or was torn down and the
remainder abandoned over the years. Situated in the shadow
of Indian Head Mountain and adjacent to the state park, the
resort has had a new resurgence. The resort is still rebuilding, but its eight upstairs guest rooms provide picture-win-
dow views of the environs, sitting areas, desert lodgepole
four-poster beds and clean white walls with colorful art; two
poolside casitas are extra private. The lobby areas and dining rooms offer the same white wall "canvases" splashed with
colorful artwork by local artists. The grounds of The Palms
also include an Olympic-size swimming pool with viewing
portals and a goldfish-shaped spa. **http://www.thepalmsat-
indianhead.com/**

THE DESERTS

LOCAL'S SECRET: TOUR FONT'S POINT

*"My favorite 'secret' destination in all of Anza-Borrego ('hidden' in plain sight) is **Fonts Point**, "California's Grand Canyon," a jaw-dropping vista point only accessible by hiking or driving a 4-mile sandy wash off of the Borrego Salton Seaway (county route S22). The Borrego Badlands stretch for miles in all directions, with hundreds of slot canyons, mud caves and washes beckoning below. No four-wheel drive on your car? No problem! California Overland takes folks to Fonts daily as part of their adventure tours (https://www.californiaoverland.com/). Sunrise and sunset are the best times of day to go, when a kaleidoscope of color and dramatic shadows cover the land. Views from nearby Vista del Malpais are equally dramatic; an even more clandestine precipice to take in the stunning desert canyon."*

– Robert Arends, Public Relations Manager, San Diego Tourism Authority, https://www.sandiego.org/

In town turn on Palm Canyon Drive to reach the **Anza-Borrego Desert Visitor Center**. At first you may not see anything of the center but the sign, but look closely. The center is built into the earth; be a desert ground squirrel and burrow deeply into the attractive chambers for a bounty of desert touring information. Exhibits include a film of an actual earthquake experience as it occurred in the desert here; live pupfish; desert stones to touch; and temperature gauges at, above, and below desert ground level. Knowledgeable advice is available for mapping out hiking or driving tours in the expansive terrain. Organized park activities, such as bird-watching walks, horse trips and historical walks, as well as campfire programs on such interesting topics as the secrets of the southern Anza-Borrego and the trail of Juan Bautista de Anza, who brought 240 immigrants overland to Alta California through the desert, are offered.

AUTHOR'S TIP:
PRIME WILDFLOWER VIEWING

*Each spring, a spectacular display of wildflowers may bejewel your hikes and excursions. To check on the status of the blooms, call the park's 24-hour "Wildflower Hotline" at (760) 767-4684 or visit the website for updates (**https://www.parks.ca.gov/**) since no one can predict when nature will offer its full bounty of blossoms, from thick forests of red ocotillo to dazzling yellow Desert Dandelions. If you miss the wildflowers, the equally brilliant cactus flower displays generally last through May.*

A trail beginning near the parking area of the visitor center leads to a hidden oasis, as well as magnificent vistas, animals (within the park live more than sixty different species of mammals), streams, washes, plants and the remnants of Native American village sites. The **Borrego Palm Canyon Nature Trail** is a mile-long self-guided trail (pick up a brochure at the center) that may also be enjoyed in part. At the end of the trail, hikers may continue a half-mile to the first palm grove and waterfall of the secluded oasis.

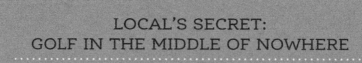

LOCAL'S SECRET: GOLF IN THE MIDDLE OF NOWHERE

*"If **Rams Hill Golf Club** in Borrego Springs was instead located in the Coachella Valley – there's no question it would track among the top three public courses. The Tom Fazio design is awesome, with highly-playable landing areas from the tees, large, swaling greens and a host of really fun holes (even Golf Boards). The fact that it's basically in the middle of nowhere only enhances the allure."* https://www.ramshill.com/golf-course/

– Judd Spicer, golf journalist and radio host, https://www.juddspicer.com/ https://www.1039espn.com/shows/the-press-box/

A driving tour along Anza-Borrego's **Southern Emigrant Trail** traverses the route of gold seekers, frontiersmen, soldiers, stagecoaches and the San Diego mail. A brochure at the visitor center will guide you through the interesting canyons and passes. County Road S–2 leads to Box Canyon, a once treacherous crossing used in the Mexican War in 1847 and in the years that followed; County Road S–2 also leads to the Vallecito Stage Coach Station County Park. Located in a green valley with bountiful springs, Vallecito was first inhabited by desert Indians and then became an important crossroad for early travelers because of the abundant water supply. The restored stagecoach station that met the Butterfield stages in the late 1800s is located here; squint into the midday sun and you can almost see a coach and team of horses approaching.

SAN DIEGO COUNTY

https://www.sandiego.org

The San Diego Coast

While this entire 900-mile stretch of California's Highway 101 gained state historic designation in the late 1990s, San Diego County's charming beachside communities straddling the coast from Oceanside to La Jolla may represent the laid-back beach and ocean lifestyle of the past the best. Instead of strip malls and cookie cutter developments, you will discover funky beach-inspired shops, locals' cafes and coffee shops, plus miles and miles of sandy beaches. It's all here from cultural treasures to surfboards. What unites them all is this historic ribbon of road as well as the surf-hugging Coaster train and the train-track bordering Coastal Rail Trail, a 12-foot-wide, 33-mile trail that has become a haven for joggers and bicyclists and a recreational destination in itself.

Oceanside

Oceanside may be straddling more than three miles of northern San Diego's summer-perfect coastline, but you have to admit that it is the less glitzy counterpart to nearby beach-going communities—a casual, grittier throwback to California's authentic beach spirit. For this reason, Oceanside has been "starring" in films and television as early as John Wayne's 1949 "Sands of Iwo Jima" and most recently as the locale for the hit television series, "Animal Kingdom." However, it was the 1985 blockbuster "Top Gun" starring Tom Cruise that really put the city on the filmmaker map. In fact, the **"Top Gun" bungalow** backed by ocean vistas has become a cinematic landmark. Although Oceanside has portrayed other locations around the world, from war-torn islands to Zorro's swashbuckling hideout, the city has a lot to offer simply "playing itself" as a true coastal town.

A natural division between town and broad, white sandy beaches is the **Coaster train** that scrambles the coast several times a day. Carrying ocean-loving passengers today, it was the 1880's transcontinental train that was responsible for establishing the town, known as San Luis Rey in the early days.

LOCAL'S SECRET: MOST HAPPENING NEIGHBORHOOD

*"The perfect "local's secret" for Oceanside is the **South O neighborhood**. Located on the Southern edge of the city along Historic Highway 101, South O is known for its quaint bungalow neighborhoods and a retro shopping district with unique maker spaces, vintage-inspired shops and a variety of popular local dining options. Here, you can rub elbows with local residents from surfers and skaters to artists and entrepreneurs at favorite haunts such as Revolution Roasters (great coffee and fresh baked goods), Beach Break Café (known for its Banana Crunch French Toast and breakfast burritos), Oceanside Urge Gastropub/Mason Ale Works (great craft beer), and Wrench and Rodent Seabasstropub (sustainable fish and sushi offerings) to name a few. Once a month, South O businesses stay open late for the "South O Walkabout," a locally organized walking event that showcases the unique shopping and dining*

experiences offered in South Oceanside and includes live entertainment, special promotions and more. Outside the main business area, there's also a retro bowling alley, fresh water lagoon with nature center and trails, a beautiful beach and a two-acre, organic farm that supplies many of the restaurants with fresh produce and has a farm stand open to the public most Saturdays. South O is also home to the historic community of Saint Malo, which was developed in 1929 and resembles an old-world village in Normandy France. The private, gated community was once a hidden getaway for Hollywood celebrities and hosted Princess Anne and Prince Phillip during the 1984 Olympics. You can catch a glimpse of it walking along the beach in South O."

– Shae Geary, Public Relations Specialist, Visit Oceanside,
https://visitoceanside.org/

The surf is always "up" in Oceanside, which is why it is home to countless professional and recreational surfers who can always find a swell. Surf shops and custom surf board shapers prevail with dozens of surf board manufacturers in a business district just a few miles from the coast called "**Shaper's Alley**."

Photo by Ann Kathrin Bopp, unsplash.com

More surfers head to California than any other state to catch the perfect wave, so it is no surprise that some "primo" surf museums have emerged to capture the history of this unique beach culture. The **California Surf Museum** in Oceanside was originally located in Encinitas, then moved to this site just 3 blocks from the pier in 1991. The museum is filled with surfing equipment and photographs that document the history of area surf in entertaining mini-exhibits. Every year the board of the museum chooses a new theme for the main exhibit in the 1,800-square-foot location. Surfing aficionados won't want to miss the gift shop here, with everything surfing-related, from key chains to videos. **https://surfmuseum.org/**

Oceanside possesses one of the longest wooden piers in the state. The nearly 2,000-foot-long wooden pier holds a Ruby's Diner at its terminus for great hamburger lunches and a popular event amphitheater at its entrance with great happenings, such as the World Bodysurfing Championships.

A handy guide to the city's history earmarks several of the surviving businesses—from the late 1800s through the 1920s—is just a stop away at the 1928-begun **101 Café**, Oceanside's oldest restaurant. A hardy breakfast is served all day in the former drive-in diner decorated in reminders of days past, from historic photos to the juke box. **http://101cafe.net/**

Carlsbad

Highway 76 connects with Interstate 5, leading to the historic ocean town of **Carlsbad**, known as the Village by the Sea. Growers' flower fields ablaze in color, and a quaint European village with boutiques and bistros await visitors in the idyllic beach town. Nestled on prime coastal property in Northern San Diego County, the city has become well known in recent years for family-friendly LEGOLAND, but its natural beauty highlighted by miles of sandy beaches, hiking trails, some of nature's freshest organic harvests and lagoons filled with migrating wildlife ensure a close-to-nature stay as well.

Carlsbad was founded in 1886 during the Southern California land boom but did not prosper as a town until the 1920s and 1930s, when agriculture flourished, especially avocados and flowers. The town grew during this period, as did many commercial endeavors. The **Smith-Shipley-Magee House** with adjacent Magee Park, located at 258 Beech Avenue, is the 1887 home of the town's cofounder, Samuel Church Smith, and is now the headquarters for the Carlsbad Historical Society. The house itself boasts circa-1900 furnishings and decor, old photos and other memorabilia and is open for touring on certain days. Plan a snack break at intimate Magee Park and enjoy its spacious lawn areas, picnic benches, barbecues and shade trees. **http://www.carlsbadhistoricalsociety.com/**

LOCAL'S SECRET:
CARLSBAD GONE SMALL

*"Everyone knows about the multiple museums in Balboa Park, but up in the northern part of San Diego County (in Carlsbad) and off the beaten path is **The Miniature Engineering Craftsmanship Museum**. Displayed are many small engines and models of things that engines make go. Complementary exhibitions include lathes, matchstick sculptures, a 7-foot-tall Erector Set replica of the Eiffel Tower and a section just for dollhouses. The machine shop offers engine demos three times a day. Admission is based on donations, as the museum is a component of The Joe Martin Foundation, established by the owner of Sherline (a Vista-based company that makes miniature machine tools) to encourage excellence in craftsmanship."* **https://www.craftsmanshipmuseum.com/facility.htm**

–Janice Kleinschmidt, Author/Editor

The town is home to three lagoons and dozens of varieties of migrating and resident waterfowl, including geese, turtles, ducks, frogs and even some flamingoes. The ecological treasures found in California's only freshwater lagoon, **Buena Vista Lagoon** and the saltwater lagoons of **Batiquitos** and **Agua Hedionda** make for rare explorations, from nature walks to some limited water sports at Agua Hedionda.

Overlooking the northern shores of tranquil **Batiquitos Lagoon**, a protected wildlife sanctuary, is the **Park Hyatt Aviara** resort in Carlsbad—itself a sanctuary for those seeking exclusive luxury perched high above the Pacific Ocean. Finding the hilltop resort is only part of the discovery that awaits. Winding upward past impressive estates leads to a hidden paradise that offers sweeping lagoon and ocean vistas. Located on 250 acres drenched in lush landscaping and populated by singing birds is the resort's centerpiece— the Arnold Palmer-designed golf course that serves as the prestigious home of the annual LPGA Kia Classic, as well as a world-class tennis facility that has been voted one of the nation's "Top 50." Although there are many prestigious Park Hyatt designated resorts in Europe and Asia, there are only five in the United States, with Aviara reining as the only Park Hyatt in the western states. **https://www.hyatt.com/en-US/ hotel/california/park-hyatt-aviara-resort/sanpa**

The brilliant, blossoming **Flower Fields at Carlsbad Ranch** are open for just a handful of precious weeks each spring, depending on the growing season. Time it right and step into an "Instagram Heaven" when vibrant Tecolote Ranunculus flowers create a 50-acre rainbow of color, highlighted by a sweet pea maze, wedding gardens, hands-on workshops, events and more. **http://www.theflowerfields.com/**

Not far from Carlsbad's fragrant flower fields is a museum dedicated to the intriguing history of music, **The Museum of Making Music**, a division of the NAMM Foundation. Located in a sleek commercial center at NAMM headquarters, the unique museum depicts the hard work, challenges and inspiration of those who have made the music through the ages. **https://www.museumofmakingmusic.org/**

Wandering the village boutiques and stopping for a bite or drink along the way is another off-the-sand pleasure in Carlsbad. Stop by lunch in one of the most unusual new eateries here—**Campfire**. If the name conjures tents and roasting s'mores over an open campfire, then you have the idea behind the innovative and rustic restaurant with teepee on the patio and a much more gourmet idea of the marshmallow chocolate treat. Adjacent to Campfire is a recently opened sister tasting room for Carruth Cellars in Solana Beach. The open-air, intimate area is perfect for a glass of wine to toast your outing. **https://thisiscampfire.com/**

Encinitas

Known for both its stellar surf and flowing fields of flowers, **Encinitas** is one of the funkiest beach communities along this stretch of coast. Popular beaches include family-friendly **Moonlight** and **Swami's Beach**—the inspiration for the Beach Boys' hit, "Surfin' USA." Interesting shops and cafes lodged in artsy cottages give downtown Encinitas its laid-back, nostalgic character. While here, checkout the still-operating **La Paloma Theater** that has a history reaching back to the 1920s.

The town served as a former 1880's train stop on the Los Angeles to San Diego route. You can celebrate the coastal city's railroading heritage by stopping at the **Pannikin Coffee and Tea** cafe, located in the charming old section of the city. The Victorian train depot, which houses the coffee and tea shop, was moved to its current location more than twenty years ago and is the hundred-year-old Encinitas station. A latticed patio on the front of the station is an ideal spot for sipping Pannikin's own freshly roasted coffees and fine teas, as well as brunching or lunching on pastries, muffins, croissant sandwiches, soups, steamed scrambled eggs and homemade granola. **https://pannikincoffeeandtea.com/**

AUTHOR'S TIP: WORLD'S LARGEST BAMBOO COLLECTION

*The **San Diego Botanic Gardens** in Encinitas is known for having some of the most exotic plants in the world, including the largest bamboo collection in the United States. Encinitas, whose name means "little oak," is actually known as the flower capital of the world. Fields of brilliant red poinsettias, begonias, fuchsias and more occupy many acres inland, and rainbow-bright springtime flower fields line the way from Carlsbad State Beach southward. The flower fields may radiate color from May through September, but visitors to Encinitas may enjoy blossoms any time of the year at the San Diego Botanic Gardens, known for its exotic plants. Ruth Baird Larabee donated twenty-five acres of her El Ranch de las Flores to the county of San Diego in 1957, and since then volunteers and the county have developed this unique garden retreat filled with plant species and hybrids from all over the world. Wander the tranquil canyons and sunny slopes of the garden; you will be treated to exotic tropicals, palms, ferns, year-round blooms and more bamboo species and varieties than can be found anywhere else in the United States.* **https://www.sdbgarden.org/**

After a movie or day of exploring, plan dinner or drinks at hospitable **Solace & the Moonlight Lounge** situated in Pacific Station, a LEED-certified mixed-use project in the heart of downtown Encinitas. Near Moonlight Beach, the rustic multi-level restaurant with magical vistas offers creative American cuisine. Oyster lovers will want to get in on "Dollar Oysters" from 3 to 6 p.m. daily. **https://www.eatatsolace.com/**

Solana Beach

Highly walkable and hike-able **Solana Beach** fills its 3 ½ square miles with everything you might want along the historic highway. In fact, most of Solana Beach is centered along the Route 101, landing visitors in town at the award-winning **Solana Beach Train Station**. Find the popular **Cedros Design District** just one block to the east. The 2 ½-block shopping mecca of brightly painted industrial buildings includes more than 85 unique shops from art galleries and home décor to spas, cafés and the famous Belly-Up Tavern—a legendary concert venue. The **Carruth Winery** along this shopping thoroughfare is an unassuming and surprising urban wine tasting stop. Named the "Cellar on Cedros," the small warehouse-style space does the entire wine experience minus growing the grapes, from crushing to bottling, within the tasting space. Settle in, watch the process and enjoy a glass or a bottle.

Start the day off right with classic-meets-creative dishes at **Claire's**, a local favorite. As you dig into signature dishes like Salmon Cake Benedict, Short Rib Hash and "Clairecakes," take in the construction and design features that made Claire's the first Platinum LEED-certified eatery in San Diego.

Grab a beach cruiser and take a leisurely pedal along the **Coastal Rail Trail**, which connects Solana Beach to the neighboring cities of Del Mar, Encinitas, Carlsbad and Oceanside. Cruise past the city's interesting collection of public art work along the way.

AUTHOR'S TIP:
SEE THE GREEN FLASH

Some call it a myth, but locals know the green flash post-Solana Beach sunset is the real deal. Pick up a burrito from the **Roberto's Mexican Food** then make your way to Fletcher Cove Park or Tide Beach Park for a front-row seat to one of the most stunning sunsets you'll ever see.

The recently remodeled **Winners Circle Resort** in Solana Beach near the Del Mar race track is like a home away from home with one- and two-bedroom suites, a new heated pool and two popular on-site restaurants. Red Tracton's here is considered one of San Diego's finest steakhouses, and the Fish Market has been offering some of the coast's finest fresh-from-the-sea specialties since 1981. **https://www.winnerscircleresort.com/**

Del Mar

A small jaunt down the coast from Encinitas is **Del Mar**, made famous in the mid-1930s when Bing Crosby and Pat O'Brien began the **Del Mar Thoroughbred Club**. Del Mar has grown through the years and became a city in 1959, but the village area still offers small-town charm and a certain elegance. If you want to witness a quiet two-mile-square ocean village rev up to race fever pitch, then head to Del Mar when thoroughbred season kicks into high gear. The racing excitement that arrives each summer is steeped in tradition, from lavish hats to parties and concerts, as well as some horseracing. **https://www.dmtc.com/**

Although the racetrack draws the majority of sports enthusiasts to this ocean community, ballooning is fast becoming one of the most visual and popular sports. The surf-filled air guides these romantic hot-air excursions, which depart at around sunrise and again before sunset.

Del Mar, which translates "by the sea," lies just twenty minutes north of San Diego and is cradled by lagoons at both ends. Long a haven for celebrities with an affinity for horseracing, you can eye their upscale estates tucked within ocean-view canyons. A quaint village of shops, notable eateries and art galleries add 1880's historical charm to the area's natural beauty.

La Jolla

La Jolla's nickname, the Jeweled City, says it all. It sparkles like a multifaceted gem, from its seven miles of curving beachfront with glittering surf to its hillside estates and bistro-and boutique-filled Village. People come to explore nature at wondrous **Torrey Pines State Reserve** and play golf on fabled Torrey Pines Golf Course nearby. Visitors marvel at undersea wonders at the **Birch Aquarium**, and they spend long, golden days kayaking and surfing. However, there is an off-the-beaten-path side of La Jolla worth adding to your stay. It might seem difficult to hide treasures in this intimate locale, but they exist—often in plain sight.

We have all heard of the **Salk Institute** in La Jolla, sequestered on North Torrey Pines Road. Famous for its explorations of neuroscience, genetics and more, the world-famous Institute is dedicated to finding cures for a long list of major diseases, from cancer to diabetes. However, you may not know that the Salk Institute structure itself is one of the world's most impressive architectural masterpieces. Completed in 1965 and now designated a historical site, the Institute fulfills founder Dr. Jonas Salk's vision of a facility with open, unobstructed laboratory interiors set in a dramatic location designed to inspire creativity among its researchers. Indeed, the Institute rests on some of La Jolla's most impressive coastal bluffs, soaring more than 300 feet above the Pacific on a 27-acre site that was donated by the City of San Diego. Guided by Jonas Salk's vision for an environment that would serve as a "crucible for creativity," the Salk Institute offers a vibrant arts and science calendar with events tailored for general audiences as well as the research community. The Institute offers weekly guided tours at noon, Monday – Friday only; tours must be scheduled online. Although there are no weekend tours, you are welcome to walk around the property and admire the architectural wonder. **https://www.salk.edu/**

One of Southern California's most interesting oceanographic museums and aquariums is located at 2300 Expedition Way in La Jolla. The **Birch Aquarium** at Scripps Institution of Oceanography challenges visitors to "walk by a kelp bed, past a submerged pier piling, and next to a coral reef without even getting your feet wet!" Large tanks and tide pools display hundreds of various underwater inhabitants. **https://aquarium.ucsd.edu/**

As you wander La Jolla's **Village**, look around for surprising artwork in the form of murals. Since 2010, more than a dozen artists have transformed the coastal seaside village into an outdoor contemporary art gallery. The **Murals of La Jolla** feature massive painted and photographic works by local artists as well as international contemporary art stars. Find a handy map on the website. **https://www.muralsoflajolla.com/Map**

La Jolla's seven sea caves are renown, filled with ocean wildlife from frolicking sea lions to colorful pools of fish. Kayaking through the caves is the most popular way to visit the caves, but if you would rather go by "foot," you can—at **Sunny Jim's Sea Cave Store**—the oldest continuously running business in La Jolla. In fact, Sunny Jim's is the only ocean-carved cave you are able to access by land in California and worth the steep staircase descent that begins inside the store. The **Sunny Jim Sea Cave** was named by Frank Baum, famed author of The Wizard of Oz, who saw a resemblance between the outline of the cave's mouth and a cereal mascot from the early 1900s.

The tunnel and gift store stand as a historical landmark today. Fossilized shell and water level marks indicate that the ocean started boring into the sandstone cliffs about 200,000 years ago. In 1902, German engineer Gustav Shultz purchased the land and, with the help of two laborers, dug the tunnel using picks and shovels, allowing visitors to tour the cave by rope. After the death of the original owner in 1912, his widow added the stairs. Although the original purpose of the tunnel and store was tourism, rumor has it that during Prohibition in the 1920s the cave was used to smuggle alcohol into La Jolla.

Take care in traversing the 145-step staircase that is often coated by seeping groundwater. As you descend, admire the mineral deposits that color the cave walls with the red iron oxide, the black, greys and yellows of vegetable matter and the pinkish-purple of iodine from kelp. Look along the right side at the bottom of the stairs for flowstone, a white waxy substance that drips down the walls to form shelf and drape formations. This calcium-based material is the same fragile substance that forms stalactites and stalagmites in other cave systems. Reaching the mouth of the cave reveals a world of sea wonder, from rock-basking sea lions to colorful fish. Not long ago, one of the cave's occupants—a curious baby sea lion—actually made its way upstairs to the surprise and delight of gift shop visitors. There is a small fee for cave admission—sea lions are free. **https://www.cavestore.com/**

AUTHOR'S TIP:
WHALE WATCHING BY KAYAK

About 28,000 gray whales follow a 10,000-mile migration path from Alaska to Baja, Mexico and back again each year along the dazzling California coastline, beginning in winter through late spring. The journey to their birthing grounds is an amazing sight to see. **Hike Bike Kayak San Diego** *offers a very novel way to catch sight of the spectacular creatures—by kayak. Launching from scenic La Jolla Shores and paddling at a leisurely pace for about a mile, the three-hour tours are offered daily through February and include kayaks, paddles, wetsuits, life jackets, a guide and after-tour warm drinks and snacks. No kayaking experience is required (they use stable, easy-to-sit-on vessels) and a brief paddle and safety lesson happens before you hit the waves. The company also offers some other incredible tours, including swimming with leopard sharks!* **https://www.hike-bikekayak.com/**

Definitely not one of La Jolla's cutting-edge bistros, of which there are many, is this popular taco shop. **The Taco Stand** may be self-serve and less than glamourous, however, that seems to make it all the more fun at this hidden gem. The Taco Stand on Pearl Street is a quick lunch spot that locals know well—never bothered by the line that forms down the sidewalk. Watch them make the taco and burrito offerings, from homemade tortillas to the generous fillings, and then enjoy the close-to-Tijuana menu creations. **http://www.let-staco.com/**

AUTHOR'S TIP: HIGH TIDE DINING

The **Marine Room**, secreted on a secluded stretch of beach in La Jolla, boasts award-winning cuisine, however, it is the wave-crashing experience of dining at the Marine Room that has been luring diners there for decades. The restaurant opened in 1941 directly on the sand with "ocean liner" views of the surf, created by floor-to-ceiling windows with unobstructed views. On a calm night, watch sandpipers scurry across the sand in between waves. Better yet, plan your meal during high tide when the waves come crashing extra close to diners. Enjoy a surf-shattering breakfast buffet on high tide dates, but be sure to make a reservation. **https://www.marineroom.com/Menus/HighTideBreakfast**

Less than a mile from fabled Torrey Pines Golf Course is a resort that exudes early California rancho charm, submerged in abundant native California gardens. The original site of the affluent Black family's 1940's estate, **Estancia La Jolla Hotel & Spa** retains the feel of a private hacienda with terra cotta tile, fountains and heavy wooden beams and doors, all framed by California Pepper trees and agaves. A complete destination in itself, the resort offers 210 privately spread-out accommodations, including ten spacious Estate Suites and a Presidential Suite, on 9 ½ lushly landscaped acres. All rooms come equipped with extra touches such as Keurig machines and Fresh toiletries, and most rooms include a balcony or patio for savoring the garden views. Plan a guided tour of the resort's gardens that feature plants from all over the world, featuring two rose gardens as well as a Mediterranean-style garden. Estancia will arrange your architecture tour of the Salk Institute nearby; and a shuttle, on demand, will take you to various spots, including the Village or beach. **https://meritagecollection.com/estancia-la-jolla**

Nestled between Del Mar and La Jolla, is a unique state reserve devoted to the Torrey pine. The magnificent and rare tree from the Ice Age clings to the sides of the weather-beaten sandstone cliffs along Torrey Pine Road; enter the **Torrey Pines State Natural Reserve** along here and follow the road up a steep incline to the visitor center, which has a museum and interesting natural history exhibits and a slide show. The precious 1,000-acre reserve stands as one of only two places in the world where the Torrey pine is found in its native habitat, the other being Santa Rosa Island off the Santa Barbara coast.

Visitors to the reserve come in the form of hikers, bicyclers or observers of beauty and history. No matter the level of physical activity you choose, a stop at the Visitor Center, the former 1923-built Torrey Pines Lodge, at the top of the entrance road is worthwhile. Here, exhibits of plant and animal life are available as well as a short film that explains the evolution of the state reserve. Learn about the Hopi-designed lodge itself that served Sunday dinners to visitors, the remarkable preservation of the lands through the years and the hidden treasures along your excursion. Take a self-guided easy, moderate or strenuous hike along eight miles of trails. Docent-led hikes are also available and worth the first-time visit. The Guy Fleming Trail is the most moderate of the hiking trails, affording a diversity of scenery from sandstone formations to ocean vistas. The Razor Point Trail follows the Canyons of the Swifts past dramatic views of the gorge, badlands and incredibly picturesque trees. **https://torreypine.org/**

AUTHOR'S TIP: TIKI INSPIRED SAN DIEGO COAST

After WWII, American soldiers and sailors returned home from the South Pacific with photographs, art, souvenirs, music and more from these tropical islands, to the delight of the American public who romanticized exotic island cultures. As a burgeoning strategic Navy town on the Pacific, San Diego was a prime destination to celebrate and recreate Tiki culture, especially on the shores of the newly developed Mission Bay and Shelter Island where the city realized it could create an affordable, closer-to-home version of the islands.

San Diego's surviving Polynesian-style buildings have been described as "fantastical" and "whimsical" representatives of the popular Polynesian lifestyle that includes lots more than architecture—really, everything from entertainment and music to clothing and cuisine. Not really an island, **Shelter Island** was nicknamed "San Diego's Hawaiian Isle." The one-plus acre, former sand bar was created in the 1930s and developed in the 1950s with hotels, restaurants and marinas that all reflected a Polynesian style. Greeting you at the gateway to Shelter Island is Trader Mort's Liquor Store, originally named the Hooch Hut, built around 1966. Mort's is famous for its Tiki hut design with a lava rock veneer and a large, tongue-wagging Tiki sculpture welcoming customers at the entrance. Even before the Hooch Hut opened, The **Bali Hai Restaurant** that opened in the mid-50s on the island became well known as a "Tiki temple" that hosted luaus in its heyday. Today, hand-carved Tiki idols like the iconic Mr. Bali Hai and Goof on the Roof, genuine Polynesian artifacts and tapa cloths adorn the popular restaurant, which got a make-over in 2010. Diners feast on Pacific Rim cuisine and island-strong Mai Tais against a spectacular backdrop of the San Diego Bay and the downtown skyline from the upstairs *dining room. If you arrive by boat, plan to "dock and dine." For those seeking a memento, souvenir Tiki mugs are available for purchase.* **http://www.balihairestaurant.com/**

Coronado Island

Situated across the bay from downtown San Diego is **Coronado**, known as the Crown City. Almost an island, Coronado is connected to the mainland by a long, narrow sandbar known as the Silver Strand and by the Coronado Bridge, an amazing structure that spans the Pacific while offering awe-inspiring city and ocean vistas. Orange, the main commercial street in the area, boasts a wide green belt between traffic lanes bordered in tall palms and cone-shaped pines. The famous **Hotel del Coronado**, an 1888 historical landmark hotel, is along here at the end of a row of small businesses and boutiques.

Coronado and its landmark inn got their real beginnings in 1884 when financiers Elisha Babcock of Indiana and H. L. Story of Chicago came to San Diego for recreation and health benefits; the two liked to row across the bay and hunt rabbits in Coronado's then brush-filled country. The idea of a hotel in this favored spot inspired them to raise the capital for the Hotel del Coronado, which when completed in 1888 stood as the largest structure outside of New York City with electric lights; none other than Thomas Edison supervised the installation of the historic lighting system. The red-roofed official landmark of the city with rotundas, gables and gingerbread, affectionately known as the Del, has become a living legend, with visits from thousands of celebrities and dignitaries throughout the years, as well as twelve U.S. Presidents. Marilyn Monroe and Jack Lemmon fans will remember the Del as the location of the filming of the 1959 movie Some Like It Hot. **https://hoteldel.com/**

AUTHOR'S TIP:
GHOSTLY HISTORY AT THE DEL

Among the Hotel del Coronado's attractions is its resident ghost, who most commonly haunts rooms 3312 and 3502. The ghost is fabled to be the spirit of twenty-seven-year-old Kate Morgan, who was staying at the hotel when she was found dead on the beach. The death was ruled a suicide, but the possibility of a murder of passion was the gossip. Guests in the haunted quarters say that Kate only haunts those who are in a grumpy mood. So, the best bet is to be happy during your entire stay here—not too difficult to accomplish.

Historic **Glorietta Bay Inn**, Coronado founder John Spreckels' 1906-built dream home across from the Del, hosts guests in its 11-guest room bed and breakfast and is also the perfect starting point for a walk through the island's rich history. The **Coronado Walking Tour** departs Tuesday, Thursday and Saturday mornings at 11 a.m. and offers an inside, 100-year look at the playground of presidents and princes, including stately mansions, the cottage of the Duchess of Windsor and the very home where the "Wizard of Oz" was conceived. **http://coronadowalkingtour.com**

Tucked away down an exclusive residential street just a stroll from the bay and the village shops and bistros, is the **1906 Lodge**—a restored 1906 boarding house that has added all the modern-day conveniences without losing any of its historical charm and integrity. The original parlor, dining room and veranda lead to the 17 guest rooms and suites located both in the original structure and in additional garden-set buildings. Suites all feature fireplaces, king beds, wet bars with refrigerators and private porches overlooking the garden courtyard; most offer sumptuous, in-room soaking tubs. Linger over late-afternoon wine and hors d'oeuvres and rise to a gourmet, hot-cooked breakfast. **https://www.1906lodge.com/**

Imperial Beach

One of the most overlooked Southern California beach towns is on the wave of a major renaissance, but despite growth, the 27,000-population **Imperial Beach** is clinging hard to its surfing roots and small-town vibe. Imperial Beach stands as the closest coastal city to Mexico, as well as the most south-westerly city in the continental U.S. The burgeoning area is one of the fastest growing cities in the county.

Much of this recent renaissance is thanks to a new, sophisticated on-the-sand hotel that opened in early 2014, **Pier South Resort**, that inspired facelifts to other businesses along the strand. Pier South Resort redefines the modern beach resort with 78 elegantly appointed guest rooms featuring beach-chic designer furnishings and luxury amenities, as well as wake-up calls to waves crashing just a few feet away. The all-suite accommodations are an ultra-spacious 650 square feet, featuring separate living and bedroom layouts with private balconies to enjoy 180-degree views directly over the sand as well as to the pier a short walk away. The LEED-certified resort has a unique coastal design with elements such as sea glass-and-seashell-embedded surfaces, a sea foam and sand color scheme, curved glass and flowing waterfalls. **https://www.piersouthresort.com/**

Imperial Beach has also welcomed **Bikeway Village**, a visitor-friendly addition to the already popular Bayshore Bikeway, a 24-mile regional bike and walking path that will eventually extend all around San Diego Bay. The Village is being constructed along the Imperial Beach portion of the bike path and will feature cafes, an outdoor deck with ocean vistas, bicycle parking and a water refill station. **http://www.bike-wayvillage.com/**

Just five miles from Mexico and a short drive to Coronado Island, Imperial Beach (or IB as locals know it), has a Mediterranean climate and some of the best surfing locations in the county along its four-mile stretch of white sand beach that still remains uncrowded on the most ideal beach day. In the 1930s the beach was used as a surfing test ground for mainlanders going to Hawaii; the 2.5-mile stretch of **Silver Strand State Beach**, trimmed with silver shells, is a favorite of surfers and kite-boarders. A salute to IB's surfing history can be found in a clever surfboard art installation that traces the long and short boards along Palm Avenue as sort of an "outdoor surf museum." Even the benches in the coastal area are constructed of surfboards.

AUTHOR'S TIP:
SUMMER SANDCASTLES

Imperial Beach's annual Sun & Sea Festival gets its name from the original public sand sculpting celebration held in 1960; IB played host to the U.S. Sandcastle Competition, one of the largest in the state attracting thousands, from 1980 to 2011. Today, the more family-engaging festival enjoys its historical roots and celebrates its own way each summer with a community parade, awe-inspiring master sand sculptures, children's craft activities, a kids' sand-building competition, an adult sandcastle building contest and much more. **http://sunandseafestival.com/**

Horseback riding along the beach is a perfect way to enjoy the scenic coast, as well as some rugged inland terrain. The route to the shoreline passes through shady groves that give way to vistas of the Mexico border, just a short gallop away.

Imperial Beach is also home to **The Tijuana Estuary**, a National Estuarine Research Reserve and State Park. The estuary, located off Seacoast Drive, is home to many endangered birds and wildlife and marks the spot where the fresh water Tijuana River enters the saltwater Pacific, making it the largest saltwater marsh in Southern California. Birders come to spy the elusive light-footed clapper rail. **http://trnerr.org/**

IB is one of the rare SoCal cities that still airs "movies" at their drive-in theater. The **South Bay Drive-In** began in 1958 with upgrades throughout the years. The family-favorite outdoor theater has experienced a grand resurgence in recent years and features the latest releases, plus family fare—all at reasonable prices. The South Bay is open seven days a week. And, yes, they also have a swap meet three days a week. **http://southbaydrivein.com/**

Inland San Diego County

Fallbrook

For a real off-the-beaten-path journey not far from Temecula, take a peaceful, rural drive that leads to "nowhere." Just a short jaunt south of Temecula on the I-15 is the Mission Road turnoff that deposits you in the tiny town of **Fallbrook**, drenched in avocados and ancient oaks. Literally on the way to nowhere because the road ends there, the 127-square-mile community is a destination in itself, promising abundant groves, white-fenced farms and an 1800's-vintage restored downtown.

An agricultural community since the early 1800s when Pennsylvania farmers settled there, the area is populated with more than 200 different crops—mostly grown on small family farms. Even though the area is best known as the "avocado capital" of the world, the fields are also robust with sweet-smelling citrus, exotic nuts and fruits, colorful flowers and, most recently, rows of grapes—following vineyard-friendly neighbor Temecula's success. Farmers' stands dot the roadsides selling the season's freshest offerings.

AUTHOR'S TIP: CELEBRATE THE AVOCADO

*Since the early 1960s, Fallbrook has been celebrating all things avocado during its annual spring **Avocado Festival**. From giant scoops of guacamole over salty chips to avocado pie or ice cream, you can partake of this versatile food of the day. Be sure to check out the popular avocado oils and products. Literally, hundreds of booths line Main Street for an endless day of fun, food and avocado-themed souvenirs. Of course, avocados and avocado trees are sold at the festival, along with crafts, flowers and fruit and vegetables. Activities include the Avocado "500" race with avocados serving as the racing "vehicles."* **https:// www.fallbrookchamberofcommerce.org/events-v2/avocado-festival.html**

Recreation is as plentiful as the crops in Fallbrook. Numerous equestrian facilities are available, a popular horse path being the Margarita River Trail that meanders through the rolling hills of the countryside. Fallbrook's Land Conservancy has done an outstanding job of preserving open space and trails for hiking. Just north the high school is the 46-acre **Los Jilgueros Preserve**, popular for walks and birdwatching. Visitors can enjoy the preserve's two ponds, a stream and an easy loop trail, all surrounded by native oaks and sycamore trees.

In town, take some time to wander the antique and collectible shops, homemade craft boutiques and art galleries along the vintage Main Street. There are several cafes lining the avenue, serving Mexican to French cuisine, for lunch or dinner.

AUTHOR'S TIP:
CELEBRITY FALLBROOK

Fallbrook's secluded and rural qualities, along with ranch land extraordinaire, have attracted celebrities through the years. Fallbrook High School's most famous graduate might be Howard Keel, the singing star of such movies as Showboat and Kismet. Other stars who have owned ranches here include John Barrymore, Norma Shearer, Martin Milner and movie producer and director Frank Capra. To look up their family histories and others, stop by the Fallbrook Historical Society's cluster of museums at 260 Rockycrest Road.

Vista

Seven miles inland from Oceanside on Route 76, between 76 and Oceanside Boulevard, lies **Vista** and a museum dedicated to furthering the understanding of early farm life in America. The **Antique Gas & Steam Engine Museum,** situated on 55 rural acres of rolling farmland, presents exhibits and demonstrations of early farm days and a collection of more than 1,000 related items. In addition, the museum collects and preserves historical gas, steam, and horse-drawn equipment related not only to agriculture but also to the general development of America. The unique "living museum" operates a blacksmith shop, a country kitchen and parlor, a one-third-scale train and a steam-operated sawmill. To really experience early farm life, plan to attend the nonprofit museum's annual Threshing Bee and Antique Engine shows on the third and fourth weekends of June and October, during which time American farm life of the past is re-created with planting, harvesting, threshing, household chores and early American craft demonstrations. http://www.agsem.com/

Experience the natural beauty surrounding Vista at **Alta Vista Botanical Gardens**, a 14-acre oasis of art and garden trails, restful vistas, ponds, herb gardens, exotic plants, native flora, an interactive Bugs, Birds & Butterflies Children's Garden and Mediterranean garden with a labyrinth. Well-known regional artist Ricardo Breceda, who created Borrego Springs' outdoor art exhibition, has produced Alta Vista's newest attraction, a collection of nine fantastical metal sculptures including dinosaurs in the Prehistoric Garden and a giant dragon-like "Serpent" in the children's garden. Special programs add to the allure of the gardens, such as art shows, culinary events and performing arts. http://www.altavistagardens.org/

Just adjacent to the Alta Vista Botanical Gardens, visitors can catch a show at an award-winning outdoor theater. The 2,000-seat **Moonlight Amphitheatre** is considered a cultural treasure in the North County, nestled in Vista's Brengle Terrace Park. The production company has an extensive summer Broadway musical line-up, but has recently added fall and winter shows. Arrive early to enjoy a pre-show picnic or dining in the Artisan Café. http://www.moonlightstage.com/

AUTHOR'S TIP:
ONE OF THE WORLD'S
LARGEST TELESCOPES

The **Mount Palomar Observatory**, operated by Caltech, is located within the Cleveland National Forest on Palomar Mountain in North San Diego County, not far from Pala at an elevation of 5,598 feet. Home to one of the world's largest single-mirror telescopes, the Hale Reflector, the observatory has been electronically enhanced into a charged-coupled device with photographic plates one hundred times more sensitive than when George Hale first designed it. George Hale also built the telescope at Mount Wilson but died before his Mount Palomar telescope was completed. The telescope was dedicated on June 3, 1948. With some exceptions, Palomar Observatory is open to the public daily. http://www.astro.caltech.edu/palomar/visitor/

San Marcos and Escondido

Not far from the coast, but inland from tourism-rich, ocean-fronting Carlsbad is **San Marcos**. Although San Marcos' history goes back to when the Spaniards settled in the fertile valley in 1797, the young city has only been incorporated for scarcely 50 years. Known more as a residential community, it is situated surprisingly close to all the action—just 35 miles from downtown San Diego in the northern part of the county and bordered by Escondido, Encinitas, Carlsbad and Vista. Embraced by foothills dotted with mini-mansions and an abundance of hiking trails and golf courses, San Marcos is best defined as a country destination that feels far removed from city life.

Hidden deep within the residential confines of the city is **Lake San Marcos**, a playground for nature-lovers. Birdwatchers have a field day with migrating species that fill the banks and marsh areas; and graceful swans, added by a newer resort, skim the calm waters. Although unveiled just unveiled a few years ago, the **Lakehouse Hotel & Resort** that fronts the lake still remains one of northern San Diego's best kept secrets. Spread on 250 peaceful acres along the shores of Lake San Marcos, this suburbia- ensconced resort underwent a property-wide multi-million renovation, reopening its doors in 2013 as the only four-star rated hotel in the area. **http://www.lake-househotelandresort.com/**

To break up the tranquility, a multitude of opportunities are just a few miles away—from Legoland to the Wild Animal Park and myriad coastal pleasures. However, a huge draw to the area is the local brew scene. San Diego County is definitely one of the hottest spots for a "cold one." Now home to more than 100 award-winning microbreweries that span the area from coast to inland areas, the brew scene offers a bounty of beer-related activities from festivals and food and beer pairing events to behind-the-scenes tours and, of course, foamy tastings. To get the full microbrew experience, consider a **Brew Hop Tour** that transports visitors to several local breweries. **https://brewhop.com/**

In fact, there are fifteen breweries within just fifteen minutes of San Marcos. For visitors wanting to really pull back the curtain and see where the magic happens, a brewery tour is on tap. High on the list should be a 45-minute VIP tour of **Stone Brewing** in nearby Escondido, where the aroma of "baking bread" leads tour-goers into the impressive enclave of brewery components—from gift shop, sampling bar and bistro to the gardens and brewing factory. Stone Brewing World Bistro & Gardens, with its distinctive gargoyle mascot, offers visitors a fresh, organic menu in the bistro paired with its signature beers that are known for bold and aggressive flavors.

The Stone Brew pub is the site of regular tastings and tours, as well as interactive classes that transform visitors to beer connoisseurs. The Bistro & Gardens has another popular location in San Diego's Point Loma area. **https://www.stone-brewing.com/**

Escondido, Spanish for "hidden," is aptly named, tucked away in San Diego County's northern area. Surrounded by high-end residential areas and encircled by scenic, craggy hills, the city which was founded in 1888 is the gateway to some rural wanderings, making it a perfect locale for venturing out to the Santa Ysabel Valley rich in mission history, pastoral wanderings and off-the-beaten-path treasures, from eateries to antiques and art. The trip is always filled with rural beauty, but spring adds fields of daffodils along the way as well as ideal weather for a roadside picnic. Valley Center Road southbound passes through Escondido Valley's lush orchard and farming areas; several open-air stands provide fruit and produce fresh from the fields. Tranquil Woods Valley Road, lined with oaks, passes a scenic mill house with pond and green pastures and leads to **Bates Brothers Nut Farm**. Set way back from the road with chain-link pens of farm animals (buy animal food in the store) and open picnic areas in front, Bates's warehouse store has come a long way from its beginnings in the 1920s, when walnuts were sold out of the ranch garage. Today the store sells a mouthwatering array of nuts, preserves and jams, vegetable pastas, trail mixes, granola, honey, dried fruit, candies and farm-fresh goose and duck eggs. The Farmer's Daughter gift shop, next door, offers a fine selection of country crafts and homemade gifts. **https://batesnutfarm.biz/**

LOCAL'S SECRET: ORGANIC DELI IN VALLEY CENTER

*"We love to get away from our city life on weekends. When **Yellow Deli** opened near us in Vista we enjoyed a fresh organic lunch with great atmosphere and unique music. We found out there was also one in Valley Center, well worth the drive to see countryside and sit right in the middle of a tranquil setting with trees, flowers, succulents, a stream to walk down to. The patio seating is covered with umbrellas for summer temps and a firepit for chillier days. The friendly staff are called Twelve Tribes and live right up the street. The menu is small but fresh and open for breakfast, lunch, dinner. You build your own sandwiches and they sell fresh organic veggies they grow on their farm on site as well as their hand-squeezed green drinks. The service is slow but the atmosphere makes up for it. It's peaceful and relaxing. Dogs are welcome."* http://yellowdeli.com/valley-center

–Cindy Wardrip, Vista, CA

One of the few remaining rural areas in North County, the **Elfin Forest Recreational Reserve** in Escondido covers more than 750 acres and offers 11 miles of hiking, mountain biking, equestrian trails, picnicking spots and six vista lookouts with views all the way to the Channel Islands and the Laguna and San Bernardino mountain ranges. The natural scape is abundant with oaks, coastal sage scrub and packed with wildlife. The reserve also sits within the Escondido Creek watershed which flows year-round from Lake Wohlford to San Elijo Lagoon. https://elfinforest.olivenhain.com/

Ramona

While passing through the town of **Ramona**, take in the historic abodes and country atmosphere. Stop on Main Street to tour the **Ramona Pioneer Historical Society** and **Guy B.**

Woodward Museum. Here you'll find the 1886-built Verlaque House, the only western adobe home of the French provincial designer still in existence and complete with furnishings, library and research center. Museum-goers will also discover Indian artifacts, an outfitted cowboy bunkhouse and blacksmith shop, a delightful rose garden and an extensive collection of women's clothing and accessories. http://www.woodwardmuseum.net/

Can you really milk a camel? You'll find out at the **Oasis Camel Dairy**, located in the pastoral Ramona Valley. The unique facility is the first camel dairy in the United States. During its monthly Open Farm Tours, visitors can enjoy exciting camel rides, petting the camels, fun photo opportunities and shopping at the dairy store which sells camel milk lotions, soaps, chocolate and more. https://oasiscameldairy1.godaddysites.com/

LOCAL'S SECRET: COZY WINERY

"As we were looking for new wineries, this cute family, cozy patio winery in Ramona, Grant James, caught our attention. We tasted the reds, our favorite. And the friendly staff kept pouring more in our glasses for no charge. A glass of wine is a large pour for $8 to go along with our picnic lunch. You can order a delicious cheese roll as well. We were told about each wine in detail. **Vineyard Grant James** *sits on the mountain top overseeing vineyards and views of the surrounding countryside. It is a very relaxing way to spend an afternoon. You definitely won't go home empty handed."* http://www.vineyardgrantjames.com/

- Cindy Wardrip, Vista, CA

Santa Ysabel Valley

Follow winding rural route Highway 78 to tiny **Santa Ysabel Valley**, on the way to historic Julian. Pass horse ranches and fruit stands to reach the bakery founded by the late Dudley Pratt in 1963. Celebrating more than 50 years as a bakery tradition, **Dudley's Bakery**, roadside in tiny Santa Ysabel, serves more than 40 types of freshly baked breads, fruit bars and pastries to lines of loyal patrons who purchase thousands of loaves of bread every day. The breads, which are now available in more than 70 stores, are baked daily and made from fresh ingredients from their own family recipes. Note that Dudley's is closed on Tuesday and Wednesday. **http://www. dudleysbakery.com/**

A slight detour off the highway leads to **Mission Santa Ysabel**, nestled in tranquil surroundings that have not changed significantly since the area was founded by missionary visitors 200 years ago. Rich in Native American and Spanish settler history, the mission still offers masses and some weddings. Visit the modest museum that chronicles the mission's history with photos and an abundance of old artifacts that chronicle its rich past, as well as the sacred Indian burial grounds. The chapel is marked by interesting murals, and alongside it sits the clappers that once graced the mission's bells which mysteriously disappeared one night in 1926. In remembrance of the bells, a carving called "Angel of the Lost Bells" stands in the mission.

Continue further up the road to **Julian Station** on the left. Housed in an original 1943 apple packing plant, the marketplace is a sprawling collection of buildings filled with handicraft arts, antique shops, a taco bar and local wine, beer and hard cider tasting bars. Be sure to sample Julian Hard Cider, a lightly colored alcoholic treat with a surprising "champagne" taste. Live music backs the outdoor shopping experience. **http://www.julianstation.com/**

Near here, Cordon Bleu graduate Jeremy Manley has transformed the former Tom's Chicken Shack into a surprising California-style bistro marked by fresh, seasonal farm-to-table cuisine. Located between Julian and Santa Ysabel, near the Julian Station, the family-owned **Jeremy's on the Hill** has garnered a faithful following since opening in 2008. The menu, which changes daily depending on locally available ingredients, wins with its locally raised bison burgers, its Julian apple salad and main dinner entrees such as chicken cordon bleu or pork tenderloin with farmer's market vegetables. The bistro is probably best known for its Sunday made-to-order champagne brunch. **https://bestrestaurantinjulian.com/**

Julian

Continue up the hill a few miles to a neighboring community rich in history. Nestled 4,500 feet in the mountains is the historic gold-mining town of **Julian**. The hidden gem of San Diego's backcountry, Julian offers an abundance of early California history, quaint Victorian streets filled with apple-pie eateries and antiques stores, crisp fresh air and friendly people. Situated in the heart of apple country, Julian's charming downtown swells with visitors during the fall apple season. A San Diego tradition "as American as apple pie" is the popular annual **Julian Fall Apple Harvest**, September through October, celebrating this historic mountain town's famous homemade apple pies and ciders. Visitors can also enjoy acres of colorful fall foliage, apple picking in local orchards, charming bed and breakfast inns, art shows, quaint antique shops, horse-drawn carriage rides and live entertainment.

At any time of the year, explore the old-fashioned downtown streets and byways the same way gold seekers may have in the I800s. The best way to experience tiny Julian is on foot. Park your car once you reach the main street of town and head in any direction. The brisk, clean mountain air around town is filled with the scent of cinnamon and bubbling baked apples; give in to your urge for a giant slice of home-baked pie by stopping in at one of the several bakery cafes. One of the most charming is the **Julian Pie Company** at 2225 Main

Street. The Victorian cottage boasts a small front patio with umbrella tables; a tiny inside eating area with round oak tables, lace window valances, Oriental rugs, country hangings and vintage wall coverings; and a large rear patio deck surrounded by bright blooms and apple trees whose apples may be "harvested" by the cafe's guests. The 1904 cottage bakery serves original, Dutch, and natural cider-sweetened apple pies as well as cinnamon rolls, caramel pecan rolls, walnut apple muffins and more **https://www.julianpie.com/**.

Julian has ample charm to warrant an overnight stay or longer. To relive the area's colorful past, stay at the historic **Julian Hotel** a few doors down from the cafe. The cream-colored, frontier Victorian–style hotel is listed on the National Register of Historic Places and is reported to be the oldest continuously operating hotel in Southern California. Built in 1897 by a freed slave, Albert Robinson, and his wife, the grand hotel was often referred to as the "Queen of the Back Country" and was visited by several dignitaries of the time. The Butterfield Stage stopped across the street from the hotel, and drivers looked forward to a piece of Mrs. Robinson's hot apple pie with cheese. The hotel was the social gathering spot for the community for many years and was operated by Robinson and then his widow alone until 1921. **http://www.julianhotel.com/**

Gold was discovered in Julian on Washington's birthday in 1870, and it's easy to imagine life as it might have been, especially once you have toured one of the area's original mines. The **Eagle Mine & High Peak Gold Mine**, about six blocks off Main Street, still offers underground tours into its hard-rock tunnel. Don't miss a chance to climb through the caverns, up a small ladder and back out for stories, history and perhaps a few "ghostly" encounters. The two mines were joined in time and became the site of the most notable disaster in the history of local mining in 1906, making it a frequent stop for paranormals. **http://www.theeaglemining.com/**

AUTHOR'S TIP: DAFFODIL GOLD

Julian survived through the rough and tumble gold mining days when other communities turned to ghost towns. But, in the spring, when the wintry ground gives way, Julian turns to "gold" again—with daffodils. The present-day bounty brings dazzling displays of daffodils on roadsides, in the ancient cemetery and myriad places in between. In 1990, local resident Sally Snipes planted some daffodil bulbs along the rural Julian roadside to honor her late father, Jack. No one could have guessed this gesture of love would eventually transform the historic town into a spring-time wonderland for nature-lovers. More plantings caught on in a grassroots effort each year, and, today, more than three million daffodils grace the area.

Back in town, stop in the **Julian Drug Store** on the corner of Washington and Main. The original Levi-Marks Building, built in 1886, was the first brick building in town, constructed of bricks made from native clay that was baked on nearby Duffy ranch. The nostalgic marble soda-fountain counter in the drugstore is still the spot for an old-fashioned malt, shake, sundae or phosphate. Just past Fourth Street on Washington Street is the town's former 1876 brewery, now the stone **Julian Pioneer Museum**. http://julianpioneermuseum.org/

Hiking and exploring is plentiful in the countryside surrounding downtown Julian. Drive just out town to the **Menghini Winery** for wine tasting; harvest some apples from the orchards nearby. For prime outdoor fun, head to the 25,000-acre **Volcan Mountain Preserve**, just north of downtown. Home to wildlife and several species of oak and pine, it actually extends to Anza-Borrego State Park; guided tours are offered on weekends. **https://www.volcanmt.org/**

If you are looking for an "Old West" outdoor adventure, stop by **Julian Stables** and "saddle up" for a trail ride through Volcan Mountain and the peaks of Cuyamaca. Highway 79 south out of Julian is a scenic backcountry route that winds through a country blending of oaks, pines and flowered meadows. The highway intersects picturesque **Cuyamaca Rancho State Park**, offering a wide range of side trips and hikes throughout the park area. The 30,000-acre state park, with peaks, forests, alpine meadows, and narrow valleys, features some 110 miles of hiking trails that penetrate the park's backcountry.

Located minutes from the town of Julian, the **California Wolf Center** is committed to the repopulation of the critically endangered Mexican gray wolves and North American gray wolves. Visitors can help support the organization's efforts by participating in one of the center's tour programs. Plan to take a private or public tour; different packages include educational presentations, intimate guided tours, individual time with a staff educator and meeting packs of wolves. **https://www.californiawolfcenter.org/about/**

Santee

With millions of boulders in San Diego County, bouldering is a local specialty, and rock climbers can free climb, sport climb, multi-pitch climb and trad climb among hundreds of vertical rocky paths. **Santee Boulders** in San Diego's rural East County is a popular field offering a full-day of challenging climbs. With thick faces and mantles, taxing cracks and steep slopes, the most skilled and novice climbers can enjoy a good climb with nothing more than a sturdy pair of shoes. At an elevation of 3,000 feet, El Cajon Mountain, nicknamed "El Capitan," offers challenging and steep climbs for adventure seekers with rewarding panoramic views of the Pacific Ocean and scenic valleys below.

Hidden in the mountains of **Alpine,** not far from Santee and about 30 minutes from downtown San Diego, is another sanctuary dedicated to wild animals. **Lions, Tigers and Bears** offers a safe haven for abandoned or mistreated exotic animals. The 93-acre sanctuary is home to 19 species including bears, cougars, tigers, lions and leopards, among others. Visitors can support the organization by taking part in one of their guided educational visits led Wednesday through Saturday. Experiences vary and include behind-the-scenes tours and animal feedings--even a two-night luxury stay at the sanctuary's White Oak Mountain Retreat. **https://lionstigersandbears.org/**

Campo

Highway 94 through the rural countryside leads you to the country town of **Campo**, boasting a museum dedicated to vintage railroad equipment and steam and diesel locomotives. Each weekend the **Pacific Southwest Railway Museum** offers a 15-mile round-trip through the rugged backcountry here. The museum is open on weekends and holidays (except Thanksgiving and Christmas); admission is free. The railway excursions are also offered on weekends and holidays. While in Campo, visit the **Old Stone Store**, one of the oldest structures in the town and now open on weekends as a museum of local history. **https://www.psrm.org/**

City of San Diego
https://www.sandiego.org/

The eighth largest city in the United States, San Diego is one of the fastest-growing major cities in the country. The city, with more than 1.4 million inhabitants, is known for its mild climate and major tourist attractions such as the San Diego Zoo and Sea World. San Diego's 320 square miles are filled with diverse facets, but those who dig deeper will discover a blend of the best of the old and new, the historic and the avant-garde, from innovative chefs to unexpected thrills.

You could say San Diego is very "neighborly." From the Gaslamp Quarter to Little Italy, you can traverse from one mini community to another in a few minutes. The variety of experiences, from food to events and stays, will bring you back again and again to explore an amazing diversity of visits just a trolley ride away.

Gaslamp Quarter

The 16-block **Gaslamp Quarter** historical neighborhood is an entertainment paradise, filled with bistros, hopping night-spots and even its own baseball field, **Petco Field**, where the Padres knock it out all season, right smack in the middle of all the action. Nightfall brings a new level of "secret" to this slice of San Diego—top secret night spots that even the locals can't find without some clues. I asked permission from each of these **clandestine "speakeasies"** to reveal these hush-hush hints to detecting those libation and entertainment nooks hidden within the confines of the Gaslamp Quarter and all walkable from the core of the historic neighborhood that has hosted Presidents since the days of Ulysses S. Grant.

AUTHOR'S TIP:
GUIDE TO SPEAKEASIES

Although the days of illegal speakeasies are past, the illicit thrill lives on after dark in San Diego's Gaslamp Quarter. The area is jam-packed with hopping bistros sharing the sidewalks, some more noticeable than others.

*One you may not notice is the Neighborhood restaurant at 777 G Street, the entre into the hidden nightspot, **Noble Experiments**. Pass right on by the diners and wait staff, heading to the restrooms in the rear. Look right for a wall of "kegs." No beer here, just a cleverly concealed entrance. Push on the kegs and a world of mystery and wonder opens up in an intimate space known for its cocktails and hypnotic décor. For those who are fans of the Haunted Mansion ride at Disneyland, you'll feel like the ride stopped and you entered its macabre interiors— accomplished by a wall of skulls, a massive crystal chandelier and changing framed art on the walls (and ceiling) that morph into bizarre portraits pairing humans with rabbits or dogs. To gain access, text for a necessary reservation.* **https://nobleexperimentsd.com/**

*The name, **Prohibition**, is perfect for this hidden nightspot—one of the locals' best known and a popular live jazz nook. You can't call for a reservation—you just need to know, but the small size means you may have to wait. Head to 548 Fifth Avenue and look carefully for a small plaque that declares "Law Office Eddie O'Hare, Esq." If Eddie meets his legal clients in this locale, they are in for a surprise. Down the staircase is a world that celebrates the speakeasy period with crafted cocktails, low lights and plentiful music.* **https://www.prohibitionsd.com/**

*There is actually a sign that signals **Vin De Syrah** on a Gaslamp corner, but don't be fooled—it is not that easy to find. When you arrive at 901 Fifth Street, walk down a flight of stairs to this subterranean place of wonder, as in "Alice in Wonderland." Push open the door covered in grass and "fall down the rabbit hole" to a spacious area filled with intimate seating nooks, princess chairs, hanging branches that give a forest-like feel and accent lights. The hidden door entrance is fun to watch from the inside since closed circuit television reveals patrons trying to find the right door to wonderland. The food is tasty bar fare and the wine list impressive.* **https://syrahwineparlor.com/**

*Unlike the other concealed nightspots, **Fairweather** is easy to spot—but nearly impossible to find. If you are in the Petco field vicinity on J Street, you might eye a lively rooftop patio where baseball games are clearly visible (on a massive screen) and audible. Fairweather patrons only need to look for Rare Form and head to rear of the restaurant. Turn right and several doors await marked "yes" or "no." Upstairs, welcome to Fairweather, a comfortable and pleasant patio bar that sports "drinks from sunny places"—from generous piña coladas to mai tais. The refreshing concoctions served under sunny skies (hence, the name) or at night for a lively vibe, are all accompanied by deli-catessen delicacies from Rare Form. You won't care which team wins by the end of the day or night.* **http://www.godblessrareform.com/**

*Created by Consortium Holdings, the group that has been populating the San Diego area with the most talked-about bistros and speakeasies such as Noble Experiments comes Craft & Commerce, blending an air of library and wild animals in a clever rustic manner that invites conversation and conviviality. Two bars are within the restaurant, and an open patio with individual fire pits is perfect for Sunday brunch people watching. Enter the reservation-only **False Idol** in the rear of the bistro through a "freezer" door; it is packed almost every night with guests seeking the total Tiki experience as only Disney could conjure, from the three-dozen over-the-top exotic drinks and wood carvings to the inspired, sporadic Polynesian-style volcanic eruptions, complete with pulsating seats, thunderous music, water and flaming torches.* **https://falseidoltiki.com/**

For all that sleuthing, you need a "home base" that is in the middle of all the action, especially for your late-night adventures. The perfect choice is a surprise hidden gem snuggled in the heart of the Gaslamp Quarter. Locating the hotel might require an extra turn around the corner to spot since the brick-fronted historic structure fuses quietly with this lively downtown center. However, once inside its multi-storied hallows, unexpected surprises await on every floor. **The Keating House by Pininfarina**—created by the same Italian design team responsible for the Maserati and Ferrari—ventured into hospitality for the first time with the 1890-built Keating Building office structure. A salute to its historic side, the five-story Romanesque building still possesses the longest running elevator in the city, powered solely by steam heat. To create a unique experience worthy of the Pininfarina name, the design team removed features you might expect in standard hotels, such as interior walls, drapery and carpeting. The final result is a design full of surprises including model cars in the hallways, whirlpool tubs in the living room, lots of stainless steel and sleek Italian designed furnishings. State-of-the-art amenities abound from Lavazza espresso machines to Alpha Morphosis Jacuzzi tubs—both Pininfarina Extra designs as well. **http://www.thekeating.com/the-keating-hotel**

LOCAL'S SECRET:
COCKTAILS AND JUMBO JETS

*"**Mr. A's** restaurant, on the top of the 13-story Banker's Hill building downtown, has wonderful cuisine. However, my favorite part of dining there is the eye-level view of planes flying directly through downtown to land at Lindbergh Field. There is nothing more exciting than having a Happy Hour while watching the jets that look close enough to touch."*
https://www.asrestaurant.com/

– John Eger

Located below Fifth Avenue is a novel way to dine: a trailer park decorated with vintage trailers and thrift store furnishings. Grab a seat on a shopping cart or perhaps in a wheelbarrow and feast on such downhome delights as Frito pies, sloppy joes or soft pretzels with cheese at **Trailer Park After Dark**. You can wash it all down with local craft beer and entertainment, from karaoke to foosball. **https://www.trailer-parkafterdark.com/**

Little Italy

We can all agree that Italians are passionate about their food. Fellow travel writer Rick Steves will tell you that cuisine in Italy is like a religion — and it's the quality of the ingredients that's most sacred. Even the most traditional of all destinations, those bursting with charm and history, are open to change and enhancement. San Diego's European-style neighborhood, **Little Italy**, is no exception. Recently, it has exploded in gastronomic adventures discovered amid the tiny area's relaxing piazzas, sidewalk cafes, bocce ball courts and icy gelato stands—all just a short walk from the glistening Pacific.

In the 1990s, the Little Italy Association reclaimed the neighborhood's Italian heritage and restored its beauty. Referred to as the "Italian Riviera" of San Diego, Little Italy's cozy, eclectic blocks are filled with vintage fishermen cottages made into boutiques, modern geometric lofts for city dwellers, highly revered eateries and local hang-outs.

Stroll down India Street past myriad cafes and Italian markets and upscale bistros to **Amici Park**. A salute in itself to the history of the area, the park has public art dressed as red-and-white checkered tables donned with "food" and the recipes that go with it, bocce ball courts and an amphitheater that stages entertainment. A block below India is **Kettner Street**, hosting the neighborhood's burgeoning art and design district that flourishes in once-vapid warehouses. The nearly two dozen shops include Architectural Salvage with a large collection of vintage pieces worth touring.

Little Italy's certified **farmer's market** is one of the most popular in the county with blocks packed with more than 200 certified farm booths, artisan foods and specialty vendors every Saturday. It is also the inspiration for many of the stand-out eateries in the area. Join the chefs and get a preview of your evening's fresh fare at the **Mercato**, held year- round rain or shine. Plan to "eat" your way through the streets sampling pastas, cheeses, olives, desserts and more in this outside neighborhood "grocery store" that perfectly complements the romantic charm of Little Italy.

The giant white chicken out front gives it away. The **Crack Shack**, Chef Blais' ultra-casual al fresco restaurant, is all about chicken—and the egg. The relaxed bistro with bocce ball court and a full beer and cocktail bar offers an all-day menu of chicken and egg creations, as well as food to go in case you want to pack a picnic. Fans love the "Senor Croque," a crispy chicken sandwich with bacon, fried egg, cheddar cheese and miso-maple butter on a brioche bun. Don't be surprised to hear the giganto-chicken actually crow. **https://www.crackshack.com/**

In every Italian village there is a quaint pensione just steps from espresso-sipping bistros and sliced prosciutto delis. Little Italy is no exception. **La Pensione Hotel** recently emerged from a multi-million-dollar urban-chic makeover of its petite but charming guestrooms. The new design features a sophisticated, clean palate of white and silver décor accompanied by vintage photography and custom furnishings. The charming and unassuming hotel features some private balconies overlooking the main India Street. Still one of San Diego's best-kept secrets, the little hotel sits right in the middle of everything worth experiencing in Little Italy. An exciting new addition to the neighborhood, the Piazza Famiglia, is directly across the street. **http://www.lapensionehotel.com/**

AUTHOR'S TIP:
POP-UP TRAILER DINING

*Located below Fifth Avenue is a novel way to dine: a trailer park decorated with vintage trailers and thrift store furnishings. Grab a seat on a shopping cart or perhaps in a wheelbarrow and feast on such downhome delights as Frito pies, sloppy joes or soft pretzels with cheese at **Trailer Park After Dark**. You can wash it all down with local craft beer and entertainment, from karaoke to foosball.* **https://www.trailerparkafterdark.com/**

Point Loma

Located northwest of downtown San Diego, **Point Loma** is a historically rich bayfront community set on a scenic peninsula. Not only is the area where "California began" and where the iconic Spirit of St. Louis was built and tested, Point Loma also showcases San Diego's rich military and naval history. However, Point Loma's recent shift into a cultural and gastronomical hub has transformed it into one of the city's hottest neighborhoods. From art galleries, concert venues and food markets to hidden tide pools and the perfect spots to catch the sunset, Point Loma will always be history in the making.

In 1542, Portuguese navigator Juan Rodriguez Cabrillo landed at the end of the Point Loma peninsula and was the first European to set foot in present-day California. Described as "the birthplace of California," a statue of Cabrillo stands tall at the **Cabrillo National Monument**, a U.S. National Park. Every October, Cabrillo's arrival is commemorated during The Cabrillo Festival, a weekend-long event with reenactments of the discoverer's arrival, music and food. Cabrillo National

Monument is also home to the **Old Point Loma Lighthouse**, San Diego's first light house, and Fort Rosecrans, where gun batteries, bunkers and fire control stations once safeguarded San Diego. However, the area's history can be traced back millions of years through its eroded sandstone cliffs along the Pacific Ocean, known as Sunset Cliffs. Here, 75 million-year-old dinosaur fossils from the Late Cretaceous period can be found, along with some of the best sunsets in San Diego.

Recently added to San Diego's Point Loma neighborhood is a local-popular destination for dining, artisans and farmer's market shopping: **Liberty Public Market**. Though still not quite on the visitor's itinerary, it is destined to be soon. The unique marketplace that opened recently is already a huge hit with locals for good reason. Like big markets in other metro areas, this site is made for strolling and dining. The former Liberty Station naval base in the city's Point Loma neighborhood still pays homage to its roots, but that is where the comparison ends. The 22,000-square-foot development offers a seven-day-a-week farmer's market where goers may sample artisan breads, tortillas, cheeses, olive oil and jams and buy from small businesses that offer gourmet pet food, arts and crafts and more. Dining either inside or out is a big draw at Liberty. **Mess Hall**, located in the former naval dining hall, is a perfect way to sample the market's various artisans since daily menus are sourced from the restaurant's Liberty Market "neighbors." It is also very popular, especially for Sunday brunch. I doubt that the prior occupants enjoyed jeweled brioche bread pudding French toast with strawberries or a wood-fired asparagus and feta quiche. **http://libertypublicmarket.com/**

Old Town

A great deal of San Diego's inherent charm is found in discovering its beginnings. The first European settlement in California, **Old Town San Diego**, is located in the city. In 1769 the Franciscan monk Junípero Serra raised a crude cross on the site of the first mission in California on a hill overlooking San Diego Bay, and the Royal Presidio was constructed. The Presidio became overcrowded as more settlers arrived, and by 1821 many had moved to the foot of the hill to build their homes and gardens. Six restored blocks of this "new" Old Town form **Old Town State Park** and offer visitors numerous historic buildings as well as specialty shops and restaurants to explore.

The only way to appreciate the history of California's founders, while following in their footsteps, is to park your car and wander the colorful plazas and streets of Old Town. The displays, historic buildings and shops and cafes of the area re-create the feel of early California life from 1821 to 1872. The state historic park was formed in 1968, and since, much restoration and reconstruction work has been completed on its buildings, especially the original adobes. **http://www.old-townsandiego.org/**

From Old Town State Park, walk a short distance to another group of San Diego's reminders, **Heritage County Park**, on the corner of Juan and Harney Streets. The nearly eight-acre historical park is a haven for the city's Victorian heritage, an area where endangered Victorian-era buildings have been relocated and renovated for future generations to enjoy. Wander the cobblestone-like plaza of the park and step into late-1800s America. The **Victorian Village** is a 7.8-acre county park with seven restored and relocated Victorian homes, saved from the wrecking ball. The Village includes San Diego's first synagogue, which now hosts weddings, receptions and bar mitzvahs. **http://www.sdparks.org/content/sdparks/en/park-pages/Heritage.html**

The **Whaley House**, which once was the County Court House, San Diego's first commercial theater and various other businesses, stands as California State Historic Landmark #65. It is also considered one of America's most haunted buildings, according to the Travel Channel. The reason might be explained by some significant events, such as the suicide of Violet Whaley in 1885, as well as the hangings which occurred on the property before the house was constructed. The earliest documented ghost at the Whaley House is "Yankee Jim." James Robinson was convicted of attempted grand larceny in San Diego in 1852, and hanged on gallows off the back of a wagon on the site where the house now stands, but many visitors to the house have reported encountering Thomas Whaley himself. **http://whaleyhouse.org/**

Balboa Park

Often referred to as the "Smithsonian of the West" due to its large number of museums, **Balboa Park** is the cultural heart of San Diego. At 1,200 acres, this National Historic Landmark is the largest urban cultural park in the U.S., beating out both New York City's Central Park and San Francisco's Golden Gate Park in size. With 17 museums, 16 gardens, multiple theaters, shops and restaurants, visitors have access to dozens of different experiences in Balboa Park. With sprawling grounds and so many venues to explore, some of the park's most interesting features go largely unnoticed by visitors. Look a little harder and enjoy these 7 unique experiences on your next visit to Balboa Park. **https://www.balboapark.org/**

AUTHOR'S TIP:
6 HIDDEN GEMS IN BALBOA PARK

Free Rembrandt: You can't really take home an original Rembrandt for free, but it doesn't cost a cent to view Rembrandt van Rijn's "Saint Bartholomew" at the Timken Museum of Art. Open daily except Mondays, admission to the Timken is always free.

Hidden Chapel: Many visitors head to the Museum of Man for its informative, interactive exhibits on the history of mankind and never realize that the museum also houses a Spanish Colonial chapel built for the Panama-California Exposition of 1915. Located across from the museum's entrance, the St. Francis Chapel features an elaborate gilded altar featuring the Virgin and Child in the center, flanked by Saint Francis Xavier on the left and by San Diego de Alcalá on the right. The chapel which is available to rent for special events can be viewed by appointment.

Historic Brass Ring: Located near the world-famous San Diego Zoo, this is a different kind of menagerie—one where all the animals are made of wood. Dating back to 1910, the Balboa Park Carousel is composed almost entirely of its original, hand-carved animals including horses, giraffes, dogs, camels and even a dragon. The carousel is one of the few left in the U.S. that still features a brass ring that rewards those who grab it with a free ride.

Scratch and Sniff Plants: One of the park's original structures from 1915, the Botanical Building houses numerous plant species, ranging from delicate, multicolored orchids to voracious Venus fly traps. The building's "scratch and sniff" section encourages visitors to rub the plants' leaves and identify the scent (chocolate mint, anyone?). It's a popular display for kids, but plenty of adults join in the sensory exploration.

Public Art Hidden in Plain View: While patrons wait for tables at the popular Prado restaurant, many don't realize they are just steps away from one of the City of San Diego's prized pieces of public art. Created by sculpture Donal Hord, the Woman of Tehuantepec Fountain was commissioned by the WPA Federal Arts Project in 1935 to capture the spirit of the New Deal. Located in courtyard of the House of Hospitality, the sculpture can be viewed 365 days a year for free.

The Land of Misfit Sports: Forget games of touch football on the lawn—in Balboa Park, it's all about the lesser-known sports. Guests can try their hand at lawn bowling on the park's west end, disc golf at Morley Field on the park's east side, or give archery a go at the 30-acre Rube Powell Archery Range.

Barrio Logan

Located south of downtown San Diego, **Barrio Logan** is a Mexican-American neighborhood established by refugees back in the early 20th century during the Mexican Revolution and rooted in civic movement. Throughout time, numerous rezoning projects slowly transformed this bayfront community into an industrial zone, until the 1970s when the construction of a California Highway Patrol Station on a local park heightened the community's frustration, resulting in a nonviolent uprising to reclaim what is now known as **Chicano Park**. Today, the resilient voices of this Chicano community are echoed throughout the barrio's murals and galleries. The neighborhood's cultural significance resulted in a prestigious designation in 2017 by the California Arts Council as one of 14 California Cultural Districts for showcasing some of the unique artistic identities driving California's culture.

Designated a National Historic Landmark in 2017, Chicano Park is the heart of Barrio Logan and home to the largest collection of outdoor murals in the world. The murals painted on the support piers of the San Diego-Coronado Bridge narrate the story of San Diego's Mexican-American community. Throughout the year, the park is the site of many important cultural celebrations like Chicano Park Day, held every April, which commemorates the park's anniversary with music, Aztec indigenous dance demonstrations, food and art. Every November 2, Día de los Muertos comes alive with the Muertos Candlelight Procession and altar blessing that begins in nearby Sherman Heights and culminates at Chicano Park. **http://www.chicanoparksandiego.com/**

Hillcrest

San Diego's **Hillcrest** area boasts fashionable, gracious residential neighborhoods as well as a quaint downtown area with a bevy of 1950s and 1960s vintage cafes and shops. Park your car and stroll down Fifth and University Avenues. Check out the marquee at the **Guild Theater** on Fifth Avenue—it may very well be playing one of your favorite flicks from the 1950s or 1960s.

Hillcrest is known as the hub of San Diego's LGBTQ community, with its symbol of diversity being the 65- foot- -tall Hillcrest Pride Flag at Pride Plaza on one end of the rainbow, and its famed and historic Hillcrest sign on the other. The rainbow flag serves as a community gathering point for special events, including the nation's third largest LGBT Pride parade. Pride Plaza also hosts the **Hillcrest Farmers Market**, which features more than 175 vendors every Sunday.

B

L

ABOUT THE AUTHOR

Kathy Strong has been a travel writer for more than 30 years, having written or contributed to more than 20 travel guide books and countless magazine features, covering all areas of the world. Her former books sold in bookstores nationally are: Southern California: Off the Beaten Path; Recommended Bed & Breakfasts: California; Driving the Pacific Coast: California; Driving the Pacific Coast: Washington and Oregon; The Seattle Guidebook; and Recommended Island Inns: The Caribbean.

Her newspaper column, GOING MY WAY, appeared in the Gannett/USA Today newspaper Travel section every Sunday in Southern California for a decade. Strong also was a regular contributor to USA Today's travel magazine, "GoEscape." She has also been a contributor to Forbes Travel Guide and USA Today weekly magazine.

Through the years, Strong has been a frequent talk show guest on both radio and television, recently appearing on "The Today Show."

Strong's latest travel reveal is a new online travel website: PS Wish You Were Here Travel (**http://pswishyouwerehere-travel.com/**) that covers both national and international travel news and explorations.

This first edition of Secret Southern California is a culmination of the native Southern Californian's knowledge and love for the off-the-beaten-path treasures of the southern part of the state, as well as "secret, authentic" finds at every turn.